Amazing Grace

By

Lee Albert

Albert Byrne

authorHOUSE™

1663 LIBERTY DRIVE, SUITE 200
BLOOMINGTON, INDIANA 47403
(800) 839-8640
WWW.AUTHORHOUSE.COM

This book is a work of non-fiction. Some names have been changed to protect the privacy of the individuals. The events and situations are true.

First published by AuthorHouse 08/05/04

ISBN: 1-4184-0289-3 (e-book)
ISBN: 1-4184-0288-5 (Paperback)
ISBN: 1-4184-0287-7 (Dust Jacket)

Library of Congress Control Number: 2004090199

Printed in the United States of America
Bloomington, Indiana

This book is printed on acid-free paper.

The Holy Grail

How at the Castle of Corbin a Maiden Bare in the Sangreal and
Foretold the Achievements of Galahad.
By Arthur Rackham.

The Italian Princess,
Whose smile inspired this book.

VIII

Acknowledgements

I wish to pay tribute to the constant motivation I have received from the one thing I truly value: the power and love of woman. The mysteries and beauties of woman are divine and God-given. How sad it is that man imposes his morality onto them, not even understanding his own nature, let alone theirs. What wonders he misses. How sad it is that man in his pride is unable to kneel at her altar. This surely is a reflection of the wasteland of modern man that has forced the goddess to flee into the mists.

I want to say thanks to Karl Naeher, who was a needed companion during the time of the events described later in these books. Through the power of e-mail, I had a lifeline to someone who knew what I was going through. I would also like to acknowledge my friend Séan who aided me during the early part of the writing process with his encouragement and constructive criticism. In this regard I owe a debt of gratitude to my friend Hans who at the eleventh hour gave me invaluable assistance in the final preparation of the manuscript. His help can only be properly described as divine intervention. Thanks also to my friend Elena for her help with the pencil drawings.

A very special word of thanks to my mother and father for the selfless sacrifices they made for our family. The pressure of work they sustained while I was growing up was phenomenal. As a child there is much one does not understand or appreciate. Through my healing work I have strengthened my links to them. I am also happy to be able to say that my father has been spiritually present with me during the writing of this book and continues to be an important source of support for me.

Everyone needs a watering hole, so I would like to thank my local Cafeteria Royal, a venue at times like a sea storm of change, where my friends, the three brothers Miguel, Santiago and Carlos, gave me a warmth of home that could only come from good hearts. I have always felt welcome there and in good company. It is a metropolis of life.

I would also have been lost without the good use of my local gymnasium, Granada Sport. In particular, a special thanks to Jose and his elemental spinning classes. They were a rush of energy and good feelings. I would like to say thanks to all the friends I made there who helped me with my faltering Spanish and made me feel at home.

Thanks also to the friendly services of Eliska and Raul of Uninet, Cibercafe. Their friendly and relaxed environment made my task a lot easier. And of course, thank you to the people of Granada and Andalusia. Your openness and warmth helped heal a broken heart. For this you will always be in my mine.

I cannot go without saying a special word of thanks to my dear friend Laura. Her friendship I can only properly describe as divine. Through her I found the support of a conscientious friend at a time when I could barely speak Spanish and was very much alone. She also helped me with the images in this book. I was very blessed to meet her so soon after my arrival in Granada. Thanks also to our mutual friend Carmen who also played an important part in my time here.

During the writing of this book I have been very fortunate to make many friends from all over Spain and Europe. Your friendship has meant a lot to me. Thank you.

Of course, a word of thanks and a big hug to my dear friend Greta. In her quiet way, she has gently guided me in my choice of writing when I was unwittingly intent on overburdening the reader with too much at once. I gave her the first couple of chapters to read, as I had another 11 in the works, and she rightly pointed out to me (but did not impose) that the chapters I gave her were a book in themselves. This extremely useful observation led me to rework what I had given her into something far greater than I had ever imagined possible. Greta, for this and so much more, I thank you.

It would be remiss of me to forget to thank all my spiritual helpers who have been ever-present and ever-caring. I have not once felt lessened in any way I did not want.

And finally to all my good friends around the world, from Dublin to Sydney, whom I met on my path, thank you for the support you gave me.

Lee Albert
Granada,
Spain.

"Two roads diverged in a wood, and I –
I took the one less traveled by,
And that has made all the difference."

Robert Frost (1874-1963),
From the poem, *The Road Not Taken*.

Intention Is Everything

The Spiral Galaxy M33.

Photo by Bert Katzung, © 2002.

XIV

Table of Contents

XVIII

Foreword by Karl Naeher

Of all the people looking for an Eboga treatment, Lee was the only one coming over by ship and from Greece at that. This triggered two flashes of thought in me: Ulysses, the man who, after a long and arduous journey, finally found his way back to his island and to love; and the Eleusi, the 2,000-year-old Greek temple where seekers were initiated into the secrets of the divine by a magic and psychedelic drink called kykeon.

Meeting Lee for the first time in the harbor of Venice, I encountered an intelligent businessman who was "washed with all seven seas," instinctively sizing you up to put some useful labels on you, which wasn't difficult for someone who had gone through years of psychotherapy.

On his healing journey, Lee embarked on a ship that cannot be appreciated by everybody. His journey gave him access to the knowledge necessary to master one's life in peace and love. It also healed many wounds. In the manner of ancient traditions, the revelations came in the form of a symbolic language, not always easy to decipher.

This journey is an invaluable contribution to show a relatively fast and exciting way to cross the wavy sea of our troubled souls and to find our way back home, where love awaits us. However, it cannot be described as a pleasure cruise. It took Lee six years of persistent adherence and trust in the way of Eboga to fully comprehend and arrive close to the end of his Process. Pain was part of that journey. During these years of persistent adherence and trust in the way of Eboga, Lee charted the waters of the Process to give us useful hints as to how to proceed successfully and what to expect with Eboga and ibogaine. He built a bridge between an ancient African initiatory rite of passage and a modern everyday world. His life story is a living example of how Eboga can change one's life for the "Good."

Like Lee himself, the reader is called to participate in the exciting search for meaning in the otherworldly scenes and beings that appear during his voyages with Eboga. To render the ephemeral appearances of these beings useful as a guide in life was and still is, an enormous challenge for Lee and for anyone willing to go beyond the barren ground of "modern psychology." It is an endeavor to give birth to a new language to encompass the vast origin of the psyche as opposed to scientific endeavors to isolate it out from the whole and analyze it as a separate entity. What language allows us to reconcile the Logos with the deep, ineffable experiences of the soul, our need for creativity and love, our "inner child," as Lee calls it?

This book – and the books that follow – mark a departure for a new way to a suffering humanity, integrating many old traditions with modern psychological insight.

Karl Naeher M.A. D.C. (U.S.A.)

www.ibogainetreatment.com

June 2004

Foreword by Lee Albert

Nothing remains the same.

Eboga has been known to the Pygmies of the Rift Valley for more than 20,000 years and in the past 300 years it has played a central role in the Bwiti religion of West Central Africa. It is a "deeply" spiritual plant. Its spirit is carried by a serpent. This book refers to the use of the eboga plant and, in particular, the principal alkaloid of this plant, ibogaine, in what I call "The Eboga Process" or, simply put, "The Process." The "Session" is at the heart of the Process.

Eboga is not a Bwiti religion, nor is it a Pygmy religion. Eboga is an "African Spirituality," which means it draws its energy and resources from the cradle of human life, Africa. "Eboga Spirituality" in a Western context expresses itself in a deepening respect for the Earth, the community, the ancestors, one's parents and, in particular, oneself and one's family. Eboga is the circle of life that brings you directly in contact with your heart, your soul and the ones you love. It is a way to God.

The purpose of Eboga spirituality is not about being "holier than thou" nor is it about blind faith. It is about being "real" and in that reality discover and connect to one's place within the greater scheme of things, drawing one's source from a higher consciousness. Throughout the book I make reference to eboga and Eboga. The first usage refers to the plant itself. The second usage refers to its spirituality.

Eboga can also be thought of as an African natural healing medicine. In that sense Eboga is a dynamic healing system dependent on the innermost state of the individual, i.e., its actions cannot be predicted other than in a general way. With time it mends and heals each broken part, finally polishing the whole. It leads to emotional health and physical well-being and a profound connection to life and God in an ever connecting continuum which brings us deeply into our soul. Needless to say, it is also a teaching plant.

Eboga can also be described as a non-addiction therapy.

An Eboga experience initially targets the physical addictions of the body and arrives naturally at the subconscious where all that we seek to avoid, expressed in our addictions, is revealed and healed in time. This however requires the unseating of the ego as the ego blocks our true state of mind – see later, The Eboga Process, chapter 1. This opens the door to what lies repressed and the healing begins. The success of the healing depends on the power of Eboga (expressed in dosage) and the willingness of the person to confront their true self. This willingness is manifested through intention. Thus, when one is ready, little by little Eboga shows us each wound, having used its power to free it from a trapped state. At the same time a release of the trapped emotional and spiritual toxins linked to the wound takes place. Eboga then helps us understand the meaning of the wound (which has been partly or fully exposed) before it cleans and dresses it, i.e., envelops it in an emotional bandage. The rest is left to mother nature, time and divine coincidence to bring about the associated emotional connection and mental acceptance we normally experience in the final stages of healing. Like a flesh wound, an emotional wound needs time once it has been treated by Eboga, i.e., a period of integration is required.

The next phase within an Eboga session involves the reeducation of the ego to a more holistic way of thinking. Afterwards, in this new state, with the passage of time and right intention, the ego shifts it allegiance from a purely animalistic relationship to the material world, to a relationship with the soul and its alternate form of "gratification" – a state where our true choices are made manifest, as these choices are the choices of the true mind, the soul. Eboga thus liberates the soul and aligns the ego to its wishes. Without this alignment we inevitably become corrupted by power and money as that is the way of the purely animalistic mind that seeks to avoid a troubled soul.

Ibogaine, the principal alkaloid of the eboga plant is, I believe, synonymous with eboga as it is the principal and, to my mind, *"the"* healing component of the eboga plant. I believe that is how it was meant to be in order that it could play a major role in this stage of man's evolution within a Western scientific model. More recently ibogaine has been recognized for its properties in the elimination of physical drug dependence. This is only a drop in the pond of its history, as its deeper meaning is not yet properly understood here in the West. The focus on drug addiction and the preoccupation with the safety of ibogaine means that its full spiritual life cycle and action, i.e., the Process, are not properly understood. The reason for this is that complete healing requires an ongoing Process that, in my case, has lasted for nearly six years, with the end or, should I say, the beginning now very clearly in sight. The ibogaine drug treatment community is mostly preoccupied with the starting posts. I have personally gone to the far reaches of the Eboga experience. My writings are focused on this second part, while paying tribute to the worthwhile and extremely important work done within the drug community in understanding the safety aspects of the first part.

My writings are therefore written within the context of safe, present-day use of ibogaine within the Process, following the medical guidelines as developed over the past number of years. (These guidelines are based on ibogaine, which is a major reason why I chose to work with eboga in this form only.) My use of ibogaine in this regard has been and is based on personal decision and responsible action. Anyone considering its use must also act in this way. Ultimately it is a personal decision and the responsibility begins and ends there. My perspective has been to interpret my experiences firsthand from the viewpoint of a rational Western scientist open to all possibilities. I see no reason whatsoever to introduce a lot of religious doctrine and regulations that do nothing but confuse the person undergoing treatment. It is a journey to the heart and there you will find everything you need to know. What counts is that your heart is renewed, healed and in harmony with the One, the All.

Eboga is probably the most sacred substance known to man. Ibogaine, its principle alkaloid, is a humble salt that, like all things humble, contains greatness. I have nothing but respect for it. I believe that, once the fuss over the use of ibogaine for the treatment of drug addiction passes, it will finally be seen for what it is, a sacred sacrament for man's benefit on his path to self and union with all. For this reason I hope in time, people will come forward, who have been healed by Eboga, to administer it without seeking payment – gifts being acceptable. The real payment belongs to the spiritual entities that help us and the person taking the eboga.

For this reason it is my fervent wish to shed light on the intensely spiritual nature of the Process, which is not a recreation but a spiritually guided process of personal transformation. My understanding has not been built on any religious framework and has been driven solely by my desire for wholeness and happiness, my quest for the Holy Grail. I have not investigated the religious nature of Eboga as practiced in Africa. I have simply explored the Process as it applied to me. In this way I hope to bring a fresh, new perspective to the spiritual use of eboga and ibogaine, leading to what I call "The Eboga Process towards Personal Transformation," i.e. the Eboga Process. I wish to expand the real meaning of the Process to open the door to those who seek its healing and spiritual powers and as yet are not aware they exist. Because of this I do not identify myself with the ibogaine community, as its aims and many of its ideas do not accord with my own. I identify with a different and what I see as an emerging agenda of real personal liberation and full self-actualization. I have no doubt that this is possible if the attitude and intention of the seeker are true. In this regard the Grail myth has a lot to teach us if we have ears to listen.

Thus, this book has not been written to promote ibogaine use as such. It just so happens that ibogaine is integral to the Process; but no one should be in the Process unless they really seek it out. Tourists are usually suffered, but most likely ignored, i.e., intention is the main engine for change in the Process – without it, change is unlikely. Clearly, under no circumstances should anyone undergo the Process who is not accompanied by a knowledgeable guide whose role it is to ensure the user's safety and comfort, nothing more, nothing less. If taken incorrectly, it can lead to death. If taken correctly, it can lead to a new destination in life in the same way a modern airplane takes many to new and unexplored places.

To say, as one critic has who warned against publication of my work, that ibogaine is an experimental medication used to treat drug addiction and that the author is advising its use for a purpose other than its originally intended use, is very misleading. Its actual use (in the form of the whole eboga plant, of which it is the main constituent) for more than 20,000 years among the Pygmies and the last 300 years among the Bwiti of West Central Africa, is for spiritual renewal and initiation. Its recent use in the past 30 years in the West has been simply an awareness of the fact that it could also cure drug addiction.

The same critic also says my book may encourage the recreational drug use of ibogaine. In light of what I have written, I take this criticism to be uninformed and thus reactionary. How can a substance that causes an elimination of the desire to take drugs encourage drug use itself? Have the scientists got something wrong? I am surprised this critic did not see the irony in this statement; or was this critic threatened by what my writings revealed?

For the record: I write this book as I am entitled to write about my experiences in any democratic society. I have the vote (for what its worth) and simply seek to share my experiences to add to the human body of knowledge. In no way, shape, or form do I seek to encourage the recreational use of ibogaine. In fact, the words "recreational" and "ibogaine" are polar opposites and anyone who carefully reads my experience will draw the same conclusion. It is an intense encounter with oneself and one's demons and not the kind of experience recreational drug users seek. Recreational drug users seek to avoid their past, not to face it. Ibogaine is of no "earthly" use to them in that pursuit. Ibogaine, with its inherent risks, has no place on anyone's list of recreational drugs. If someone decides to run out and take eboga or ibogaine I do not accept responsibility for the outcome. Information about ibogaine has long been available within the drug community. This is simply my story and my understanding. What anyone chooses to do is ultimately their responsibility. Laziness is not an excuse for being misinformed.

In this regard, however, it is accepted by many that ibogaine is relatively safe once the guidelines are followed. It is very powerful and thus, like anything powerful, if handled incorrectly, can be very dangerous, in fact lethal. Like all substances, there are specific conditions for its use. These conditions have been outlined on the principal Web site for drug addiction treatment, *www.ibogaine.org,* where a comprehensive manual is available, mostly designed for the treatment of drug addiction. There are also specific dose ranges and specific preconditions for its use. The most important of which is to be of sound heart and reasonably good health (good liver function), as the experience is physically demanding, i.e., not everyone is physically capable of taking it. It also causes a lowering of blood pressure. Ironically, from the spiritual viewpoint of its use, which my writings are mostly concerned with, the best results are also obtained with those of sound heart but in the emotional sense. Given that it is a totally internal experience, these guidelines are equally valid for spiritual use as they simply seek to ensure the safety of the user.

In time, I hope to record my growing understanding of the subject of eboga, spirituality and healing, for which I have created the trademark "The Eboga Process"™ to protect its integrity, into its own book. For now I have included a number of the principles of the Eboga Process in the latter part of this book and refer to "The Process" throughout. I have also included the corresponding safety information. However, conscious of the reactionary criticism I have received, I have decided at this stage to leave out my recommendations regarding actual dosage. In any case, this information simply seeks to enhance the understanding of the factors involved and should not to be considered as a do-it-yourself self-help guide. An experienced facilitator is highly recommended, if not vital.

As my healing has deepened, my eyes have opened and I intend to write about what I have learned on each stage of my journey toward wholeness, the stages of healing, my understanding of pain and finally the real possibility of everlasting joy and peace, the Holy Grail. You could say I have become an investigative healing journalist who has actually experienced real, deep and tangible healing, much like a journalist recounts the effects and stages of war and peace, having been there.

You may ask yourself why I did not undergo this process many years earlier. The answer is two-fold. Firstly, I did not know about it. Secondly, I have always had a fear of mind-altering substances and chemicals in my body. I rarely take pharmaceuticals. I see such things as poison to the body. I never take aspirin. I see cigarettes as the devil's own invention. I also have a keen interest in fitness and well-being. But I guess the real reason is that I had my path to follow and, if I was not aware of it, my soul was. I would not know what I now know had I not needed to take eboga in order to save my own life. If what I now know saves the lives of others, then what I went through will have been worth it.

The Process will draw interest from genuine spiritual seekers and from the countless millions suffering from trauma and pain. If handled correctly and in the right frame of mind, it can go all the way to advancing one's spirituality (grounded in one's sexuality) and lead to a complete remission of psychological trauma.

We are on the edge of a great shift of consciousness. The Eboga Process is but one way. There are others. The end point of such a journey is a mending of the split between our nature and our spirit, the return of the divine feminine, which is the quest for the Holy Grail.

Lee Albert M.Sc.

Corpus Christi 2004
www.myeboga.com

Preface

Once we begin, as each day passes,
The old wall of resistance crumbles,
Believing not what is past but what is yet to become.

This book has evolved out of the persistent efforts I have made to heal myself, driven by a vision of one day realizing my dreams. I write from my own experience and accept that there are those whose experience is different. However, although I am Irish, I believe the essence of my story is a universal one and I hope that through it others, like me, will make the same journey from the emotional wilderness to the emotional highlands. This book points to a new way to do this, one of many, which the universe in its wisdom has given us.

I believe, in order to understand the Irish psyche (and thus better understand my story) one of the essential keys is sexuality. In this regard I am inclined to equate sexuality with self-knowledge. Full sexuality brings awareness, clarity and knowledge and thus with its onset the turmoil of adolescence, i.e., that which we sought to ignore can no longer be ignored. Sexuality is also, I believe, the basis of relationship. So if sexuality is suppressed we suppress knowledge and relationship and produce a frightened and confused individual, unable to relate properly to life and to others. We also repress a potent source of healing power quite often leading to deep depression and psychosomatic illness, not to mention the self hatred and disgust that accompanies the repression of unmet desire. By embracing our sexuality we embrace life.

Thus, one of the reasons why, as a child, I lived in a state of confusion – I grew up in a sexually ignorant society. It was only after many years of conventional healing methods and in desperation, that I "stumbled" into the world of Eboga, an African spirituality. It opened the door to the healing "Eboga Realm" and brought me into "The Eboga Process." In my opinion it is the most powerful process for personal inner transformation known to man today. Through it I achieved clarity of mind based on a realization of my personal history and its effect on my mental processes, resulting from a catharsis of my innermost self. But perhaps more importantly, through Eboga, I achieved a liberation in the area of personal relationships reflected in a deeper connection to my own sexuality. Also, it guided me to an inner peace that results from a perspective that goes beyond the purely material and connects me to the universe and its untapped potential – a potential the animal orientated mind is unable to grasp. Thus, through my healing process, I have learned much about man and his "spiritual" and "physical" evolution and have had my mind opened on a level I never imagined nor expected.

In reading my story you will see how, having started out as a precocious happy child, one day without knowing why, my ability to restore my ebullient nature died. In its place arrived the hidden wasteland of Irish culture and Irish history. A wasteland handed down through generations, resulting from the years of abuse Ireland had suffered in one form or another, suffering which it then inflicted upon itself, was then successfully passed onto me. I became withdrawn and confused. I was unable to stop it taking hold. However, I knew how it tasted to be whole and I loved it dearly. All my childhood dreams remained intact. I resolved to restore myself; to somehow find the key to unleash the waters within once more. But first I had to rely on an almost non-existent ego in order to survive and function, as the other (the child, the soul) was pained and dysfunctional. And as my ego grew so too did the pain of separation I felt from my true self, my soul, the child. As a means of surviving and learning, the ego served its purpose. However once the other (the soul) was ready to be restored, my entrenched and strengthened ego had to be usurped from its seat of power. My story explains how I did that, or should I say how it was done to me, in a manner I can only properly describe as a full blown African exorcism.

My story also entails the dying influence of the Irish Catholic Church and the emergence of modern affluent Ireland. While I may appear critical of both, perhaps I am not critical enough? Power comes with responsibility, whether it is the power of the Church in a poverty stricken Ireland or the power of the government and groups of individuals in a modern affluent Ireland. The wealth of modern Ireland is a "wonderful" thing for the material freedom it brings, as is all wealth, but it becomes a curse when it is used to hide the problems of the old and ignore the responsibilities of the new. Make no mistake, I would never wish to return to the poverty of the past – it was not a pretty sight and it was the source of much abuse. However, materialism can never be a substitute for spirituality. It can however be enjoyed within spirituality. In attempting to replace spirituality by materialism many in modern Ireland are masking their hidden pain. Their mentality is also feeding into our influence on world affairs, with negative consequences. We live in an ever inter-connecting planet which, without proper governance along with escalating abuses of power, is on a collision course towards environmental disaster and a third world war. Should one tip-toe around the issues given that today it is possible to carry a nuclear device in a suitcase?

When I started this book three years ago I did not imagine that I would write anything like this. There were times when I had to stop and deal with what emerged. In fact, I stopped writing for almost a year, as I was not convinced of what I was writing and if I was not going anywhere myself I saw no point in bringing anyone else along. In the end though I recovered my faith. I then rediscovered my way and better understood the Process I was going through. This book has thus been an integral part of my healing journey, driven by a vision of something very beautiful born out of a deep faith. It comes from the crucible of my very soul. In the end it was the dream that brought me through and a burning love in my soul.

Through trial and error I have learned and continue to learn, the way of the Eboga Process. In so doing I have poured its healing waters over my opened wounds. I succeeded in my quest simply because I tried with all my heart to succeed. I can only describe my great good fortune as nothing short of "Amazing Grace". In my writings I describe this Process and the optimum conditions under which it works. Many fail because they reject out-of-hand the spiritual dimension of healing, a rejection, if you like, of soul. They do this in the same way as they reject the dreams of their true heart. However, I did not pursue healing with a spiritual agenda. In the end, though, I could not avoid it, as pain and soul are intrinsically intertwined. Pain reaches down into the very fabric of our being, our soul, as a form of possession. Is it any wonder then that healing and spirituality are intertwined?

In his book *The Alchemist,* the author Paulo Coelho asserts that, when you really want something, the entire universe conspires to help you achieve it. The only thing that you need to do is be aware of the omens and follow your heart. Coelho singles out four reasons why we do not follow our personal dreams or "Bliss", as labeled by the distinguished mythologist Joseph Campbell. Firstly, prejudice built since childhood in every one of us about what is possible and what is impossible, perhaps also a sense that we do not deserve our dreams. Secondly, fear of hurting those we love, because following our personal dreams might require abandoning them. Thirdly, fear of defeat on the path and, finally, the abandoning of courage at the last moment after a long journey. Perhaps these reasons can be put into one: namely, the pain of the unhealed state that following our dreams uncovers. In other words in order to keep an open heart and access the knowledge and wisdom that it gives us, we must allow ourselves to feel the pain that is evoked until we are healed, otherwise we resort to the protective mechanisms of the ego which cut us off from life and the soul.

In my own struggle for freedom I have spent a lifetime battling with the voices of my childhood instilled in me by a system that was threatened by anything outside itself. I also, at one point, was afraid of what effect my dreams would have on those I loved, afraid to excel too fast for fear of losing them. Needless to say I was also afraid of defeat, but deep down I truly believed I had something great to achieve that would fulfill me and lift me up. I did reach a point towards the end where I lost all hope, but my faith in life and the realization that I had no other choice made me pick myself back up again. Ultimately, personal death was never really an option, even if, for a time, I prayed for it. The choice was simple, really: either I go up or I go down. I chose not to go down.

I have chosen the Holy Grail myth as created by Wolfram Von Eschenbach in the late 12th century or thereabouts in order to illustrate my story as it is entirely appropriate to this book. Without it I feel that not everyone would appreciate what I was trying to say and would simply imagine it was all just a matter of taking a pill; which couldn't be further from the truth. The use of myth also helps to invoke the spiritual dimensions of the healing process which inevitably my book encompasses. In order to get that message across I needed something of the order of a myth. The Grail Quest in particular describes the state of mind necessary for someone to succeed in their desire for wholeness and the consequent happiness which ensues. It is a state of mind fundamental to the Process I describe in this book.

In reading the interpretations of this myth I was delighted to see that the universal truth of a medieval myth, written about the quest for wholeness, is equally applicable to a Process born from an age-old African tradition, as employed by a modern man struggling with the problems of everyday modern life. But that is not surprising really, as truth is universal, no more so than in myth, whether it comes from Africa, Europe, Asia or wherever. Just like archetypes, it is shared in common by all man. So in realizing that the myth of the Holy Grail described my experiences and my ideas, I concluded that the myth was actually a living myth. One that I was in. Furthermore I had reason to believe that, on a spiritual level, one does actually drink from the Grail Cup and the Waters of Life it carries leading to a deeply profound experience of the divine feminine. Thus, without realizing it, my whole journey from an early age has been designed to drink once more from this cup and, in so doing to know that I have overcome and healed my wounds, as many as a thousand perhaps. We, all of us, have our wounds to heal and I hope in my writing you will be able to identify with some of mine and draw strength from the fact that I did succeed. By "succeed" I mean the complete clearing of specific wounds (not all wounds, as all is not necessary – the other, i.e., the soul, plays its part) right down to the genetic code in my body. I did it because I loved life more than death and I loved my family, my friends and, in particular, one special person.

According to Joseph Campbell "Wolfram starts his epic, *The Holy Grail Quest*, with a short poem saying that every act has both good and evil results, every act in life yields pairs of opposites in its results. The best we can do is lean toward the light, i.e., intend the light. And what the light is, is that of the harmonious relationships that come from compassion with suffering, (i.e.,) understanding of the other person." To intend the light is exactly the state of mind required to succeed using the Eboga Process, i.e., intention to good. I would also add that, once we begin to see the pattern of a higher presence in our lives, we realize that it is action born from the intention to good that paves our way to personal fulfillment and happiness. Any adverse results of our actions, which we unwittingly cause, are part of a different process in the path of another's life. We, at times, are the unwitting helpers in a greater plan to try and bring all of humanity to perfection. Life is a tapestry that, at times, is not explicable.

Ultimately it is through our own intention that we are healed, not through the intention of another. All another can do is guide us to the door. The door only opens when we connect with the part of ourselves that holds the key, i.e., our compassion for self, which in turn becomes our intention to heal. Once we connect with this we begin to heal the split between our nature and our spirit, body and soul. This in turn allows the spirit (our soul) to help in healing our wounded nature (our ego and emotional body), as the soul has been empowered. This empowerment acts as a counter weight to the difficulties encountered in the natural healing process. A balance between our physical and our spiritual nature emerges. This leads to an awakening of consciousness – perhaps what Krisnamurti refers to as an awakening of intelligence. The compassion described in the myth is not enough. Yet it points the way, as compassion for oneself is one with intention to heal. The next step for me was the Process.

I hope the three books that form the trilogy of my story are of help to the many who right now seek answers to the more meaningful questions in life, depressed by the seeming lack of regard for such questions in the highest offices of our lands. We appear to live in a world of double-speak driven by economic and ideological necessity and not very much sincerity or integrity. In truth we are living in the wasteland of modern man's soul.

The Divine Feminine

Madonna of the Stairs.
C. 1490 Marble. Casa Buonarroti, Florence, Italy.

By Michelangelo.

1. The Goddess, Myth & Modern Man

Sometimes you have to find hell,
To know the way to heaven.

It is a very lonely existence if all you have is your ego and your body, in a world you cannot leave and a life you cannot keep. So we search for meaning and find it in the myths of old as they appeal to a part of us where we know we are not alone. All we have to do is to see, not with the eyes of the ego but with the warmth of the heart and through the heart right down back where we started, our most sacred child.

How sad it is that so many have abandoned their child. What has taken its place is little more than a mouthpiece that started to believe that it (the ego) was "it" (the soul) that it (the ego) was talking about. The poor child looks on in horror, his hands folded, his head in his hands. In truth the child is the soul and the soul is the center of who we are. If we want to live a truly "happy" life it has to be a "whole" life. The natural laws of the universe apply and, when we are natural, to know what to do comes naturally. Otherwise we reap what we sow, much like the law of Karma.

Joseph Campbell says that myth is the edge, the interface between what can be known and what is never to be discovered because it is transcendent of all human research. It comes from the source of life. One of the functions of myth is to show us how to live life under all circumstances, i.e., deal with the situation we are in or if you prefer, the path we are on. Myths are thus designed to bring us into a level of consciousness from which we know intuitively what is right action, i.e., the function of myth is not to show us our path in life but to understand our way through it. As in myth, when we decide inwardly to undertake our own quest to wholeness the opportunity presents itself. The adventure that manifests itself brings us to our interface. We leave behind the safe world we know and it is then that we encounter the dragons and eventually the wasteland of our inner world. This is a sign that we are near our goal. We would not have been called to this unless we had the strength and support to succeed. The darkest hour is just before the dawn.

There are many myths but probably the most famous are those of the quest for the Holy Grail, of which there are many. These myths grew out of a host of new ideas brought back from the Holy Lands by the Crusaders, who perceived the Saracens as having a culture which seemed much more wonderful, civilized and enticing than their own Christian culture, whose stifling grip they sought to pry off. Because of this stifling grip the religion of the goddess was retreating into the mists. The Grail myths were an attempt to salvage some of what was being lost. They are myths of loss and renewal, heroism and transformation and, in effect, were a reaction to the patriarchal Christian tradition that was so brutally imposing itself upon the world. This in part manifested in the burning of innocent people at the stake when their only crime was to use the wisdom of nature to heal others. It is still manifested in the constant uphill struggle women have to endure to receive basic human rights.

For many the Holy Grail is a metaphor for the divine feminine, the goddess and as such a cup does not exist. (However on a spiritual level I believe it does as a symbol of the divine feminine.) According to Dan Brown, in *The Da Vinci Code,* the Grail resembles a cup or vessel, which resembles the shape of a woman's womb. This in turn communicates femininity, womanhood and fertility, i.e., the sacred feminine, that which has been lost. Also, according to Dan Brown, the star Venus has always been associated with the divine feminine, the goddess, as it traces a perfect pentacle across the ecliptic sky every eight years. The pentacle is the symbol of the divine feminine.

In the patriarchal world, woman, the sacred giver of life, has become the enemy as the patriarchal mind is threatened by the divine feminine. The patriarchal mind is in effect a misogynist mind as it refuses to acknowledge the goddess and what she represents. This then translates into the subjugation of woman, the projection of that fear. In a world filled with the goddess, to be a misogynist is a perversion. In a world dominated by the patriarchal, it is a tendency. Those of us who accept the divine feminine are looked upon as "lacking" in some way. What is not understood is that the divine feminine brings with it creativity, depth, relationship, joy and a living sexuality. In the world, as in the individual, crisis is often needed to turn one's attention from an over-dependence and perversion of the patriarchal (as typified by the over-indulged ego) to an understanding of the divine feminine. Given the calamitous path present day events are taking one has to ask: is the world on the brink of a seismic shift in outlook? If so, is this part of the Age of Aquarius, the Age of awakening?

Many rebuke these ideas regarding the patriarchal nature of God based on the notion that God is everything, which of course is true. The problem is, once said, we quickly revert back to the patriarchal view of God as that is what we are conditioned to believe by a patriarchal society born from a patriarchal Church. This conditioning at a subtle level filters our experience of life and introduces many prejudices – not least our understanding of woman.

For me wholeness is about a deep emotional and spiritual connection to the divine feminine, the goddess, rooted in a relationship to the god, leading to inner peace centered on loving relationships. This is only possible once we acknowledge and hold onto that connection, in her name, which comes about by the removal of fear and the opening of the mind, the door to the universe. We need to restore what has been lost and unless we identify it and give it a name our ego cannot focus on it. I imagine for a lot of early Christians it was the same.

Like all myth we tend to dismiss the Holy Grail myth as something fanciful, as I once did. When I came to study the myth of *Parcival and the Holy Grail,* some 10 years ago in Australia, I must have turned off as I don't recall very much of what I learned. Perhaps I was so far from my goal I simply could not relate to it. The myth which stood out for me at that time was *The Hero's Journey,* as I felt I was on an adventure with no real end in sight, and I wondered if it shared similarities with that particular myth. I guess I thought of the Grail myth as simply too fanciful to be true. In that sense myth speaks to us when we are open to its message, i.e., it reflects back our situation to us. The hero's journey ultimately leads to the quest for the Holy Grail, which is the quest of the individual struggling toward wholeness or perhaps, as Jung calls it, Self-Individuation. We are all called to be heroes in our own way. Each journey is a step on the path to wholeness. The adventure we are ready for is the one which manifests in our lives, i.e., the landscape matches the condition of the hero. It is a manifestation of his character.

Within all of us lies the quest for the Grail. The search for the Grail leads to eternal life and love. It is the search for the meaning of self, all that we are, all that we were and all that we are to become. The Grail can only be found by those who seek it with a pure heart, which in turn leads to love and compassion, as that is the natural state and it is in the natural state that we become worthy of the wholeness of life. When we succeed in our quest, we arrive at a state where the split between our nature and our spirit within is healed, thus arriving at our whole and natural self. It is in this state that we drink from the Grail Cup, i.e., access the divine feminine within, as it is only in this state that we can properly access its meaning. It is then that we properly understand the bible teaching, "I tell you the truth, anyone who will not receive the kingdom of God like a little child will never enter it." Luke 18:17. The Grail quest is therefore one of the gradual mending of the split between our nature and our spirit.

The Grail myths emerged at a time when the ideals of romantic love (which preceded the Grail myths) were being developed in the courts of Europe during the 12th century. With the arrival of romantic love, "The courage to love," according to Bill Moyers, "became the courage to affirm against tradition whatever knowledge stands affirmed in one's own experience," i.e., the validity of the individual's experience of what humanity is, what life is and what values are. In other words, the individual must have faith in his own experience instead of following the monolithic tradition, simply repeating what has come from another's mouth. This is what defined the Western world's accent on the individual and is probably the greatest and most important hallmark of Western culture today. Prior to the emergence of romantic love, marriage had been based on arrangement and it was this union the Church blessed. Any other union was considered akin to adultery.

At this time the forerunner of romantic love was known as courtly love. Courtly love idealized "a spiritual" relationship between a man and a woman whereby the knight and the lady were never involved sexually. It was a means of lifting themselves up spiritually. It was a place where one was vulnerable, a place where the soul could break through the ego's armor and go beyond the ego to experience the ecstatic, the divine. We thus see courtly love as a love that is greater than pain, greater even than death. The most famous courtly romantic myth is that of Tristan and Iseult.

However, it was through Wolfram Von Eschenbach's myth of *Parcival and the Holy Grail* that the ideal of courtly romantic love was transformed. As Wolfgang Spiewok states (Ingrid H. Shafer, *The Holy Grail*), "Wolfram transforms courtly romantic love into genuine, conjugal love: the foundation and fulfillment of marriage" whereby "God is not encountered through denial of the world and asceticism but rather through meaningful social relationships in the world." That is why this myth became so widely accepted. Thus, while courtly love was the major turning point in modern man's journey to self, away from religious persecution of the individual in this period of history, the Grail was the confirmation and completion of that journey.

To my mind the Grail myth represents the real maturity of modern man. It was a brave step forward to recognize the fullness of a person at a time when nature and sexuality were divided by the Church almost by pain of Hell. In courtly love we still see man castrated from his nature. Courtly love expressed the highest form of love between a man and woman possible in the absence of a conjugal relationship. It channeled the sexual impulse onto a purely spiritual plane which is to some extent, unwittingly, what the emasculated Roman Church sought to do. But that is a form of spiritual practice (as is everything) and is most definitely not for everyone. In any case, sexuality is not simply about the sexual act. It is primarily about the sexual force and the spirit it channels which leads to the full psycho-spiritual maturation of the individual. Its presence leads to a deeper connection to life and the hidden knowledge this brings, which is necessary to make us whole. Celibacy is a choice. Sexuality is not.

Sexuality between partners often opens the Pandora's box of relationship. This is not a vindication of the orthodox Christian view, though perhaps not admitted, that sexuality is intrinsically evil. It is a sign that we are not whole in our nature and, consequently, we are unable to be comfortable in our sexuality or its expression. Once our broken nature is confronted by our sexuality it buckles under the strain of its blinding light as full sexuality requires a whole nature to enable it to emerge without trauma. Initial sexual attraction between a couple is often driven by the animal instinct and thus encounters few problems in its expression. However subsequent encounters require an awareness and openness that goes beyond instinct and requires a wholesome nature, i.e., an ability to relate as a whole person to the right person. Thus sexuality in its proper manifestation exposes our weaknesses as it is the finest expression of who we are. How can the spark of life be evil? It's the most beautiful sharing a couple can have. Sexual abuse is certainly evil and it is probably this and the Church's inability to relate properly to sexuality that has left it fearful and reactionary towards it – which is not surprising as it worked to wipe out the cult of the goddess from which it sprang. In turn it has demonized sexuality, thereby perverting the individual from reaching full physical and spiritual maturation, leaving in its wake a torrent of confused feelings and insecurities. You could say the Church shot itself in the foot. Its own fears a testament to its failure.

None of which is to say that man is driven solely by his "nature." He also has a spirit; but he is not driven solely by this either. One is working with the other. The body needs nourishment and nurturing and, in turn, the soul receives the warmth it needs to function properly. Unfortunately what some take as a natural impulse is in fact an impulse born out of a broken nature. So the question is how do we know when our nature is not broken and our impulses are pure? Perhaps the answer is this: when our nature is in "perfect harmony" with our spirit we are perfectly natural. Perfected nature is, I believe, an intelligent and compassionate being which acts when its spiritual equilibrium is in balance, i.e., when one acts in a state of wholeness all action is natural and we see a harmony of body and soul. The journey of man to wholeness is one of the development of harmony between his soul and his nature. For myself this is fostered by the removal of underlying pain, fear, trauma and neurosis as these block the relationship between the two, in other words via the Process I describe in this book.

The Grail myth that thus emerged from the courtly romantic legends was a search for the union of what had been divided, nature and spirit, the peace that comes from their joining. The loss of the Grail and the water it contains, symbolizes the loss of magic and mystery in our world, the loss of the divine feminine, the loss of a potent means of healing and renewal. The element water has long been associated with the soul and the unconscious, as well as sexuality and the emotions. This implies that sexuality and self-actualization are interconnected. The recovery of the Grail thus symbolizes a return of the divine feminine and is the reward of an authentic life lived in terms of its own volition.

Thus, we see, embedded within a 13th century myth, ageless wisdom for those who seek their way to wholeness and the happiness which ensues. Why is it that I need to repeat these ideas in the 21st century? The answer of course is that modern science lives in the wasteland of modern man and what is obvious to natural man is a mystery to modern man. Perhaps the Grail was a myth in the 13th century but, with the help of the Process I describe in this book, it is a reality in the 21st.

2. The Grail Myth

When you realize you can no longer live in the darkness,
It is then that the light appears.

In the most famous and widely accepted version of the Grail myth as created by Wolfram Von Eschenbach in the thirteenth century, *Parcival & The Holy Grail,* the Grail is presented as that which is attained and realized by people who have lived their lives by their own volition, i.e., by the use of their own will in making their own life decisions.

The gods speak in symbols and what better way to speak than through a myth that was clearly divinely inspired. It is a myth that grows in significance with time. It is a myth that contains, I believe, a living truth, one which is attainable but is somewhat hidden. It is a phenomenal piece of work, written in medieval times by someone who apparently could not write but had it transcribed. It is also entirely appropriate to this book both literally and figuratively. It draws many of its motifs from Pre-Christian Irish Celtic legend – see Ingrid H. Shafer, *The Holy Grail.*

When I began to write this book I had not considered the Grail myth. Then I began to have certain experiences and fancied I might somehow refer to it. On more than one occasion, a sacred cup was presented to me during my spiritual encounters in the Eboga realm. These occasions I detail in the subsequent books of this trilogy. I therefore decided to take a closer look at the Grail myth and as I did, I began to realize, little by little, that I understood it and that it reflected back to me the situation I was in. In other words, I was living the myth. I began to realize that the Grail Parcival had drunk from and which I had once dismissed as fantasy, was in reality a spiritual Grail, not a physical one. It served the purpose of replenishing the soul which in turn replenishes the body. I realized that this could only come about after a great deal of self encounter, after passing through the wasteland of one's life, a wasteland I was passing through myself. I realized that once the questions had been asked and the healing applied, the Grail Cup containing the Waters of Life appears. It is as if it somehow adds a seal to the soul of the one who drinks from it. It also symbolizes the return or the arrival of the divine feminine into the life of the individual. This leads to the union of what was divided, nature and spirit. Hence, as the individual heals, the Grail's appearance increases in frequency marking the progress of the individual. The individual begins to feel, more and more, the life force flowing in his or her being. It was this and the experiences I was having, that drew me to the myth. It made me realize my journey to restore my inner font of well-being, a journey started in early childhood, was nearing completion. We all have our own journey to make.

The stories regarding the Grail myths originated in Ireland among the Celts, with their ancient and magical myths of renewal and regeneration. The Celts laid down guidelines as to how kings should behave, outlining their responsibility for the health or sickness of their kingdoms. They elected their kings, who ultimately were there to serve the people and the land. Sovereignty was seen by the Celts as an immortal goddess. If the relationship between man and this immortal goddess was bad, a wasteland would result. In Celtic mythology a ruler was connected through his or her body to the body of the land. That is the meaning of mystical sovereignty, the connection of our physical being with all life on Earth.

In the Grail myth we see that Parcival (meaning: "naïve fool") spent most of his life in the forest along with his mother who is in hiding. He is completely ignorant of the outside world. One day five knights in shining armor ride through the forest where he lives. He is so amazed and overwhelmed by their appearance that he determines there and then to become a knight. When asked, after leaving the forest, what his name is, he replies, "Good son, dear son," as that is what his mother had called him. He did not know his own name and only later, when he was recognized as the son of a king who lost his lands in a battle to save them, did he receive it. His first arrival at Arthur's court was in fool's garb, as his mother did not want him to be accepted and hoped he would return to her. He was blissfully unaware of his condition, as he was a simple and natural man and, thus, a natural healer. Yet his beauty and bravery endeared him to the court of Arthur where he found refuge and became a knight.

It was around this time that the knights of Arthur's court expressed a desire for an adventure (a personal growth experience). Then, much to their surprise, a vision of a floating, veiled chalice appeared. Before each of them there appeared food and drink that they liked. Each saw the chalice differently. The hall filled with music and flowery perfume and their hearts overflowed with a feeling of love and unity for each other and all of Creation. The chalice in this vision was thus a symbol of the divine feminine which nourished every body in the way they loved best, blessing each one with their own vision of beauty and love. The court of Arthur there and then determined to find this chalice, the Grail.

It is said that the first taste from the Grail is free and that it causes the heart to leap with joy and the mind to be filled with untold possibilities. It gives us a taste of what could be and creates a hunger that reveals our illusion of complacent satisfaction. Without the first taste we would not have a vision of the quest and so it has to come at a time when we are ready to begin. It is part of the initiation. The second taste is another matter and comes with a price. For this we must enter into an unknown world in search of a dream of wholeness we have learned to live without. It exposes our wasteland and we must ask the question: what ails thee? We must learn compassion for one's self. To drink once more from the cup means we must change our old ways of being, as they keep us in the wasteland of dissatisfaction and, quite probably, pain.

Thus with their first taste the knights of Arthur's court, along with Parcival, rode forth in search of the Grail. Each entered the forest at a different place, a place where there was no path. Each had a unique quest to make, one that had not been taken before. Each in their own way was following their bliss, their own call to fulfillment. Each one of us, in our search for the wellspring of joy that brought us first to spiritual awakening, our first taste, is following the same knightly quest.

At the time of their departure the Grail King, also known as the Fisher King, lay wounded in his castle. Because the Grail King was one with the land, the land and all in it were sickened as well. Legend had it that the king and his kingdom could only be healed by a brave and worthy knight who asked the right question: "What ails thee?" So the king and his kingdom waited for the arrival of such a knight.

We are told that this likeable but foolish and unsuitable Grail King, as a young man, rode forth one day from his palace with the war cry "amor" on his lips. As he rode forth a Mohammedan warrior came out of the woods and, on seeing one another, they attacked with their lances. The lance of the Grail King killed the Mohammedan but the lance of the Mohammedan castrated the Grail King leading to a wounded and impotent sexuality.

The Mohammedan in this myth is considered a person of nature, a pagan and on the head of his lance is written the word "Grail." This implies that the pagan or nature chooses the Grail as its motif, its "intention." Thus we see that spiritual life (the Grail motif) is the bouquet of natural life and not a supernatural being imposed upon it. The impulses of nature give authenticity to life, not obeying the rules that come from a supernatural authority. We therefore see in this act of the foolish, young Grail King the Christian separation of matter and spirit. In other words, the separation of the dynamism of life from the spiritual. The ailing Grail King embodies the Christian predicament whereby nature is castrated from its proper expression and thus nature is oppressed. Life has been emasculated by this. The true wholeness that would have come from nature and spirit in harmony has been killed by the belief that nature and spirit are separate. The fact that the Mohammedan is killed probably reflects the slaughter of "pagans" by the Christian Church and the resultant castration of the Christian psyche.

In his quest Parcival comes to a castle in the middle of a desolate wasteland where no crops grow and darkness has descended on the hearts of the people. There is a sickness on the land. He enters the castle and is brought to the room of the ailing king. He does not realize the king is also the keeper of the Grail. His impulse is to ask him out of compassion: what ails thee? This one spontaneous act of compassion is all that is required to heal the wound and, therefore, the land. Parcival is a natural healer and, although this question comes to his heart, he is afraid to express it as he has been studying the ways of the knights and feels that this is not something a knight would ask. Tired, he eats and then goes to sleep. When he wakes up, the castle and the Grail King have disappeared. He therefore, without realizing it, has failed the first time in his quest.

We learn from this that the way to wholeness or the Grail requires that we ask the questions that begin to heal us and, in so doing, we are brought into the healing waters of life. Here, we are shown our wounds in order to have them washed and healed. We have to ask in order to learn, to understand and to acknowledge who we truly are, devoid of all pretension: our most sacred child. That is the point of the journey: to ask the right question, i.e., to be prepared to look four square at what ails us. It is then that we receive the right answers and resolve our ailments and thus grow spiritually from our experiences. Our controlling ego is diminished allowing us once more to reconnect to our simple uncomplicated self, the natural child within, our soul, empowered by what we have learned. "Ask and it will be given to you; seek and you will find; knock and the door will be opened to you. For everyone who asks receives; he who seeks finds; and to him who knocks, the door will be opened. Which of you, if his son asks for bread, will give him a stone?" Matthew 7:7-9. Eboga is the bread that empowers us to face what ails us.

For Parcival it is a further five years of searching and challenge before he has a second chance. The memory of his wife and his deep love for her sustains him in these wanderings. By now he has learned wisdom so that he can judge for himself what is knightly and thus, this time, he asks the question that comes spontaneously from his love and compassion, i.e., he is not blocked in his nature by his own unresolved issues or lack of self-worth. This heals the king's wound and returns the wasteland to bloom. He then discovers that the wounded Grail King is also the guardian of the Grail. He informs Parcival that he is, in fact, his grandfather and places the Grail, the castle and the kingdom within the care of Parcival, the new Grail King. Parcival then becomes the new guardian, able to offer the Grail's blessings to other seekers.

The myth therefore tells us that in looking at what ails us we heal ourselves and in doing so we also help others to heal. When we undergo deep healing we inevitably learn much about ourselves and the suffering of all man. The healed state by default brings with it greater compassion for oneself and for others, i.e., we naturally show the way. We learn to become Grail guardians and help others to come to that place of compassion for their wounds also.

The way to the Grail is not a simple affair and requires taking a journey into our own wasteland. It is a long and arduous journey but it is doable. However, as we heal and transform, we are shown visions of the unveiled Grail, the divine feminine, who nourishes each of us in the way we love best, blessing us with visions of beauty and love. We sip from the Grail Cup. These visions and gradual transformations sustain and strengthen us to complete our quest. For many, like me, these visions encompass visions of romantic love, the beauty of what is yet to be once the cup's contents have been sufficiently tasted and the true power of relationship restored. The gradual healing during the quest empowers us to reach down to our deepest wounds, to confront them and finally to heal our broken nature. The world in turn is renewed by this mending of the split within.

In the right hands and with the right mind, a mind we can learn from the example of Parcival, one can and does ultimately drink from the Grail Cup. However, the effect of drinking from the Grail Cup is not instantaneous. In the same way as a wasteland recovers with time, the split between our nature and our spirit also mends with time. It is as though the cable between our nature and our spirit is reconnected, restoring what was lost. It is a process of rediscovery. Much like a child first discovers life, at times stumbling, but eventually becoming a coordinated whole. There is a movement towards one's center, where one acts knowingly, naturally. In this new state one is a part of life, not apart from it. The divine feminine flows within.

It is intention that helps us to look at what ails us, but it is with the help of a higher force that the healing waters are poured over our opened wounds, as we require great strength to confront them so that they may be healed. The higher force I found is the subject of this book. It works through what I call the Eboga Process. Without it I could not have found the Grail.

Each one of us is the wounded Grail King. Once we begin to face what ails us, it is then that we see our first vision of the Grail Cup.

Subsequent visions come at a price. However, they act to sustain us in our quest until ultimately we "drink" from the cup and our inner wasteland is restored to bloom. To turn away from the quest after an initial taste of perfection is to live in a state of perpetual dissatisfaction. The first taste of the Grail brings initiation. It is the subsequent tastes that bring transformation.

3. The Island of Destiny

He who forgets his past is doomed to repeat it.

A person is at the very least the sum of his or her parts. Even at that, we are neither one thing nor the other. One needs to understand the other. That is the human condition. Hence, in order to understand my story, we need to go back and explain some of the influences that made me who I am, as I see them. I do not claim historical accuracy but I doubt if many Irish men or women would be able to tell you the date St. Patrick arrived in Ireland, either. What they will tell you is how much Ireland suffered under Britain and how it is still reaping the bitter fruits of its harvest.

So what defines an Irishman? Well, when I first left Ireland and traveled overseas I was accused of not loving Ireland, as I was taking on the strange ways of foreigners. At times I thought that maybe someone might hit me. I find it a strange irony that here I am now writing about Ireland. Education is about change and inevitably I have changed. Remaining a frightened, subdued and emasculated individual is not what being Irish is about, even if there are some who would prefer it that way.

So what does it mean to be Irish? I like to think it has to do with an attachment to the Earth and the generations that have gone before us. However, being Irish is a troubled state, as there is so much pain in our history. Therefore, to recall the generations is to recall the history also. But this we must do if we are to remain faithful to our fathers. They still live, if only on a different level. There is a Book of Life being kept and it contains all the details of past actions. Everybody in the end will have to face theirs – peacefully. In this way the suffering of humanity will not have been in vain.

The Celts were not the first to come to Ireland. Apparently the first colony of Irish people was led by a man called Parthalon.

He and his followers died of a plague. Then another group, called the Nemedians, arrived. They left but their descendents returned and were known as the Fir Bolg or Bagmen, as it is believed they had been forced to carry leather bags filled with earth in a foreign country where they had been in captivity. It was into this the Tuatha De Danann arrived prior to the arrival of the Celts. Thus, we see that before the Celts, Ireland was inhabited by other groups, smaller in stature, who had landed there and made their homes along the coastline, afraid to enter the interior which was populated by wild animals.

In the days when I was growing up every child in Ireland knew of the fairies and the little people. They were spirits that wafted their way through our psyches, giving us a sense of benign comfort and protection. According to legend the Tuatha De Danann, who arrived in Ireland before the Celts and who believed in magic, were defeated in battle and were only allowed to stay if they remained underground. They then became known as the Celtic fairies. It is said the Tuatha De Danann were the last generation of gods and goddesses to rule Ireland and that they possessed magical abilities and great skills in the arts. Legend has it that they were given the island of Tir Na nÓg, the land of the Ever-Young, by the goddess Danu, who protects them with her powerful magic. It is also said that Tir Na nÓg is a land of eternal springtime where all is peace and happiness. It lies to the west of Ireland and is only seen by humans through a sea-chill mist. It is only by the will of the fairy folk that a human can enter there. The fairy folk themselves spend their time making love, having feasts, hunting and playing. Sometimes they step outside their kingdom to bring back a human to strengthen their bloodlines.

As a child I believed the fairies and the little people lived in the forests and one had to be careful not to desecrate a fairy ring, which could be found from time to time in the countryside. There was magic in the country I roamed as a boy. It had nothing to do with the Church. It was like a secret we kept to ourselves. In fact, the only thing I learned about priests was that they were a step away from God. In time, of course, we learned about Jesus and Mary and, from what we were told, they lived in the little box on top of the altar which was a place of shining light, filled with sanctity and goodness.

Then they built a new church in my parish, even though the old one was well loved and afterwards they used the old church for bingo. Now it is used to sell furniture. I wondered how that could be done. What about all the prayers and devotions and all the light that had shone there? Clearly, they knew something I did not know. That was my only answer to the conundrum of how being one step from God allowed you to use this old, lovely building, where so many of our forefathers had worshipped, in such a careless manner. The truth is they were protected by the authority of the Catholic Church and the Catholic Church, unlike the Celtic Church, was more interested in pen and paper than it was in hearts and minds.

The Celts arrived to what was then called "The Island of Destiny" from Central Europe around 300-400 BC, apparently drawn by the stories of gold and the sight of Irish gold ornaments. The Celts also settled in other parts of Europe, including Great Britain. They were big, fair-haired people who believed in gods whose images they saw in the foam of the sea, in the sun and in the lightning. In those days gold came down in abundance from the streams of the Wicklow Mountains and was traded to buy tin. Tin was needed to mix with copper, which was plentiful, to make bronze. Apparently, no other country in northern Europe has unearthed the quantity of ancient gold ornaments that Ireland has.

The Celts brought with them weapons of iron which were no match for the weapons of bronze and arrows of stone they encountered among the older peoples who were smaller and dark. There are many ancient burial places that still stand as a testament to these older peoples and their respect for the dead and their ancestors. The most common are called dolmens. A dolmen is a large stone that was placed on three or more upright stones to form a kind of rough table. It was a pagan custom to erect these above the graves of important persons. In those days and for some time to come, Ireland was called "The Island of Destiny." A name that aptly described a country filled with legend, much love for music, for friends, for family and for spiritual greatness. Yet that was not to last.

Through intermarriage there emerged on the island one people called the Gaels, or the Gaelic people. Ireland is thus a country of mixed race. History and legend spoke of the early Irish as one country, one people. I can only assume that the differences in the Gaelic language, as compared to the languages of other Celtic groups throughout Europe, were partly due to the influences of the groups who had preceded them, reflecting in part their integration even though the Celts had initially enslaved them. The Celts were a fighting people and intertribal wars were not uncommon. However, their redeeming features were their love for the arts and love of hospitality. Over the years the country was ruled by various kings. The most important being the High King situated at Tara. Nevertheless, it was to be many centuries before a High King existed without opposition, i.e., with the consent of all the kings. The kings of Ireland would meet to agree on laws and regulations which eventually gave rise to the Brehon Laws, "Brehon" being the Gaelic word for "judge."

Written history only began with the arrival of Patrick and the conversion of Ireland to Celtic Christianity. Hence, much of the stories of early Irish history are, in part, legend. Poems and stories were handed down by word of mouth. Out of these came the Ulidian tales, stories from the pagan period of Ireland that came from the Ulaidh of Ulster. This was the same period of Irish Celtic folklore that gave rise to many of the elements in the Holy Grail myth. It reveals how much at odds the Celtic Church must have been with the sanitized Roman Church, which viewed God as masculine, women as inferior and sex as deeply suspicious and dangerous.

In those days it was not unusual for Irish women to take part in war. During the pagan period the most famous was Queen Maeve, a tall woman with blue-grey eyes and a very fierce temper. Perhaps that explains in part why Ireland is, in some respects, a matriarchal society today. In any case, the most famous of the Ulidian tales tells of how two friends, Cuchulainn and Ferdia, were forced to do battle due to Maeve's desire to possess a bull located in Ulster, outside her domain. Cuchulainn's feats were legendary and, though they fought for five days, he was the more able of the two. It is said that at night Ferdia would send food and drink across the ford to Cuchulainn and Cuchulainn would send doctors across to him. Even in battle they remembered their friendship. It is a sad story, but one filled with honor and respect. We are told that the early group of Irish was given to quarrelling and fighting and in battle cut off the heads of their enemies. But the moral of this story is how they also admired courage, self-sacrifice and fair play.

During this early period of Irish history a group of men existed known as the Fianna, a paid force of fighting men renowned for their valor and great deeds. To become a Fianna one had to – among other things – be able to stand in a hole in the ground up to the chin and defend oneself against nine men throwing spears. On the other hand, a knowledge of 12 books of poetry was required, as well as the knowledge of how to make a poem. Their motto was: "Truth in our hearts, strength in our arms and faith in our tongues." As a child I felt somewhat inadequate listening to these stories as they were sometimes taught to emphasize how lacking one was in manhood. They were also scary, as one could not imagine passing their tests. On the other hand they sometimes inspired a sense of bravado and a fantasy of being a great warrior. One thing they did instill, though, was a strong sense of a code of honor and at least this one could try to uphold. If one didn't, a great sense of personal shame would follow. It's quite amazing how such stories influence young children. The Fianna continued to exist until 284, when they were disbanded, as they had become unruly and were in some ways a threat. One of the legends to emerge from the Fianna is that of Oisin, a member of the Fianna who fell in love with Niamh of the Golden Hair, one of the Tuatha De Danann, and went to live with her in Tir Na nÓg. After 300 years Oisin wished to return to see his family. Time had passed so quickly he did not realize they would all be dead. He was warned not to touch the soil, as he would age immediately. On his return to Tir Na nÓg he bent down from his horse to help some farmers move a large stone. He slipped and fell to the ground where he began to age. He never returned to Tir Na nÓg and it is said that St. Patrick looked after him. He refused however to take on the new Christian beliefs, preferring to remain with the old ways.

Into this world stepped Patrick, a slave boy who had been captured on one of many raids made by the Irish against what was by then a weakening Roman Empire. By the middle of the fifth century the Romans had left Britain. Patrick was born around 389 in the western part of the Roman province of Britain and was 16 when he arrived in Ireland. He was a Celtic Christian, as the Celtic Church was well-established in Britain at this time. The Celtic Church was considered orthodox by the Romans and was well-organized. They conducted their services in Latin and their hierarchy consisted of bishops, priests and other ministers. They differed from what was later to become Roman Catholicism. For instance, they took bread and wine in remembrance of Jesus and saw it as a symbol, not as a miracle. Hence, the laity also received wine. Also, marriage was common among the clergy. At the same time there were monasteries with monks sworn to poverty, chastity and obedience. Many of the pagan festivals were incorporated into the Celtic Church, allowing a smoother acceptance among the Celtic people.

After Patrick's arrival as a slave boy, he worked as a sheep- and cow-handler for his Irish owners. He writes that after six years he heard a voice say to him in his sleep, "You will soon return to your fatherland." A few nights later another voice said, "Your ship is ready." He left, walking 200 miles to the coast, where he managed to obtain passage home. Soon after returning, he writes that in a vision he heard the voices of the people of "The Island of Destiny" begging him to return. Thereafter he adopted as his mission in life the conversion of the Gaelic people to Christianity. He studied for the priesthood and returned as a bishop with a small party of priests and laymen in 432. There were already some Christians in Ireland at this time from an earlier Roman mission that was short and unspectacular and had fizzled out. Thus, Patrick founded the Celtic Church in Ireland.

It is written that Patrick so impressed the High King that he was allowed to preach the gospel among the people. It is said the High King also took his advice from time to time. The High King remained pagan but other kings, with his blessing, converted. According to tradition Patrick used the shamrock to explain the meaning of the three persons in the one God: Father, Son and Holy Spirit. He focused a great deal of his attention on the powerful in order to expedite the conversion of the masses. By all accounts, Patrick seems to have been a likeable character and not the fastidious Catholic I thought he was when I was a child. The Druids were the spiritual leaders at this time. Many of them converted to Christianity and became priests. At Christ Church Cathedral in Dublin, I believe it is possible to draw a line of continuity between the present-day clergy of the Cathedral (not Roman Catholic) right back to the Celtic Church and their predecessors, the Druids, at this same site of worship. Now that is what I call a Church.

Patrick died in 461 after 30 years of missionary work in which he founded more than 300 churches, consecrated many bishops and ordained many priests. Slavery was being practiced in Ireland when he arrived. He himself had been one and it is thought he had a benign influence on the laws of a country that, at times, treated people brutally. Slavery was not part of the message of Christianity. Schools and organs of government had existed for centuries in Ireland, but with the advent of Christianity, the history and tradition of the people was written down and more schools were founded. The only form of writing preserved from pagan times is a system of lettering on wood and stone called "Ogham" which would not have been suitable for books.

By the time of Patrick's death, we are told, most of the Irish had converted to Christianity except some druids, nobles and kings including the High King and possibly two of his successors. A period of great religious fervor ensued where the Irish were no longer known as Fierce Scots (an earlier name for the Irish) who had plundered and ravaged the shores of Britain and Gaul (France). Instead they became known as "The Land of Saints and Scholars." The national spirit now showed itself in works of piety and in the arts of peace. The men and women responsible for this were sometimes called the "Three Orders of Saints." The first lived in the time of Patrick, or soon after him and completed his work of conversion. The second and most numerous were those who, from the sixth century onwards, founded schools and monasteries. The third were the hermits who retired to lonely cliffs and islands for a life of hardship, prayer and contemplation. St. Brigid was of the first order and was born in 453 A.D. From her came the rural tradition of making St. Brigid's Crosses with reeds.

Both the history of the Fianna and the history of Patrick were taught with equal fervor. It seems that the proud, fighting spirit of the earlier Irish was required to instill a rebellious nature still deemed necessary to rid Ireland of an English presence, still considered unacceptable in the days when I went to school. And so we see part of the Irish nature emerging. On the one hand, one should be noble and able to fight like the Fianna and on the other follow the way of Patrick and practice the arts of piety and peace. It was a little confusing for a young boy to decide what to do and many unscrupulous men took advantage of this history to enlist young boys into their cause. Fortunately for me, I decided against it. It would be fair to say that, in some ways, the religious schools of Ireland in the twentieth century encouraged and fostered a rebellious nature against England, but not without some justification. Unfortunately, the Church did not understand the meaning of Christianity and bartered away our lives on the never, never, i.e., it was okay to endure all types of deprivation, as everything one day would be miraculously taken care of. In conclusion I feel that, while they probably believed, they did not understand the message. It was a religious civil service. Like a taboo, everyone ignores the obvious. Of course there were exceptions, men and women who had given their life to God inspired in part by the memory of St. Patrick, by all accounts a good and kindly man.

According to the Venerable Bede, an English writer, in 664 "many of the nobility of the English nation were in the island of Ireland." The school of Armagh, at the height of its fame, is said to have had 7,000 scholars divided into three sections, one of which was called "The Third of the English." Many other scholars came from Europe. One modern French writer has written: "In these times Armagh, the religious capital of Ireland, was the metropolis of civilization." The Bible was the principal subject of study. The classical Latin poets and prose writers and the history and literature of Ireland, along with music and astronomy in some schools, were also studied. Every pupil began by learning the Latin alphabet and grammar. All Irish words connected with writing come from Latin, because it was from Latin scholars that the Irish learned how to write. This was the Golden Age of Ireland. During this time every monastery had its scribes occupied with copying manuscripts, the most famous being *The Book of Kells,* now housed in the library of Trinity College, Dublin. This book, like many others, is adorned with beautiful designs in color. Education was at the heart of Irish life and continued to be so in the generations to come.

Ireland has three patron Saints. Along with St. Patrick and St. Brigid we have St. Columcille, born in 521, who, it is said, was eligible for the kingship of Ireland which he refused in order to follow God. After building numerous monasteries in Ireland he went to Scotland at the age of 42 where he and his followers built another 60. He was famed for his piety and wisdom and belonged to the most powerful family in Ireland. He was known by many names, including "Dove of the Churches," "Lesson of Truth," "School of Virtues" and "Abbot of the King of Graces." He died in 597 at the age of 76 and it was said that "his face remained so wonderfully brightened by the vision of the angels that it seemed not like the face of one dead, but of one alive and sleeping."

After Columcille, his followers continued their work in Britain. It is written that by 662 there was not one bishop in England who had not been consecrated by an Irishman as a result of his work. However, in 596 the pope sent Augustine along with 41 missionaries to the Saxon kings with the intention of establishing the supremacy of the Roman Church in Britain to replace the Celtic Church. Augustine called a conference of some of the Celtic bishops. They replied, "We desire to love all men and whatever we do for you, we will do for him also whom you call the Pope." The Celtic Church took many of its influences from the east and saw itself as independent of Rome The Celtic Church would not accept any man as supreme. However, by 664, the Synod of Whitby declared Rome as the inheritor of Peter's commission in Britain. Some accepted the new order of things. Many of those who did not, returned to Ireland.

Many of the ancient Britons had been Christian. However during the sixth century, Britain – in the absence of the Romans – had been invaded and occupied by pagan tribes from Germany called the Angles and the Saxons. These tribes exterminated Christianity and sank Britain into a period of misery and cruelty. According to the Venerable Bede, bishops and people were indiscriminately slaughtered with fire and sword. The Celtic Church only survived in the northern and western districts of Britain, i.e., mostly Scotland and Wales.

Patrick's arrival in Ireland in 432 was fortunate for Europe, as it was about to enter the Dark Ages and was in turmoil from 500 to 800 AD due to the collapse of Rome. Scholars and students found a safe sanctuary in "The Island of Destiny." It became, according to Dr. Samuel Johnson, "The School of The West, the quiet home of sanctity and literature." Compared to Europe at this time it was a peaceful and thriving country, even if some local kings and princes looked on war as a sport to prove their status. Fortunately, wars only took place when crops had been attended to and hostilities ceased when the leader of either army was killed.

During the Dark Ages (500-800) Irish missionaries traveled to Europe, where the towns founded by the Romans as well as the monasteries had been overrun and destroyed by the various groups of people who sought to fill the gap left by the fall of the Roman Empire. It was a very primitive time in history and conjures up images of half-naked warriors chopping off heads. The Irish monks undertook the task of converting the new peoples to Christianity. Even from a non-Christian perspective, it would be hard to dispute the impact these missionaries had on education, coupled with the effects of a teaching that preached peace and justice. For this, at least, these men should be acknowledged. Kimo Meyer, a German scholar, wrote of Ireland's services to Europe during the Dark Ages, "Her sons, carrying Christianity and a new learning over Great Britain and the Continent, became the teachers of whole nations, the counselors of kings and emperors." By the eighth century, the literary men invited to the court of Charlemagne were chiefly from Ireland. One cannot say the Celtic Church did not serve Ireland and Europe well. There was definitely something good about that period in Irish history and I think it must have been the charisma of Patrick that fueled the fire.

I would have to say that this was the part of Irish history I enjoyed learning the most. It was hopeful, it was blessed and it was kind. It was not arrogant, violent, or angry. That latter part of history was filled with one disappointment after another – an endless stream of stories that always ended in tragedy and hardship. It left one feeling that we were trapped in some kind of endless depression and quite often it was due to the endless squabbles among the Irish themselves. Unfortunately it was this latter part of history that dominated our young psyches, except of course for the one day in the year when we celebrated St. Patrick's Day. In the same way that an individual needs to heal the hurt in his psyche and integrate it into something greater and wholesome, so too must a society. Ireland has yet to do this and denial is not the way. Our education did not and, I imagine, still does not teach history in this way.

Tragically, this golden period in Irish history came to an end with the arrival of the Norsemen in 795 who, arriving in longboats, burned and looted monasteries. They thus hastened a great movement of scholars to the Continent, many carrying their manuscripts with them. Even local Irish princes showed little respect for monasteries in their local tribal wars. It seems that Ireland's greatest weakness has been its inability to build lasting peace among its various factions. It is a weakness that still survives today in Irish politics and in the temperament of many of the people within family life. Is it a Celtic trait? Why should it persist? I think it may be linked to the culture that sometimes placed people in an impossible position where they had to carry and hide many wounds. In other words, under the banter and laughter lies dormant unresolved pain and such pain was not accommodated for within the Irish cultural ideal – as its source was often taboo. In the times of the Celtic Church such problems might possibly be resolved through wisdom, patience and love. But with the demise of the Celtic Church and the imposition of the Roman Church, we saw the spiritual heart of the people enslaved. God became that man who lived in a little box sitting on top of the altar, all bright and brilliant – the civil service was in charge.

Ireland was the safe keeper of learning during the Dark Ages for Europe. When Europe was coming out of the Dark Ages, Ireland was in some measure returning to them. What was a disaster for the Irish was a stimulus for continental Europe at a time when it needed it. It was as if Patrick, in advance of the Dark Ages, had prepared a safe place for the scholars and the learning of Europe. There was a great irony in all this. Rome was the greatest empire the world had known. Yet it was one of the smallest countries never occupied by Rome that played a major part in restoring its lost civilization. Who was it who said that the pen is mightier than the sword? And what is mightier than the pen? The spirit, of course.

Just like the Celts before them, the Norsemen began to arrive at the end of the eighth century, lured no doubt by tales of its wealth and grandeur. They were a different temperament from the Irish, who liked music, literature and dance and valued hospitality. At first they began with what were known as the Viking raids. They would arrive in their longboats, attack communities near the shore and retreat. With time they began to build settlements along the eastern and southern shores, the principal and most important being Dublin or "Black-Pool" in English, named after the dark color of the river Liffey that flows through it. In time, they became peaceful traders and merchants and, like the Celts before them, found their place in Gaelic life. They had many colonies along the coast and for a time many of their fellow Norsemen arrived in these towns intent on war and plunder. By 1004 the Norse towns had become part of the Gaelic state and their kings were half Gaelic by blood and paid tribute to the High King. Conditions improved and literature and art flourished once more.

In 1002 Brian Boru was elected High King. A change was taking place in Ireland toward becoming a unified nation-state. He was the first to be a king without opposition. This meant all other kings paid him tribute. He was held in high esteem and, according to Norse legend, "He thrice forgave outlaws the same fault, but if they offended again he let them be judged by the law." However, some kings were not happy and called upon foreign Norsemen to help overthrow Brian. They failed, as the Irish had learned the ways of war used by the Norsemen. However afterwards, while praying in his tent, Brian Boru was attacked and killed by a Norseman. This was 1014 AD; Ireland's first and perhaps most-loved High King without opposition was killed. This was unfortunate for Ireland as it delayed the establishment of a unified force to protect the country, as it had no force similar to the long-disbanded Fianna.

In 1167 the High King of the time set about establishing a central monarchy whereby no other king would exist in the country in order to create a more united country which was more prosperous, more respected by foreigners and more able to defend itself. At this stage the Norsemen had become integrated into Gaelic life. However, before this new and united Ireland took hold, another event took place that would cast its long shadow across Ireland's history to this day. I am of course referring to the Norman invasion of England in 1066. Those who settled there became known as Anglo-Normans. The Normans descended from the Norsemen who had earlier invaded and settled in France, in the area known today as Normandy.

The Anglo-Norman King Henry II (1154-1189) asked permission from Pope Adrian, an English pope, to invade Ireland to enforce the laws and rights of the Church of Rome. This was simply an excuse. Ireland was well into the process of adapting to the Roman way of things. Henry II had his eyes on Ireland due to its long-standing reputation. Thus began a series of invasions that led to a Norman presence in Ireland which, in time, integrated.

Meanwhile, what had begun at the Church Synod of Kells in 1152 was completed at the Synod of Cashel in 1171. The Irish Church was finally aligned with the Church of Rome, which signaled the end of the independent Celtic Church in Ireland. The papal legate proclaimed Henry's title to the sovereign dominion over Ireland, i.e., Lordship of Ireland and took the oath of fidelity to himself and his successors. The native liturgies were abandoned and the liturgy of the English Church was adopted. Perhaps one of the reasons the changes were accepted is that it meant local Irish chieftains no longer had control over the clergy. Under the old system the ancient chieftains were absolute masters over all their followers, including the clergy. Under the new system a new order was introduced by Henry II whereby the local authorities no longer had authority over the clergy. However, in order to maintain sovereignty over the Irish clergy, the English Kings henceforth filled the vacant Irish sees mostly with Englishmen. Thus began the first major and lasting occupation of Ireland: subjugation to the Roman Church; followed by the second major and lasting occupation: the Anglo-Norman or English invasion. Together with Henry the Roman Church initiated some of Ireland's worst history. In time however they would go their separate ways and the Catholic Church, ironically, would become aligned with the people in its struggle against the English.

It was around this time, 1210, that Wolfram Von Eschenbach wrote down his now widely-acclaimed poem, *Parcival and The Holy Grail*. It seems, disillusioned by the Papal Crusades, there existed among some an aspiration for a religious tolerance leading to a new spiritual synthesis, a genuine search for wholeness. What was taking place in Ireland at this very time was more of the same Catholic intolerance that had given rise to the Crusades and which was now undoing the indigenous Irish Church. It was also around this time that a small stone church was built in Ballinasmale in the west of Ireland. This would become the final resting place of my mother's family, the Brennans. At the same time, thousands of miles away, the Karanga Empire was building a town of "houses of stone" ("Zimbabwe" in the local language) at a site now known as Great Zimbabwe. One day a direct descendent of the Brennan line would stand and marvel at the engineering genius of Iron Age African man.

It was not until the time of Henry VIII (1509-1547) that English interference began to have a lasting toll on Ireland. The English had a presence before, but it was a small one and had suffered many defeats. There was a time when they even paid tributes to local Irish kings to safeguard roads. They had by and large become integrated and the Gaelic life continued to thrive. After a time the Anglo-

Normans became more Irish than the Irish themselves and by and large ignored London; but Henry VIII was intent on having absolute supremacy over Ireland. Thus we have a history of brutal legislation introduced to divide and conquer the Irish people.

Rather than go into all the details of Irish history from that time onwards, I will instead focus on some of the points that stand out. In truth, I find it painful to write about this part of our history as it has not resolved itself and even to this day leads to the most brutal and savage acts known to man. The brutality of the past 30-odd years is a painful reminder of our troubled history. The Catholic Church in Ireland, unlike its predecessor, the Celtic Church, that submitted to Rome, was not prepared to submit to Henry VIII, who had broken from Rome and established himself as the Defender of the Faith in Ireland. So, ironically, the people began to equate the Catholic Church with being Irish and Gaelic.

Henry VIII was responsible for much suffering. His soldiers destroyed and plundered the sacred places. They melted down the chalices and crosses and made money from them. Yet the report he received said that "neither by gentle exhortation, neither by oaths solemnly taken, nor yet by threats of sharp correction, can I persuade any, either religious or secular, to preach the Word of God or the just title of our most illustrious Prince."

Had the people accepted Henry, it would probably have meant a great deal less suffering for the people, but the Catholic Church would not allow that. It was not written in any schoolbook I read that the people were told to remain Catholic on pain of hell, but in my heart I can imagine that this is what took place. If the Church had the welfare of the people in its hearts, it would have encouraged them to accept Henry's Protestantism.

Henry wanted to subdue all of Ireland in order to have absolute and unchallenged control, as he had in England and realized he did not have the army to do so. So he proclaimed himself King of Ireland, a title the pope had not given him to use and by gentle persuasion he took the lands of the Irish chieftains and returned them with an English title. In doing so, he also asserted his independence from Rome. From this point on Ireland was mortgaged. It was only a matter of time before the debt would be called in. For one thing, by accepting Henry's proposal, the Irish nobles and the people who elected them lost control over their own destiny, as the title automatically went to the eldest son after the noble's death. They were thus deprived of their ancient rites of election. The noose was beginning to close.

It was under the reign of Queen Elizabeth I (1558-1603) that military conquest established English rule over most of Ireland, except for the province of Ulster where the Ulster Clans succeeded in overcoming their rivalries and created an effective defense. The discovery of America meant that England by the sixteenth century became very prosperous and the English – fearing a Spanish presence in Ireland – hired large numbers of soldiers to subdue the island. Even though Ulster had resisted this conquest, the famous flight of the Ulster Earls to Europe took place in 1607, due to concerns for their safety. This marked the end of the power of the Gaelic chieftains.

The campaign by England to ensure that no part of Ireland was beyond the Pale (a part of Eastern Ireland under English control) was driven by its global concerns rather than its concerns for Norman integration. Ireland was its first colony. England did not want an enemy on its doorstep. Spain was Britain's main competitor in the imperial game. According to Bill Rolston of the *New Internationalist,* in his article *"The Riotous and the Righteous"*, the Elizabethan view of the Irish as "beasts, void of law and all good order... brutish in their customs" and, as pagans, a legitimate "sacrifice to God," was based on a book entitled *The History and Topography of Ireland* written in 1183 by a Norman monk called Giraldus Cambrensis. Rolston states: "It was a work of fiction designed to justify the Norman conquest of Ireland," in which "Cambrensis accused the Irish of various vices, including laziness, treachery, blasphemy, idolatry, ignorance of Christian beliefs, incest and cannibalism. This book was the mainstay of English views of Ireland for the next 500 years." According to Rolston, this fictitious view of the Irish was also applied to the Native American people and later to Africans and Asians.

By 1654 the Lord Protector of Great Britain, Oliver Cromwell, a puritan and anti-Catholic who had launched a bloody massacre in Ireland, issued an order from the Parliament of England:

> Under penalty of death, no Irish man, woman, or child
> is to let himself, herself, itself be found east of the River
> Shannon.

Thus the famous saying: "To Hell or To Connaught." Drumkeen, the home of my mother's family, is in the heart of Connaught, Ireland's most western province. The land in this part of Ireland was inferior, ridden with rocks and difficult to farm. Connaught basically served the purpose of keeping the "wild savage" Irish caged by their "sophisticated" English overlords. The Irish, who had owned no land prior to the Cromwellian conflict, were allowed to remain as a servant force for the new English settlers. The orphans of this conflict were sent to the English colonies in the Indies and America as slaves. Young girls became very popular among some plantation owners. When the supply of orphans ran out, children were kidnapped from their families.

Eventually Ulster was subdued so that by 1703 less than five percent of the land of Ulster was in the hands of Irish Catholics.

What made Ulster unique was its plantation of colonists from Scotland, England and Wales. Here the seeds of modern Ireland's problems were sown.

In 1729 Jonathan Swift, the dean of St. Patrick's Cathedral in Dublin and author of *Gulliver's Travels,* wrote a satire called *A Modest Proposal* which proposed a scheme to solve Ireland's economic problems:

> A young healthy child, well nursed, is, at a year old, a most delicious, nourishing and wholesome food; whether stewed, roasted, baked or boiled; and I make no doubt, that it will equally serve in fricassee or ragout... I grant that this food will be somewhat dear and therefore very proper for landlords; who, as they have already devoured most of the parents, seem to have best title to the children.

Starting in the late seventeenth century a series of laws called the "Penal Laws" were introduced, designed to strip the Catholics of any remaining land, positions of influence and civil rights. The centuries-old Brehon laws were pushed aside. The Irish were being slowly wiped out. Catholics could no longer practice law, run for elected office, purchase land or own property valued at more than five pounds. During the time of the Penal Laws Catholics were not allowed to pass on a farm to one child, instead they had to divide it among all the children. It was a cynical piece of legislation. Other laws barred them from parliamentary representation or from holding important office. Life was a constant uphill struggle. Furthermore the native language was outlawed and, in the space of a century, a spoken language which imbued the culture and heart of the people was all but gone.

By 1778 Catholics were left with five percent of Irish land. The Catholic educational system was outlawed and priests who did not conform were branded on the face or castrated. It is hard to imagine that many Protestants supported these laws. In fact, less harsh laws were also passed against Presbyterians. Some fought alongside Catholics for repeal of these laws and enabled some Catholic families to retain their status during the height of the Penal Laws. By 1829 Britain passed the Catholic Relief Act which overturned the Penal Laws and allowed Catholics to hold political office. Not long after a tragedy unfolded, which not only had a major impact on Ireland but a profound impact on the world: The Great Hunger or Famine.

The Great Famine of 1846-1850 came about by a combination of potato blight, i.e., a fungus that destroyed the potato crops, and British arrogance. It saw a decimation of the population from eight million to six million people in the space of five years, a million of whom clawed their way onto what became known as coffin ships that left from the western coast. Heading out into the cold Atlantic, they made their way to the eastern fringes of Canada and America, sometimes arriving with every soul on board dead or about to die. By 1801 the population of Ireland was circa 4.6 million. By 1961 it was 4.2 million.

A report in 1849 stated that "the people say the land is cursed." Indeed it was. In spite of this mass evictions took place during this time as the people were unable to pay landlords. In response to widespread criticism, Lord Broughman in a speech to the House of Lords on March 23, 1846 stated that it was a landlord's right to do as he pleased. He said, "otherwise property would be valueless and capital could no longer be invested in cultivation of the land, if it were not acknowledged that it was the landlord's undoubted and most sacred right to deal with the property as he wished." The British government passed a law reducing notice to those to be evicted to 48 hours and made it a misdemeanor to demolish a dwelling while the tenants were inside. In response to criticism that tenants were dying of exposure due to winter expulsions the British Home Secretary, Sir George Grey "rejected the notion that house-destroying landlords were open to any criminal proceedings on the part of the government." There were, of course, some good landlords.

It has been noted by some academics that the British support for the absolute rights of landlords during the Great Famine years came very close to being a policy of ethnic cleansing. Between 1849 and 1854 over a quarter million people were evicted and 200,000 small holdings were destroyed to make way for the grazing of cattle and sheep. Consequently, the idea of English state-sponsored genocide of Irish people became a part of the Irish psyche. Many believe the actions of the British government were, in effect, a continuation of the policy of Cromwell to bring about the elimination of the Irish people, i.e., a policy of ethnic cleansing. Mortalities recorded in the sanctuary of the work houses alone in July 1849 came to 2,500 per week.

As most of the people sowed potatoes to survive, it meant they had nothing to eat during the famine years. They depended on the potatoes, so impoverished had the Irish become. If they ate any of the other crops destined for the landlord they would face eviction and a life of homelessness, considered an even worse fate. Farmers were forced to pay their taxes, which in effect meant to hand over their non-potato crops. Ironically, there was plenty of food in Ireland, but it was destined for England.

According to the same article by Rolston mentioned above, the Quakers made heroic efforts to relieve the famine. He also states that the Choctaw Indians of Oklahoma, who had lost 14,000 members 15 years earlier when forcibly moved from their traditional lands to a reservation 600 miles away, on hearing of the plight of the Irish, sent $710 for famine relief to Ireland.

The consequences of this famine are with us to this day. The huge presence of Irish in America is a testament to that, as is their traditional antipathy towards the English. Even now, in a pure Irish setting where the old sense of being Irish returns, an Englishman is considered an odd animal. Further, the Great Hunger invigorated the movement for change among the rebels in Ireland and ultimately led to the 1916 uprising and partial independence.

With the repeal of the Penal Laws, a shift took place within the Protestant community away from independence to union with Britain, as they now felt threatened by the new power bloc of the Catholics. When eventually independence did come in the twentieth century, they began to fear the retribution of the indigenous Irish and the loss of power and influence. For this reason a split occurred between the North and the South of the country in 1921. The North was the location of most of the industry and the shipyards. It was the most prosperous part of Ireland at this time. The area chosen was essentially the largest area that could be comfortably held with a majority in favor of the union with Britain. The minority were the Catholics, the rest a mix of different Protestant beliefs whose loyalty was secured by a leadership whose political philosophy was one of racism, sectarianism, manipulation of election boundaries and job discrimination. It didn't matter that in times past some of these groups had also been the victims of English discrimination. The prevailing myth of the Irish as sub-human helped maintain the split. This left the South practically penniless. So the split was not just motivated by concerns of living under a Catholic majority.

Northern Presbyterians had also suffered under England and did not feature that much higher on the social scale than Catholics. However, they were Protestant and thus were exploited to support the Protestant ruling classes in keeping the Ulster Catholics down, who now became the common enemy. Out of this division of Ireland grew Ireland's modern-day problems. Before 1921 there existed an English-Irish problem. After 1921 it became a Northern Ireland-Southern Ireland problem. More recently since the Northern Irish civil rights movement in the 1960s and the arrival of British soldiers to Northern Ireland in 1969, it became a Catholic-Protestant problem within Northern Ireland, the crucible of centuries of brutality.

England, it seems, screwed us first one way and then another and finally left us to screw ourselves. We were taught that, during our history, the Irish rebelled in one form or another every 50 years. It was quite depressing as they never, for one reason or another, succeeded until the aftermath of the 1916 rebellion. It was the execution of the leaders of this rebellion that enraged public opinion and forced the British government to grant a form of self rule which had been promised prior to the outbreak of the 1st World War. That then, depressingly, led to the Irish Civil War as the terms of the Independence Treaty were contested between those for and those against. This bloody war pitted many former family and friends against one another, including brother against brother, leading to many deaths. It ended in 1923. In this way the mark of Cain was visited upon the Irish people. It was a tragic scar on Irish history and a reminder of our flawed nature. It was natural then for a young boy to conclude that the troubles which started in the '60s were simply a continuation of Irish history into the modern day.

Fortunately today English policy towards Ireland in the twenty-first century is an enlightened one, as England itself underwent a worker's revolution over the past century which has fed into the political establishment. Ireland's policy towards England has also mellowed and is now one of "Good Neighbors." Let's keep it that way.

As children we were taught a confusing cocktail of history and religion, but something we were most definitely not taught was sexuality. In its absence, its substitute, the pain and anger of history was allowed to flourish. Had we really known our true spiritual past, we might have better known our sexuality. But our past was chosen to fit the political expediencies of the day, not to arrive at a person fully equipped for manhood and his place in society. Sexuality was raped both literally and spiritually from the Irish people. At best it was looked upon with grave suspicion. Nobody spoke about it. The idea that one could have high expectations of it, discovering a hidden paradise, did not exist. One was left to take example from the animals in the fields and some did copy their ways. It would be true to say there was a sickness on the land.

In this regard, from its unquestioned position the Catholic Church failed the Irish people because it's hierarchy were seduced by their own power and wealth and the illusion of perfection they promulgated. They were not willing to say or do anything that might harm their position – least of all naming and shaming sexually deviant clergy. Instead they passed on the problems (perhaps believing their own actions to be charitable) and contributed to a national epidemic. Their sexual ignorance promoted by their own nonsensical understanding of sexuality precipitated a crisis of sexuality in Irish life. Sexual deviancy ran amok in the Ireland of the not so distant past as the subject was completely taboo. Individuals and groups clandestinely satisfied their sexual desires, ignorant perhaps of the consequences as they were never discussed. Hence an innocent child, full of the carefree nature of life, could one day have that world completely and irrevocably shattered by some unaccountable individual or group within the community protected by a wall of silence and fear.

It was into this crucible of Irish history that I was born, an unwitting spectator in a repeating act of history as it once more unfolded throughout the '60s in modern Ireland. Was it possible to understand the birth of modern Ireland out of the seeds of its past?

Or did I have to look deeper to uncover the full story, to learn how the seed becomes the planted and the planted once more the seed?

4. The Wasteland

It is not enough to hoist a flag and cry freedom.

What else has a country but its history and religion when it has little else? And history Ireland has. As children, we learned of the great feats of our ancestors and their long struggle for freedom. That in the end the people should turn on one another in a bloody civil war in the 1920s made little sense, after the shared brutality of hundreds of years and the devastating famine of the 1800s. Why after sharing the suffering of the people did the Church then use its freedom to inflict more? It is no wonder that there is such a sense of bitterness among so many Irish the world over towards the events of the not-so-distant past; pain does not go away, it only waits for its moment to express itself. However, like the road to personal freedom, the road to national freedom lies in understanding, forgiveness and acceptance.

As a small boy growing up in the '60s, I was taught the importance of our heritage and how we were all one under God. You might be forgiven for believing that life was lived in some kind of socialist utopia. Unfortunately, not. Ireland was a schizophrenic society that taught with equal passion the deeds of our forefathers and the fight for freedom and yet allowed itself to be controlled by a backward-looking Church that looked with admiration at those who grew wealthy and spoke with stern warning to those who did not.

As children, all around us lay the remains of an ancient past. A past that was taught but not lived except under special circumstances. It was after all a pagan past, a testament to the power and soul of our ancestors and apart from the few remaining festivals incorporated into the Church calendar, mostly forgotten. As each year passes, more and more of these remains are destroyed to make way for land that is used less and less as the European Union expands. Each of these remains is all the more appreciated amidst the rains and mists that find their way over these lands; an inspiration to look back and remember an earlier time. A time when the people had a spiritual connection to the land. A time when Ireland was considered a land of saints and scholars, An Island of Destiny. A time that also included the Great Hunger or Famine of 1846-1850. The evidence of this past could still be seen untouched when as a boy I played in the deserted, overgrown poorhouse in my town. It was a place where children explored and wondered at the old manuscripts left in the deserted offices. It seems we are now forced to forget this time as the new order takes hold and one size fits all.

It is easy to be equal in poverty and to share the same high ideals. However, when Ireland had more to show for itself than poverty and myth, the real nature of the inequalities among the people finally emerged, as did the emptiness of the national rhetoric. Who would have known that what was once considered the Garden of Eden to so many Irish the world over would one day be turned into a business park and sold off to the highest bidder? Was this not the reason why we were better than the rest, because we appreciated what was really important? Or was the real reason that we had no other choice? When we did have a choice, did we not turn to greed rather than the power of the soul, no longer deemed necessary in a rich and progressively more selfish society?

It seems that those entrusted to guide the people in the healing of their pain failed in the same way that they failed to heal their own pain, preferring instead the power of dogma rather than the power of soul. How can you help others to be free if you are not free yourself? In their desperation the people have turned to the only alternative: greed. Today they live in a state of material addiction with apparently little real value for anything. Where possible, problems are swept under the rug or exported. Meanwhile, the shadow of Ireland's past hangs like a specter ignored. The dam of pain is held in place by the wall of addiction. The new society is becoming the worst of what a material society is: selfish and insular. We have swapped one prison for another. The baby has been thrown out with the bath-water. A culture which was centered around family, friendship, arts and sports tragically held in place by poverty, is fast disappearing. Meanwhile, nothing has really changed at a deep level. Like Prozac, this new comfort solves nothing. Similarly, the government reflects the addiction of the people in its desire to spend ridiculous amounts of money on vanity projects while the streets are littered with heroin addicts, abused by a society unable to examine pain and provide loving care, preferring instead to maintain the straitjacket of dogmatic hypocrisy.

It would be fair to say that what we are now seeing is the outward expression of a culture that for centuries has been oppressed, brutalized, abused and starved. Is it any wonder that this hidden cultural scare should now, more than 150 years later, express itself in a society hell-bent on acquisition, showing at times an almost pathological obsession with wealth? The thirst for money among many of the new and old entrepreneurs is staggering. It's all a sad parody of a country that is trying to buy itself out of its past instead of facing it. Consequently, the emerging problems are really the old problems in a new guise. We have not really examined our past, preferring the easy route of material wealth. But there is never really any easy route and in the same way that an individual suffers for a past hidden and repressed, so too does the society of which he is a part, the society being an organism in itself. It seems we have yet to learn the real lesson of suffering: not to create more and to heal what has been created. If we remain conscious of our past we are less likely to contribute to the horrors of the present.

In the space of 20 years we have gone from a society that met regularly through the church and the ballot box, to one where the church is disappearing and the ballot box is being replaced by a computer. An Irishman today is more likely than ever to feel as though he were a stranger in a strange land, alone and irrelevant. Elderly people are more likely to die alone. Young people are more likely to commit suicide and marriages are more likely to fail. Murder has increased, as has drug addiction. The god of money is indeed a god of Ireland. How exactly have our new economic policies furthered the vision of our founding fathers? They certainly have furthered the visions of the greedy.

While Ireland may have been a British colony, it was also a Roman Catholic colony. The piety of the Church amounted to little more than effective control of a subservient but proud people. Both empires thrived when the people were subject to Lords and Governments and had no free voice, unlike the early Gaelic people who voted for their leaders and chose their own religion. That is not to say the Church did not bring comfort to many in its daily rituals or did not lend a bending ear where needed. The Church had many good priests, brothers and nuns, but it also had many who hid in its shadows, parasitically feeding off the goodness of their bone fide colleagues and the goodness of the people.

Once there was the Celtic Church which was close to the Earth and to the natural cycles of life, much like the people themselves, but it was removed. Like the story of the Holy Grail, a split occurred between spirit and nature brought about by the corruption and legalization of Christendom, which viewed nature as evil. However, unlike Parcival, the Roman Church did not seek to find a Holy Grail to mend this split. It believed instead that it was the wrath of God that kept us out of the Garden of Eden. It did not understand that the Garden of Eden might in fact be a garden of the soul, yet to be uncovered. Such thinking was not permitted in our land and so the Church effectively closed the door on the soul, the very thing it sought to save, and lived in a rational ego-driven self: a self that justified a great deal of suffering for a people with little other choice. It did not realize that such an ego-driven self begins to atrophy and to grow deeply neurotic with the passage of time. From its unquestioned position the Church visited its neurosis on the people. However, the message of God does not exist in fear; it thrives in freedom and today we see the Irish Catholic Church fast disappearing as within today's freedom the lack of any real message is self-evident.

The time will soon come when the fabric of the Irish community, which was built around faith in the Church, will be destroyed. Not because the Irish are not people of faith but because what faith they have, has been hijacked by those who have little. With it will go our priests and our focus of community life where anyone could meet anyone. With it will go the opportunity to kindle real spirituality in the people. And what will we be left with? I am afraid the answer is a spiritual wasteland. That's the problem with conquerors. They want to own what they despise.

An "Irish" Childhood

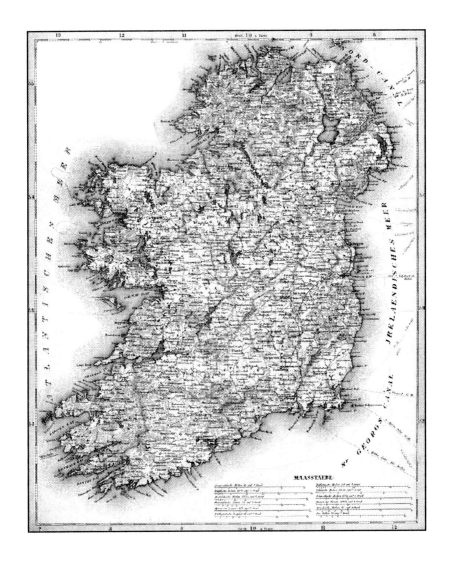

The Island of Destiny.

Source: Neueste Karte von Irland, 1844.

1. Into the West

A family that prays together stays together.

My mother's family, the Brennans, were the spiritual heart of my family; from them came the traditional Irish devotion to Church, God and land, in addition to a sense of belonging to an extended family which had its roots in the past. My father came from Dublin and as such was less influenced by the traditional Irish ways, although he was a devout Catholic. As children, we all knelt down as a family in the kitchen and said the rosary. This, for both of my parents, was in addition to a hard day's work. It was the way families stayed together. The saying my mother used to say was this: families that pray together stay together. My mother continues to say the rosary to this day.

The Brennans were the authentic Irish, born of a deep and troubled past but with a warmth, determination and simplicity that typified the Irish spirit. At least that's how I perceived most of them. In my mind, I never thought of them as ever having been British. They were just pure Irish. They started out in the early 1800s living in a small house on five acres of land about one mile outside Claremorris, in the far western county of Mayo in the heart of Connaught. Clearly within them lay a fighting spirit, as they jumped to the task of drawing stones from the land to help build the town hospital in the 1830s. It was not long before the Catholic Relief Act was passed, which gave Catholics the right to advance themselves in all areas of life. However, there was no money anywhere at the time and this work must have seemed like a godsend. With this money they bought Drumkeen Village, a Town Land, which consisted of 180 acres of land and one home. The family settled this land, dividing it into smaller sections as each started his own family, a small group of families working together. One of the sons, my great-grandfather Martin, was born in 1833. That was 12 years before the Great Famine.

During the seventeenth century, the British government had evicted the landed Irish Catholics from their lands in the North and sent them west of the river Shannon to the province of Connaught, where the worst land was and where the Brennans lived. Many of these landless people survived as farm laborers. Payment consisted of a small cottage with one room and a kitchen along with a half acre of land to grow their vegetables. When the famine hit it was Mayo that suffered the worst. Is it any surprise then that the real Irish spirit is to be found in the West?

People say, as though in surprise, that they never talked about the Great Famine of 1845-1850. How could they talk about it? The ones who survived were the ones who had food and the ones who died where the ones who starved on their doorstep. If the world marvels at why Ireland has shown leadership, it is not because of any deliberate policy to develop it. It is because of the hardship the people suffered and the soul that was kindled from it.

Fortunately, from the Brennans I acquired a deep respect for their almost missionary love of the land as well as a conviction that money was to be used with great care. Perhaps that was a little much for me having been born into a different time when there was not an active policy to keep people poor. My mother's brother Martin spent his whole life animated when talking about the land and the people he knew. I bet he could have drawn a family map of the West of Ireland from his memory. He was nicknamed the Smiler Brennan. I have never seen a man smile so easily or cry so easily without any sense of shame. It made him a very gentle man and much loved widely, even if he shouted hellfire and brimstone from time to time. I was certainly proud to tell people he was my uncle. My mother would tell me how he would sing all the way home to the West of

Ireland on his visits there. It seemed that somewhere in the town land of Drumkeen a deep love of the land was forged and a deep connection to those on it.

During the famine years, while my mother's grandfather Martin was a boy, each day six carts would travel the six roads out of Claremorris, picking up the dead and the dying from the sides of the road, putting all into the same cart. Those lucky enough to be alive might survive from the soup and bread they received in the workhouse, formerly the hospital. The hospital had been made into a workhouse for the poor, the destitute and the dying. My mother's family saved themselves from the worst of the famine by helping to build it. What a strange turn of events that was: building the hospital, which later became the workhouse, to buy the land that saved them from the famine. In the space of six years, the Irish population went from 8 million people to 6 million people. One group that suffered deeply came from the poorest of the poor, the landless peasants, now long forgotten. God have mercy on their souls.

David, my maternal grandfather and son of Martin, was born in 1870 and emigrated with his brothers to Rochester, New York. In 1897 he returned to the family homestead of 30 acres, a division of the original 180 acres. It was the year his father Martin and brother Tobias passed away – his father in April and his brother Tobias a month earlier in March. Someone had to take over the land and it fell to David. When my mother told me this I felt a sense of loss for him. He made a match with a wonderful woman called Annie Walsh nicknamed Annie Bán (pronounced Bawn), meaning "white" in English, as Annie was a very popular name at the time. My granny, the only grandparent I ever knew, seems to have come from a relatively prosperous family as her brother was a priest, her sister was a nun and another brother was a vet. David's mother had a sister, whose son Jack later became Primate Cardinal of all Ireland.

A match between my grandfather David and my grandmother Annie must, I imagine, have seemed a good match at the time.

Annie Bán had a mind like a continuous film which recorded everything, much like her son, my uncle Martin. A good, clear mind that can trace the past like one developing canvas is a sure sign of a healthy soul. I remember her from my boyhood. She was a short woman and always wore black, as was the way of widows in those days. Her hair was always worn under a net with clips. She had very soft skin and her face was round and had a look of the ancients. She rarely said anything but kept her eyes open and her ears pricked. She knew many things but said little. She would rise every morning and head straight to the kitchen where she would busy herself in preparing the needs of the day. She was a tower of strength. I remember once how, after saying goodbye to one of her sons and his family in Dublin Airport – I think maybe it was Jack, who was visiting from America and was on his way to visit his sisters in England – she was so sad to see them go, she went and bought a plane ticket to follow them. She had never been on a plane in her life and was nearly 90 years of age.

David and Annie had 12 children. Two died in childbirth and one from an accident on a lorry. From time to time the children would have picnics on the brow of the hill across from their home, which consisted of two bedrooms, another room, a parlor and a kitchen. Near the house was a little well with a stone wall, from which my mother collected water. Each day she and/or her brothers or sisters would walk the cattle along the path that ran from the main road around the edge of the fields and on into the milking parlor beside the house, where the cows would be milked by hand. One can imagine how a family of 12 must have survived around a kitchen table with Annie Bán giving out instructions and the one helping the other. There would have been very little room for airs and graces.

Instead you would have had authentic, genuine, salt-of-the-Earth people with the fire burning and a large pot of potatoes ready to meet the daily hunger that the land instilled. And within all of them, a sense of their allegiance to the family and the hope of a better life. Wealth would not have been seen as a personal possession to amass, but as something to be put back into the family so that the family could become stronger for it. Unfortunately now we have a philosophy of individual wealth, which does not share, which sadly further separates us from who we really are: a family.

The men emigrated to America and settled around Rochester, Oregon and New Orleans. My uncle Martin was the only son to stay in Ireland, possibly because of his love for the land. My Uncle Jack was a radio operator in the merchant navy and met his wife in Montreal. They then moved to New Orleans. Most of the girls became nurses. Two emigrated to England while the other two girls stayed in Ireland. My boyhood was therefore filled with the returning Americans. It was always a delight to see them as they brought some of the flavor of the West into my young East Coast Irish life.

2. A Taste of Freedom

We blame the innocent and become victims twice over.

I remember, one peaceful summer's day, standing outside my father's grocery shop preoccupied with the thought: can I swallow the chewing gum in my mouth? What if it sticks in my throat? Thinking on it made me a little excited and scared at the same time. Overcome by the emotion, with one gulp and a moment's hesitation, it went down before I had time to back out.

I was curious. I wanted the thrill of doing something that pushed me beyond my boundaries. I felt immediately relieved knowing I had survived. It was a moment close to the edge for a small boy. Little did I know then that, some 25 years later, I would re-experience the same moment but this time with something that might not choke me, but could in its own way kill me. I am still not sure which of the two was the more dangerous. What I can say is this: I don't regret either.

We are coming to the end of the '60s. Mine was a small country town not far from Dublin, yet in those times far enough to seem an age. It was an ordered town set in the country, with 3,500 people, a church, a convent, primary and secondary schools and lots of places to roam and roam I did. In fact, you could say I was born under a wandering star.

The town itself is located in what was once called the Pale. The Pale was the name given to the area which went from the south of Dublin right up to the present-day border with Northern Ireland. It stretched inland for about 30 miles at most. My town, which is not far from the sea, was on its border.

The Pale is a small but important part of Ireland. It is and always has been a melting pot for Ireland, our own international reception area, a colony of sorts. Through it came the pre-Celts, Celts, Vikings,

Normans and the English. Today, in one of the great twists of history, the sub-Saharan Africans have found their way also. Some of our forefathers moved inland but most chose this area for its relative security and prosperity. Since their arrival in the twelfth century, the English have maintained a presence there. The English presence only really became national from the time of Henry VIII in the sixteenth century. In other words, Ireland suffered English dominion for 400 years and not 800 years, as is popularly accepted. Dublin is in the Pale. It may explain why there is such a division between the country people and the people of the city of Dublin.

In this time, as I was growing up, the streets were mostly quiet. Not so in the years to come. My father used to refer to it as a sleepy place. Not much excitement after all his years of work. Each day, he would let me choose something from the sweet counter before returning to school. Some days I had to dodge him and get my prize from my mother. I could never be sure what humor I might find him in. Nor, for that matter, my mother. They both worked hard eking out a living to ensure an education for each of their five children: my sister, the eldest and me the third of four boys. Apart from my sister and eldest brother, who differed in age by one year, there was a two-year age difference between the rest of us. Of the five I was the only one to have been born in the town. So in more ways than one this was my town. The day my mother gave birth to me, she put down what she was doing, walked out the front door, down the town and into the hospital. My father carried on doing what he did best, making a living for the family. He had no other choice. They lived in a big house – big for the town – part of which had been made into a small business premise. Out the back was a secure yard and lofts where bales of cotton and the like were stored, from time to time.

The church's life permeated my family and evening rosary was mandatory. When my granny came to stay she seemed to be a hopeless addict completing all 15 Stations of the Cross before the rest of us had finished the first. She seemed to be in some sort of reverie. I didn't mind really, but we usually only said one rosary and she went for the whole pack: all three. It was hard to refuse her when she asked us all to kneel down in the kitchen to pray. I assumed it had something to do with indulgences whereby one Hail Mary was equal to three days' remission from Purgatory. Such was the power of the Church.

My earliest childhood friend was a little girl called Breda, who lived nearby when I was still a child and she little more than a baby. I remember her first as a baby all wrapped in white. As she began to crawl I started to play with her. Her house was by the river and had a fairy-tale garden at the back with a round pergola in the center. On a summer's day we would play in there. How much closer to God I could get, I do not know. Over the years my trusted friends would mostly be girls.

My father did not marry young; his wife, my mother, was at one time the district nurse. Together they bought a shop and set about building a future for themselves and their family-to-be. What his dreams were I did not know. I only knew that they both worked hard to achieve them. My father had served his time as a shop assistant in Dublin and later worked locally. Neither came from this town: my father a Dubliner and my mother from the rural west of Ireland, two very different worlds; my mother an Aquarius, my father a Gemini and I a Scorpio. They had lived through the war and never forgot the value and use of everything. This they instilled in me.

This was a time when money was not plentiful and each item in my father's shop carried a small return. Often I watched as he washed the shop window and with white chalk, painted the prices for the coming week's specials. He would then build various columns and pyramids of goods made from tins of beans and packets of corn flakes and other goods to entice the customers in and to give them something to look forward to. He knew his business and he took care of it. He was an independent man and he valued his independence.

In truth, many people lived in near poverty. Potatoes were indeed the staple diet, much like rice in India. Even in some of the better houses, it was said, they were counted out. It seemed natural that all damaged goods made their way to the kitchen table. Damaged fruit was always a good omen, as they could not be sold and I would have the chance to taste the juicy, tender fruit of a pear on a summer's day. Failing that, I had a craving for chocolate biscuits and would stand in front of my father's counter where the biscuit tins with their little glass doors were situated. While looking up at my father, as though in idle curiosity, I would stuff my pockets with chocolate-coated biscuits. My poor father was never sure what was going on, but when he did catch me he chased me the hell out of there.

It was an amazing shop selling everything you needed for the house. There was a fascination in that. I would fill the brown bags of potatoes to the nearest ounce and the little bags of sugar and salt almost to the ounce as the grains were so fine. I mostly avoided these tasks but, apart from filling endless bags of potatoes out in the yard away from everyone, I quite liked helping my father in the shop and greeting with a smile each customer who came to purchase there.

When it came to bath time, every Saturday night, there was a time when each of us children took turns to use the same bathwater. With this instilled, wealth was going to be something I would have to come to terms with if I was ever to make my "own" way in life. Sometimes my parents were not in the humor for my high spirits. The world of adults was a bit of a mystery to me. I tried to understand, but couldn't. It seemed to me that adults were the way they were because they chose to be that way. How could I begin to understand that with time a person loses their spontaneity, being overcome by the many thoughts that refuse to go away? I was much too young for that and my mind functioned perfectly well. Naturally enough, I expected it would be different for me. I felt special and excited by the world around me and relished being a part of it.

I knew little of their early life. All I knew was, they worked hard and I assumed they had always been that way. I did not realize that my mother had been a carefree country girl who would happily rise up early in the morning to deliver the milk from the family farm with her brother on the family horse and trap to the neighbors in their small, rural, west-of-Ireland farming community. Her own mother was only a generation removed from the years of the Great Famine and probably did not talk much about the coffin ships that set sail from the western shores not far from where they lived. Those were times nobody wanted to return to and all probably wanted to forget. I wonder what shadow it cast on the family. Those times were evidence of what hell had in store. The Great Famine left an imprint deep in the community psyche that lives to this day but is not often talked about.

Her family lived just outside the town on a small farm and enjoyed the simple way of life Ireland was once renowned for. Everyone worked; everyone did his or her share. So now with the responsibility of a large family my mother did what she knew best, worked, even if she did not retain the pleasures it once gave her. Growing up my mother told me many expressions handed down through many generations. I have not forgotten them. She still tells me new expressions to this day. The most recent and interesting one being: rub a stone long enough and it will wear.

My father, on the other hand, had grown up in a leafy suburb of south Dublin, his own father the chauffeur and his mother the nanny of a knighted Anglo-Irish family. He occasionally rode around in the early-style horseless carriage of the day. This experience probably motivated him to do well for himself and to have ambitions which others did not share and which he kept to himself. I imagine there was a lot of pressure on his father to maintain certain standards among his children. My father's brother Willie was probably the gentlest and most reserved man I knew. I loved to be near him. His goodness radiated. He and my father were pensive in one another's company as though sharing a great wound. Any relatives from my father's family I ever met were all gentle and intelligent and held professional positions. There was something enigmatic about my dad's family, as though he had run away from them, or they were all running from something. My dad rarely spoke or boasted about them. My uncle Willie, sadly, was an alcoholic and tried many times to stop but in the end he died young. I never thought any less of him. In fact, his situation endeared him to me terribly. His own father was buried in one of the finest graveyards in the south of Dublin, with a headstone made with quiet, old-world taste.

I never really experienced the delightful and amusing though self-conscious man my father once was. Somewhat shy, but gentle by nature, he had become serious and somewhat distant, preoccupied as he was by his responsibilities and the mountains of work he had to do. I do have some earlier recollections I cherish enabling me to reconnect to who my father really was: a caring man. Both he and my mother worked very hard, never missing a beat. Often I would watch as he prepared himself in the morning. Once washed and shaved, he would don his white coat and open the shop exactly at 9:30 a.m. Each day, he took a half hour for his lunch and spent 15 minutes of that asleep in the living room. He was a man of the siesta.

One thing that I did know about my father was that his father's mother had been Protestant. I was quietly proud of this fact, especially whenever I felt sickened by the ignorance and brutality of the Catholic Church. It was as if it treated its people as peasants. I would fantasize that I was not truly Catholic and so I was better than what the Church tried to make me out to be. My father's mother, who I never knew, turned Catholic out of love and apparently was disowned by her family. In fact, the only grandparent I actually knew was my mother's mother, who always impressed me with her occasional use of an Irish word or phrase. It impressed me because I lived in the most anglicized part of Ireland. It was as though I was Irish but culturally neutered, afraid to connect to the roots, as these roots brought a sense of instilled shame. And shame was one thing I sought to avoid. My father, interestingly, had a first cousin who as it turned out appeared every Monday night on Northern Irish TV for 15 minutes, giving the thought of the day in between the Monday evening double thriller I watched avidly every week – usually a double feature of Frankenstein or the Werewolf followed by Dracula. My father's first cousin, who looked just like my father, was a canon in one of the most staunchly Protestant areas of Northern Ireland which was wholly loyal to the Crown and hated anything to do with Catholicism. How surreal was that? I detected a sense of quiet reflection in my father for this relative. Was it because he symbolized a refinement which seemed to be lacking among some Catholic men who sometimes suffered from a perverse form of male chauvinism which at times seemed to extol the crude and the cruel? Or was it that he couldn't understand why his cousin was Protestant given that Henry VIII had clearly broken from Rome?

Apart from the civil disturbances in Northern Ireland, the 60s was the time of Cassius Clay, my beautiful hero and a multitude of pop bands: the Jacksons, the Beatles and the Monkees to name but a few and of course Michael Jackson, another hero. Not to mention Bob Dylan, the great libertarian, or Cat Stevens, a man with beauty in his voice.

My dad would often have a reason not to give me pocket money, but that didn't break my stride. I found my own ways to make money and to make it quickly. One day my friends passing by asked me if I wanted to go to the pictures with them. Of course I did. I ran into the shop, grabbed a book of tickets and in one hour had sold them and headed off to meet my friends. I definitely had a way with selling tickets, garnering the seller's commission. Another time a group of American tourists dropped coins in the river. Together with my friend Peter I waded in and collected them. Unfortunately I fell in and dried myself by a wood fire. My mother could not understand why I smelled like a gypsy.

During the summer months, with a sandwich and a Fanta, I would walk the two miles to the farmer's fields to pick strawberries and potatoes. With the money I earned I bought my first record player. It was a big event and my father seemed quiet, yet pleased when we went far away into the country to buy it. He had clearly done his homework. I was delighted with the choice. It was a thing of great beauty and perfection.

There were other ways I had of making money, including once saving the flags with tiny pins from one Sunday collection and, with my unsuspecting younger brother Noel, selling them the following Sunday after Mass for all of ten minutes before beating a hasty retreat. It amazed me how so many rushed forward to buy these flags – perhaps imbued with the priest's sermon. Once in an attempt to get ahead of myself I stole £5 from my father's till. It was probably in exasperation at the lengths to which I had to go to get pocket money. It was also probably, in part, rebellion. Whatever it was, it also hurt me. I felt I had let him down. At the same time, a school acquaintance blamed me for money he had stolen. Intimidated by the policeman I accepted responsibility for both crimes.

This episode led to all kinds of problems, including forgetting the right way to make confessions and being told by the priest to go away and learn the proper way. This left a deep impression on me. So much so that I became obsessed with the need to be utterly scrupulous in my dealings with others over money. In fact, I kept a mental record of what I stole in order to confess it properly and not leave any sin unaccounted. As each confessional day passed, I would calculate how much I had confessed and how much I had left outstanding – in this I was like my father who never left a bill outstanding. I was afraid of shocking the priest by telling him all at once. Apart from confession the church had other uses. One of them was to light the butt of a cigarette – picked up from the ground and revived to its roundness – from the candles that burned continuously with the prayers of needy people. Before the Virgin Mary I would kneel as though in prayer, hands together like an altar boy, cigarette held in place between their palms. From her I would seek the light provided by the rows of candles burning their wax onto the wrought iron trays of tiny spikes. Once alit I would exit the church quickly, much to the approval of an occasional neighbor who might see me leave, hands still in prayer.

I was quick to seize an opportunity when one presented itself. In this my father said nothing. He simply let me be in my own little world. It amazed me how quickly people parted with their money. Some years later, at the age of 16, my father told me how one Irish businessman had left school at the same age and built a large business empire. Perhaps my father sensed an ability in me. He told it in such a way so as not to seem like a suggestion, just an interesting fact. He rarely interfered. It seemed in this poor country, my father was not all that impressed with education.

My mother, on the other hand, came from a traditional background where education and the Church were the keys to a safe and secure future. She pushed my father to secure a full education for each of the children. Each, in time, would graduate from University. For this he worked a long life, rarely, if ever, complaining. Even in his final years, when he was suffering greatly, he never complained and always put on a smile. He knew he had made mistakes and wanted to heal the rift between us. He turned to prayer and prepared himself for death. He turned his illness into a time of penance and preparation to meet his maker. He was a man of example and few words as he was a self-conscious man. Once he took me to an artist's exhibition in a local town. We both stood quietly watching a man paint with his toes. I was amazed at what one could achieve if one put one's mind to it.

Our home was situated in the narrowest street, the entrance to the town. At one point we even played football in it, stopping occasionally for the odd passing car or when one of the more contrary neighbors came out and complained. There were only about ten houses on the street. Of those, three were large and contained business premises. The others were small row houses with out toilets and housed young families. The children would all gather in the shortcut behind my family home, which was a way to bypass the main street and connect with the bridge which marked the end of the territory of this little band of warriors. By and large they were good, friendly children. Every day after school and before tea time we would meet and play football between the two walls of the shortcut, one of which was the wooden gate to my family home. As each goal was scored, it would rattle its last. In that shortcut I learned how to make a catapult and build tree houses, as well as the dangers of homemade fireworks. Once I copied the older boys and engraved my name on the old mason-styled bridge along with the year 1971. It is still partly visible to this day. That was not the only indignity the bridge had suffered though. The British, in a bid to outdo the

Old IRA, drilled two small, perfectly round holes on each corner, large enough to place dynamite. They never blew the bridge. It still stands today with its perfectly round holes waiting for someone, I suppose, to blow it up or else just nursing its wound privately to itself. Of course, the street would not have been the same without Molly, a beautiful down-to-earth woman who shared my love of cats and who I often shared a cup of tea and a chat with.

Family life centered around the shop. It was Daddy's pride, but I am not sure if it was his joy. Every space was used intelligently, every part of the shop laid out to perfection. He knew what he was about. Even now it marvels me to think of the millions of items he had in the shop including a meat counter, a sweets counter, first aid section, mineral counter, ice-cream counter, household cleaners and on and on. Within each section he offered the best variety one could get at the time. For this he made two trips a week to the Cash & Carry to fill his car. I was always impressed when I entered his shop. It was a universe of life, all seamlessly interconnected and exactly to the point – no hint of greed or unfair play. Outside hung a little metal sign that said, "licensed to sell stamps." He also had a room at the back of the house he used for storing sweets. In this room the walls were filled with neat shelves filled to the last space with all kinds of sweets of different shapes, sizes and colors. I would look in amazement at the way everything was so completely ordered. It was a testament to complexity and simplicity. Perhaps it was this influence that contributed to my skill in mathematics and made me quite adept at computer programming. It was the work of a very ordered mind. The detail of his work and the manner in which he earned every penny fairly and squarely was a reflection of his greatness. Yet he never wanted any of us to go into the business after him. I guess in later years the business became tougher and tougher with the opening of supermarkets and he felt it was no life for anyone. Yet he stuck at it because that was the choice he made and he never ran from his responsibilities. He even worked past retirement age to see my younger brother through University. He never complained. I remember once he received a letter that touched him deeply. I could see this because my mother was almost in a state of silence, the kind of state when something important happens that requires placing life on hold. I asked her what it was about and she told me a customer who had left a long time before and to whom Daddy had given credit, had sent a letter with a £5 note inside to pay his outstanding bill. The envelope was blue and looked a little worn. The letter itself was very simple, written by a simple but devout man. My father kept that letter. It had an effect on me. It was a testament to those who do believe in honor even when others seek to cheapen and ridicule it.

My father never spoke to me about sexuality, but I did notice a couple of small blue booklets appear in the bookshelf very clearly outlining all the principles of male and female sexuality. At the time I took that to be his way of passing the information on, clearly recognizing its importance. That for me, counted for something. He was a thoughtful man.

One of the interesting aspects of standing in my father's shop was the view of the world it permitted. The shop was located at the mouth of the town and everyone passed up and down each day going about their business. Each year I watched the change in fashions. In particular, I can remember the year when minidresses were all the rage. As the summer progressed, the girls who passed by seemed to cut their skirts shorter and shorter as though becoming braver and braver in their daring. Then as though turning a corner, it went the other way. The dresses grew longer and longer until, eventually, they were cleaning the streets with them. For the boys, I watched how the style of shoes changed and how the pants became wider and wider. I, myself, wore black bell-bottoms that were as wide as public water pipes, along with a multi-colored tank top and beetle boots. It was a lot of fun and brought gaiety to the town. Clearly, a new age had begun and the Church was not as powerful as it had been. I was part of this new age and determined to live it to the full. I thought I had just escaped the horrors of my past history for a new and brighter age. I was confident. Unfortunately, my love of fashion led me to buy shoes which were too tight for me and led, years later, to developing two crooked feet.

Another interesting thing on my street was the little watchmaker's shop next door, run by a man called Hugh who seemed to struggle with his eyesight through the bulbous glasses he wore. I would watch him mend a watch and noted the intricacy and delicacy of all the moving parts. I learned a thing or two about how watches would stop working mostly because people would wind them up too hard and the spring had to be released. But most of all I learned about a world where everything was interdependent, each moving part feeding into the other. That fascinated me. Everything had its place and nothing was redundant. Thus began a lifelong love of watches.

The town itself came alive every Tuesday as the local farmers walked their cattle to the fair. My mother's brother Martin had a farm a few miles outside the town. He had moved to this part of the country years earlier as a result of the allocation of land by the Land Commission, although he missed the West terribly and would go back at any opportunity. After the country became independent the government bought back large farms and redistributed them. Those who had money could, of course, buy their own farms. My uncle did exactly that, but it caused some envy in his local community. The Land Commission stepped in to stop the dispute and offered good farmland to my uncle on the East Coast. That is how he came to live nearby many years ago, before my mother arrived to the town.

The land he had been given had a large, stately home and a quarter-kilometer driveway. They actually knocked down one wing, plus the central part and kept the remaining wing as their home. Even that was impressive and so I was very proud of the house my cousins lived in. At the time my cousins moved to the area my mother was working as a district nurse in Kildare when a position became vacant locally as a district nurse. She was asked if she would go. She decided to give it a go for a year, at least. I guess her brother being a few miles outside the town affected her decision. It was probably this that brought her to the town.

Whatever the case, I was proud to see my uncle among the many farmers who brought their cattle to the fair and, in the best of Irish traditions, haggled over the price of a beast. Once a bull, while passing my father's shop, went out of control and ploughed through the front window. Although I was not there to see it I was enthralled by the aftermath.

Apart from the Tuesday marts, on special occasions the town also came alive when the local Brass & Reed band played in the town after Sunday Mass. They were later renamed the Military Band. What the difference was I was not sure, but it did seem that more pride was attached to the band and they took themselves a lot more seriously. It was traditional to march behind the band and share the energy of this little band of musicians as they beat their drums through the town. All of the boys in my family at one time or other played in the band. My brother John was very good on the clarinet and I had a go at the trombone. I am not sure why. It seemed an odd instrument and perhaps that is why I chose it. We had a little social club that met in the band room every Wednesday night. John at one time was the chairman, I the secretary. We ran little fundraisers, the best being a flag day for which we received a license from the police.

I have many good memories from this time of my life, including taking the milk truck on a Saturday morning to visit my cousins' farm. I had to be on time or else my cousin would go without me. The truck would come into town early each morning and on Saturdays I would climb out of bed to meet it and jump on the back, the wind blowing my hair back as I perched over the top of the cabin, the milk churns rattling. One of my fondest memories is taking in the hay one summer's day with my cousins and playing afterwards in the barn. I always felt good at the farm. It seemed relaxed and natural. We even once played a kissing game. I would also help my cousin Gerry milk the cows. With the sheepdogs, I would go to the top of the field, whistle to the dogs, who would then gallop the half mile down to the next field to round up the cows and march them up the fields towards the dairy parlor. After the milking, Gerry and I would retreat to his little office where he kept records on each cow, particularly those who were coming close to calving, as it affected their milk. We would have a cigarette. He smoked Major, a strong cigarette and we would have a few relaxed moments sharing a joke. Once he had a sick cow that he had to milk by hand in its stall. He asked me if I wanted to milk her. I offered. Next thing I knew it lifted its back leg and landed it in my old tweed jacket pocket. Gerry laughed his heart out, as he knew it would do that. That frightened me. Another time we made petrol bombs and smashed them off the outside wall of the dairy. It was quite simple, really. We filled a couple of old bottles with diesel and stuffed cloth and straw into the neck, set them alight and flung them against the wall. I guess Gerry was watching a lot of Northern Irish demonstrations on the TV at the time.

One of the fascinating things I liked as a boy was the number of cats we had. Because of the back stores, my father had obtained one or two cats to keep the rats at bay. With time, the cats began to multiply. It was fascinating to see a cat give birth. The way the mother would lick them clean and they would lie, eyes closed, looking as though drenched with sweat, all sticky. Because nobody tried very hard to give them away there came to be 15 of them. Perhaps the special, almost healing spirit which cats sometimes carry was carried by these cats. Who knows? It certainly added life to the place.

The oldest of the cats I called Fluffy, a Persian cat with a kind of brown orange coat with different shocks of shade throughout, one of two my father had brought home. There had been other cats, but they had not survived. I looked on Fluffy as my one. She was the great mother of all the cats that now freely roamed the yard and the stores. They were never let inside being much too dirty for my mother to allow in the house. I was proud of Fluffy's offspring and the way she seemed to thrive among them – a quiet cat that seemed knowledgeable and never demanding. I loved her. I also had a dog called Bell, who I found one day as a ball of white fur curled up next to the oil heater in the kitchen, alone and lost. I immediately became attached to him and looked on him as my own. As he grew, he often created pandemonium among the cats but they were well able for him, especially Fluffy.

I had a way with people and could easily make them laugh by making a fool of myself. This didn't seem to bother me. I was not in any way self-conscious. On occasion, as a small boy, I would amuse my relatives with a full-throated version of Al Jolson singing "Mammy," which I enjoyed immensely. I also enjoyed very much listening to the music of Edith Piaf and the Strauss Family, not to mention watching Charlie Chaplin, a genius of comedy. Many times after a day's work my mother would go to the drawer at the sink and take out the hymn song cards made with white paper pasted onto cardboard and ask me to sing for her. Her favorite hymn was "Amazing Grace."

Amazing Grace

Amazing Grace! How sweet the sound
That saved a wretch like me!
I once was lost, but now am found;
Was blind, but now I see.

'Twas grace that taught my heart to fear,
And grace my fears relieved;
How precious did that grace appear
The hour I first believed.

Through many dangers, toils and snares,
I have already come;
'Tis grace hath brought me safe thus far,
And grace will lead me home.

Words by John Newton (1725-1807).

I was always a little reluctant to sing but the truth was I enjoyed these moments standing in the kitchen while my mother entered a reverie. I did not realize back then how significant this hymn would be in the sound-track of my life. I too one day would find myself on the verge of death, but not on the high seas like John Newton, begging for divine intervention. Instead I would find myself in desperation and a high degree of danger, the recipient of an African medicine which would melt my conscious mind and leave me begging from the depths of my soul for whatever divine help I could find. It would only be then that I would begin to understand the things that change a man like John Newton, things which we only imagine but never expect to happen.

Saturday was my favorite night of the week. The shop was full and bustling, filled with happy and excited customers, the lights glowing, my father and mother busy but content. I liked this night very much. The town had a happy air, flushed with the wages of another week waiting to be spent. The pubs which littered the town full and alive with music. My father content, as all the orders were in for the weekend. This pleased me, as I knew he had a sense that his time was being well spent, earning the money he had set his business up to earn. I had great empathy for my father and it bothered me whenever I saw the shop empty and him lost in his thoughts. He would sit behind the counter smoking. Above him, on the ceiling, the yellow of the nicotine. More than once I painted the shop ceiling and it pleased me to see those marks disappear. Often I helped him fill the grocery boxes. Food went into one box, cleaning materials into another. When all the boxes were ready I would pack them into the back of his car and together we would drive to the house of each customer on the list. I liked this, as it was always a nice time to see my father relax with his customers. The women were fond of him and always had a nice word to say. He enjoyed the flattery and I enjoyed watching him being flattered.

At that time everything seemed possible to me. I dreamed of what I might be when I grew up – perhaps a very rich businessman or indeed, perhaps the president of America. Then there was always the Church and the job of the pope! Or perhaps I might become an astronaut! The Apollo missions were happening at this time. The pageantry and the beauty of the badges that depicted each mission mesmerized and inspired me. I collected each one and watched with admiration and delight the first man stand on the moon. I also shared in the silence at the assassinations of the Kennedy brothers. Each Irish home had a picture of JFK and his wife with the sacred heart of Jesus. It seemed the day JFK was assassinated, democracy died in America. He was not just the president of America. He was the president of what Ireland felt it could have been, had it not been used and abused by the British. He was hope for a broken people. A symbol of what we truly were. The day of his assassination was a day of great loss for Ireland and for the world. Darker forces were intent on having their way and thwarting the great democracy America once was. Much like Rome collapsed in on itself after reaching its zenith as the bad took advantage of the good. Perhaps the good do not really understand that true spirituality does not equal trusting everyone and that sometimes, we have to be on our guard.

So I gave a lot of thought to what I would be when I grew up, as I wanted to make the most of my life. Around the age of ten, having tempered my plans and changed my outlook, I felt I had found the answer to a happy life. I wrote it in a letter I put behind the American-style mirror in the living room: a testament to our deep link to America. Some years later, on a visit home from boarding school I went to look for it and it was gone. The decorator, it seems, had thrown it away. That was a bitter disappointment and seemed to reflect the general direction my life was taking at that time. Being away at boarding school my childhood was slowly disappearing from under my feet. In the letter, I had written my fantasy of running an agency for theatrical people. I had an image of an office full of artists milling around. Among these, a clown dressed up with a red nose. What a happy life, I thought and indeed this is what I was looking for, hoping to keep the magic moments of my boyhood intact. In my childhood innocence one of my boyhood dreams had been the thought that one day I could walk through the town and be liked by all and feel the surge of happiness and well-being that I knew would fulfill and inspire me. But, try as hard as I could, this would never happen. There seemed to be some impenetrable wall in my community, or perhaps within me.

The happiest moments in my boyhood came with the church choir, in particular the Sunday evening Benediction. Not many children cared to turn up. So, on occasion, I was the only boy there. Great! This meant the organist played softly and I sang my heart out in Latin. And what a beautiful and wonderful feeling that was. My whole body was transformed for one moment in time. Every care and problem gone, replaced by an overwhelming sense of well-being. Words cannot describe the feelings I had. I knew from this how important it would be for my future happiness not to be dragged down by any problems I might encounter. And this I was resolved to do. In fact, the church offered a respite from the cares of the world. It was a place to meet friends and neighbors and to feel connected to the bosom of the community. Once, while waiting at the back of the church as an altar boy in a procession along with two others, I set the hair of the altar boy in front of me on fire with the candleholder. For a moment I thought it would not go out, but luckily it did. It gave a great blue flame! I had to control myself from cracking up with laughter.

Each week I bought the weekly *Top of the Pops* album. *Top of the Pops* was the highlight of the week. Everyone watched it. Each new artist brought a window of light onto the world. In the beginning I would buy a single record, but after a time I realized the weekly album did not cost much more. Although they were not the original singers it was hard to tell the difference. With record in hand I would lock myself away in the upstairs living room and sing my heart out to my favorite songs. In fact this was a favorite pastime of mine. When I had enough money I would also buy a new crisp comic. In fact, I was so addicted to these I spent hours reading the hundreds my friend Noel had collected. It's hard to describe the pleasure of buying a freshly printed comic, each page filled with different-sized segments full of color and characters that all seem alive. I would follow them on their little journeys and adventures and draw from the energy I found there. It was through comics I learned to read. In school I actually developed a kind of mental block towards learning. It filled me with pain and I simply passed the time as best I could. Hence my punctuation in English was never very good. Each week I would go up to the sitting room with my new album, lock the door and sing my heart out. These were great moments. I had bought the record player with my father after spending a summer picking strawberries for a local farmer and selling my old bike for £5. It was my father who also found the bike for me. The record player was a truly wonderful purchase. It was also possible to play old gramophone records by flipping the stylus over and changing the speed to 78 rpm. LPs worked off 33 rpm and were 12 inches. The singles played off 45 rpm and were 7 inches. Years later I gave it in near-perfect condition to someone as a symbol of my love only to find it destroyed some time later. This saddened me deeply, as I felt the record player and I had been betrayed. It seemed not everyone cared for things the way I did or understood the value of a personal gift. I would like to have it still as it brought much love into my life.

Singing was not my only passion. As a small boy I attended a disco and danced 'till I dropped. I was a completely free spirit and I intended to stay that way. I was not inhibited. The other children looked on somewhat shocked and laughed. I felt a little awkward but I was having the time of my life and decided there was no reason to stop. I guess they thought I was a little crazy. Perhaps I was. When selling flags with another kid, I once placed a flag on a nice, cheerful girl right in the center of one of her huge breasts. She laughed herself silly. I had a burning desire for life and I wanted to taste it. Unfortunately, I gave up Irish dancing lessons even though I enjoyed them, as my other siblings had left and I felt stupid for staying on. I was only a child and knew no better. I regret that decision a lot.

During the summer months, after working in the fields, I would come home on a Saturday evening, wash, buy a ten packet of Carroll's cigarettes, crisps and a Fanta drink and make my way to the cinema. This was a favorite pastime of mine. Cinema was a passion for me. Once I spied a girl I liked and sat beside her. It was common custom among the kids to do this and, if lucky, place your hand on her shoulder. Maybe even get a kiss.

Smoking gave me a sense of freedom and a hit to the head. At one time I experimented with the strongest cigarettes available, Churchills. There was another cigarette called Sweet Afton, Virginia Cigarettes, Filterless, but I viewed it with suspicion. I saw some men smoke it and their fingers were yellowed to the bone. I tended to avoid it. Sometimes we would smoke in the bushes, or else there was a big tree at the school where the foliage was so great you could sit inside on its branches and look out without being seen. It was a favorite hideaway of mine. Other ways we had of amusing ourselves included fishing for eels in the river using a broom handle and a fork. Once or twice we climbed over the walls of the neighboring pub and ran off with a bottle or two of corked beer for fun. In those days Guinness came in wooden casks and the publican would fill each bottle and then punch a cork into the bottle before selling it on to his customers.

Across the street from my house was a draper's shop. It was run by Jimmy, a portly man, with the help of Brege and Mary and, some time later, Jimmy's niece Marie. Every time I entered the shop Mary would look me straight in the eyes and smilingly ask me how I was. Her smile was filled with gentleness and love. She was a lovely girl who lived a couple of miles outside the town. If I was not greeted by Mary then I was greeted by Jimmy and if not by Jimmy then by Brege. They were always happy to see me come in for a chat. Jimmy was a happy, portly man with a warm heart. He always drove a Morris Minor. When I would enter the shop often I would find him leaning against the shop counter looking out towards me with a smile and a big hello.

It was a place of warmth. When the time came for the changeover of the old money to the new, what was called decimalization, Brege brought me to the back of the shop and had me give her a little lesson on the mathematics of it. It was a little confusing as one new penny equaled two or three old pennies, as five new pence equaled twelve old pennies. The deal was: if you bought something for two or three old pence you paid one new penny. Otherwise if you were due change of two or three old pence you received one new penny. Many of the children took advantage of this loophole, while they could, when buying sweets. I felt sorry for some of the older owners. There seemed to be a lot of little shops in the town selling sweets and cigarettes.

Mary had a nervous shake in her hand. I did not really understand what it was until one day she had to stop working and began moving around in a wheelchair, unable to control the use of her limbs. She still continued to smile at me but I sensed she was a little embarrassed by her condition. I liked Mary very much and missed her when she was eventually transferred to a nursing home in the Phoenix Park in Dublin. Once, nervously, I visited her there, not knowing what to expect, not sure if I could handle what I might find. I was probably only about eight or nine at the time. I entered her room with Brege and some of my family. Dad drove up for the day. Mary smiled and was very happy to see me. She had tears in her eyes. I summoned up the courage to talk to her. It was a very difficult moment and I was glad, though I felt guilty, to leave. It was not long after that Mary died. Why, I did not know. It must have been something to do with the shake in her hand. In a way it was a relief, as it meant I could return to my simple routine. The fear of the outside world once more locked away. I actively forgot about Mary. It was a great shock to me to see how God could allow such a beautiful person to suffer so much.

The highlight of the year was probably the Carnival. It arrived in town and parked in the boys' school field. Up would go the big tent, a white canvas pavilion held up by one huge tree trunk in the middle and smaller poles around the edge. The floor consisted of large, interlocking wooden squares. Sometimes when it rained they would become wobbly and the muck from underneath would squeeze through. Afterwards it was always a big task for Brother Anthony to sort out the field. He seemed to be the one who did most in that regard, having a keen interest in hurling and football. Into the tent would arrive various country and western bands and each would give out small 5-by-3-inch photos which we would collect with signatures. However, when it rained, the Carnival became a mud bath.

When the Carnival was not in town the Circus would come, announced by speakers that blared into the homes and kitchens of the townspeople. Most children like me hoped to be picked by the clown to come down into the ring and be part of one of his pranks, usually involving a circle of chairs in a kind of musical chairs. It was events like these and the life around the church which held the community together. Nowadays much has been lost.

As a child I spent a lot of time outwitting the life I was expected to live. My poor father and mother despaired. "Go to your room!" Yes and from there I would climb out onto the shop roof and out the back yard to meet with a chum and play along the river, then return the same way in time to make an appearance downstairs when supper was ready. My parents were either too busy to know or simply glad for the moments of peace my absence gave, moments they used to continue working hard to keep their dreams together. It all seemed a little hard for me to understand but this was the way things were and nothing could change that. How could I understand their situation? Once, about the age of 10, I did suggest to my father to close early on a Sunday. I explained that not many people come to the shop at that time and it would be time well-spent relaxing. My father said nothing. He was a man of few words. Not long after this, my father appeared to take my advice – something that surprised but pleased me.

One of the most interesting challenges I undertook was around the age of 10 or 11. I noticed the wires in the top of the house were starting to smell, as was the case in old houses in those days. I was using a heater in my bedroom and was worried about the danger. I decided to rewire the upstairs and bought new, modern sockets and wire with money from my mother. The idea was simple, really. I disconnected the fuses for the sockets, tied the old wires to the new, pulled the old wires out of the floorboards and the new wires followed. I then rejoined the new to where the old had been and hey, presto! We had new sockets with new wires. I slept better for it.

My father's ways didn't help me to grow close to him, even though I wanted to. Years later, he suggested I write about my travels. No longer a boy and on the way to becoming a man I dismissed the idea. Deep down I felt my time had not come and I was unable to share this with him. I could see my father felt slightly rebuked by this, even though I had not meant to rebuke him. He was a sensitive and gentle man. Our relationship was one of misunderstanding and pain. I did not realize how beautiful a man he was. That is the saddest part. But that is the way of life and the saddest part of the damage done. I reach out to him now in my heart and I find him there with a knowing and caring smile. We blame the innocent and become victims twice over.

At other times my father, in good form, would entertain the family with a rendition of a song, his favorite being "Oh, Danny Boy."

Oh Danny Boy

Oh Danny boy, the pipes, the pipes are calling
From glen to glen and down the mountain side.
The summer's gone and all the flowers are dying.
'Tis you, 'tis you must go and I must bide
But come ye back when summer's in the meadow
Or when the valley's hushed and white with snow.
'Tis I'll be here in sunshine or in shadow
Oh Danny boy, oh Danny boy, I love you so.

And if you come, when all the flowers are dying
And I am dead, as dead I well may be
You'll come and find the place where I am lying
And kneel and say an "Ave" there for me.
And I shall hear, tho' soft you tread above me
And all my dreams will warm and sweeter be
If you'll not fail to tell me that you love me
I'll simply sleep in peace until you come to me.

Words by Frederick Edward Weatherly, 1913.

Others he also sang seemed to come from an earlier part of the century, perhaps the thirties or the forties, songs I loved to hear him sing. When I listen to Louis Armstrong or other male singers from that era, I am reminded of my father singing. Perhaps my father had a secret dream of one day being a singer, too? Reality, of course, was a different matter. From time to time I would see him sit at the piano and pick out a tune. He did not know how to play but he tried. There came a time when he gave up. Perhaps in his earlier days he had worked hard hoping to get ahead and afford himself the possibilities of time to learn the piano. Whatever the case, with five children to care for and a mother who insisted on education his tasks were clearly cut out for him. He served his family and he served them well. His annual holidays consisted of mandatory public holidays and one trip each year to a different part of Ireland. He would leave after he closed shop on his half day, Thursday and return the following Monday. He would take a small black case and on his return would place it on the kitchen table from where he would give us, if we were lucky, a little something from his trip.

3. The Unholy Trinity

Keep your eye on the light,
And you won't get lost in the dark.

As a boy I had been taught to believe in the Church and God. Indeed, once I reasoned with my friends that if God exists and the church is his house on Earth, then no expense should be spared to make that house as wonderful as possible. This seemed perfectly logical to me, as I firmly believed a priest was God's voice in this world and someone to be revered. This was a time when I would go under the bed sheets with a plastic statuette of the Virgin Mary which lit up in the dark. I would squeeze my mind as hard as possible and believe the Virgin was present. I had been told it took only a small amount of faith to have one's prayers answered. Out of this faith came a commitment to acknowledge my wrongdoing when confronted with it.

As time went by and things started to go wrong in my life, I suddenly realized one day that this state of affairs appeared to be one-way. I would say, "Yes, I have been wrong and I am sorry," and expect the other to say the same. Instead, what I got was a self-satisfied look from the other child and a rebuke from an adult. I would find myself left alone, mystified as to why the other child had not done the same. On top of this, when I was wronged, I noticed nobody willing to be sorry to me. It seemed everyone expected me to be sorry, as I was in many ways the black sheep; but the same rule did not apply to them. Maybe they were ashamed to be sorry to me. Who knows? Then I began to change. I was no longer willing to accept my fault without arguing the fault of the other also. I wanted fairness and equality in humiliation. And humiliation is what I got.

At the same time I also began to realize that all was not right with the religious Brothers who taught us. They had their ways and by and large I accepted them. Each day the bell would ring for the start of class and immediately hundreds of highly energetic boys would fall into line without a sound and march double-file straight into class to their allotted places. However, once at the commencement of third class, about the age of 9, a young Brother entered the class and sat cross-legged on the teacher's table. He proceeded to pick out individual boys he named as bold and unruly and asked them to make a new start by saying they would behave in the coming year. Much to my surprise I was singled out. Not wanting to make matters worse I went along with this little charade, but for the life of me I could not see what I was supposed to have done. I saw myself as a good soul not seeking to be malicious in any way. Clearly, all was not well with the religious Brothers. I felt humiliated by this little routine which I took to be somewhat stupid, staged and clearly unfair; a staging post on the road to shame and guilt which these religious sought to instill.

I also noticed that things were not right in class, either. I was baffled when the teacher, Brother Anthony from the farthest reaches of Ireland, gave me 100% on my math exam (my best subject) and then gave, much to the embarrassment of my fellow student sitting next to me, 104% for the same test. It was a contest and clearly I was not meant to win. There were many more incidents like this that left me baffled. It was towards the end of primary school and I had failed in my efforts to win the affection of this teacher whom I liked very much. Instead, I had incurred his wrath many times and on one occasion had the leg of a chair broken over my head. It, having been used many times before to hit other children. Another time a photographer arrived in the class to take class photos. I think the photographer had a little extra time on his hands from the previous class and was filling in a few other kids. I was wearing my worst jumper and had ink on my chin – we used inkwells and pens with quills and often I would drink the ink as it had a soft, interesting taste. My appearance didn't really bother me. I was sent up to have my photo taken which was to be put into a key ring. I was delighted and thrilled to be going up first.

Even now I look on that photo as the most beautifully authentic photo of my childhood I have, the real me. When I see myself as I was before my life went off the rails and I realize I am now returning to that person, my heart is filled with a great peace and joy and, quite frankly, relief. However, now I cannot help but wonder if it was not just another snub, given that the rest of my class were able to have time to clean themselves up. My mother had to do with a key ring of her child clearly unkempt. It only hurts me because of the way it insulted her. However, she loved the key ring and saw nothing untoward. Neither did I, until I came to write this book.

Another time, the time of year when a special week of morning Mass was being said, Brother Anthony asked for volunteers to be altar boys. He said that the Mass would either be at 7:00 a.m. or at 9:30 a.m. If it were the later time we would be allowed to come to school late. If the earlier, we would arrive as normal. I put my hand up and was picked. It turned out that it was the earlier time. One morning, while kneeling on the marble altar listening to the priest drone on, I started to become dizzy and before I knew it I had fainted and banged my head off the altar. In those days men were on one side of the church and women on the other. The church had an air of historical sanctity, the faith of our fathers – I have an idea that the front rows were quietly kept for the important families in the town. A neighbor of mine, a lovely woman called Alice, a sister of Brege, stood up and said, "Someone help that boy!" I came to as two other altar boys were carrying me by the legs into the sacristy. Once I realized what was happening, I quickly shut my eyes again.

The same week we received news before going out onto the altar of someone who had died while on the toilet. We overheard the sacristan Jimmy telling the priest. I am sorry, but the altar boys could not stop laughing. It was too much to bear at that time of the morning. All of this took place in the old church and the interesting thing about the old church was that once the sacristan cleaned the chalices used for the Mass, which contained the crumbs of the Eucharist, he disposed of the water down a special well at the side of the church. At least, that is what he told me. I asked him, because I was wondering what happened to the water, which clearly would have come in contact with some part of the Eucharist. From that time on I imagined there was a well that somehow went to a very sacred place deep in the Earth, close to God's world I thought. (In fact it was nothing other than a drain.)

For some reason though, I continued to love Brother Anthony. I never once suspected any foul play. I was innocent of his ways and walked repeatedly into his traps and little games of degradation. I was honestly confused and wondered what I was doing wrong. I saw in him a rugged, solid, earthy individual with a warm heart. This greatly appealed to me. So much so that each time I was hit I would bounce back and try again to please him. To hate him never entered my mind. But, try as I might, I could not get close to him. Once, while standing on the sideline of an under-12 hurling team, waiting fruitlessly to be taken on, Brother Anthony asked me when I was born. I said November. "Ah, you will be two months too old for the team next year." Implied in this was the assumption that I would have made it. I felt crushed. I had yearned to be part of the team and to become part of the group of boys I saw as the center of my existence. I had begun to feel as if I were on the outside, as well as a little frightened in this small community and this was one way to get in. Not only that, but I had a fighting spirit and longed to show what I was capable of with a little guidance. Another time, I created a map of Ireland about six feet by four with some other boys, out of papier-mâché and paint. It was my attention to detail that gave it its authenticity. I had already a lot of experience in using newspaper, water and glue for making paper-based objects at home. It was beautiful and contained the contours of the lakes and mountains of Ireland in appropriate colors and in appropriate proportions. When Brother Anthony saw it he simply grunted and walked away.

Not that any of this affected my decision to adopt the name of Brother Anthony as my confirmation name. When the day arrived I was excited to receive my new name, as is the custom when one is confirmed in the Catholic Church. The Bishop came to me as I knelt before the altar and to my surprise I was not given the name Anthony, but another name: Joseph! In the end it was just as well, as Br. Joseph was one of the few Brothers who took the time to talk to me and show me a little of what his clerical calling was about: listening and helping. He was a good man, considered odd by many, but with a solid heart of integrity. Oftentimes we would meet in the schoolyard, where on spying him and wanting someone to talk to, I would go up to him and engage him. I loved the radiant soul that shone through him. Meanwhile, the other kids would gather round and start tugging at his robes until eventually he would pull out a stick, crunch down like an old witch and chase after them at the speed of light. It was like watching a flock of geese suddenly disappearing after the shot of a gun.

Now I can happily say that Joseph is my confirmation name, the other would have been a cruel reminder of what I had endured. Years later, at the time of writing this book, I had a dream where I was told that Brother Anthony had died an old and lonely man. That's quite sad, really. For all his faults, he was a good man who gave his heart and soul to the community. Many people remember him with deep respect. Even now I still remember him with affection, if not with disillusionment. When I like someone it's hard for me to stop. Something about me disturbed him and I am not sure what it was. Whatever it was, it placed him on a mission to keep me down. He really was a nice man, but it seems, like all of us, he had a weakness I could not have understood or, more importantly, he could not understand, being as he was a product of a more repressive culture than the one I grew into. Indeed there were Brothers the children loved dearly but it seems it didn't stop the others from doing bad things. However, Brother Anthony was not a bad man.

There was another Brother, Brother Fintan, whom I had the misfortune of knowing during my first days in the primary school. Now he was a right bastard, if not an out-and-out psychotic. He delighted us four-year-old babies with his tricks getting each child to repeat what he had done. He then instructed us to put our finger under our mouths, push upwards to release the tongue, turn on the ear to retrieve it and so on. At some point, something went wrong. It seemed as if Brother Fintan was having a psychotic break. He called me out, asked what I was doing and then beat me for being rude. Such were the sadistic ways of some Brothers. Frighten a child at an age when he is pliable and forever have him in your control. Many boys suffered badly at the hands of this "man of God" who could not be called a good man. Oddly my time at school had started well, being taught music in the first few weeks by a kindly woman teacher, later replaced by Brother Fintan – but only for a time. It was as if he was sent in to lay the groundwork: the bulldog of the religious, the sadistic face of the Church, a secret weapon they kept quiet and used as their initiation of babies into their society of control and fear, the bogeyman behind the door or, if you like, what the devil will do to you if he gets you. Once in the corridor during break I saw my brother John holding his hand in agony after being hit on the palm with a stick. John was only about six or seven, two years my senior. I was in the Babies' class at the time. What kind of a place had I entered? A place I had looked forward to joining? It was a sick joke and some of the people who administered it were the sick and broken of Irish life whom we as a society endured. They epitomized the separation of nature from spirit by relying on the perverse reasoning of a mind dictated to by a dogmatic Church cut off from the heart, not to mention the genitals! Is it any wonder then that some of these babies would grow up and in later years take out their aggression via the bullet and the bomb, transferring their aggression away from its real source to an outside source – which is always safer. It's never easy to look at the truth or to look the real aggressor in the eye because the real aggressor scares you. That is what makes you angry. But it is easy if you can pick on the innocent and vent your rage on them or, failing that, beat the crap out of your partner. That's the unspoken Irish religious legacy – cowardice and brutality and, of course, education.

Once things had settled down in Babies', or perhaps it was High-Infants', we started learning from our first books. I took home a small book in Gaelic as part of my class work. As my mother tucked me into bed I read her the first page which I understood completely. I enjoyed this learning. Unfortunately I missed a few days at school and fell behind. I could not catch up because I was afraid the teacher would beat me for not knowing my homework and I was afraid to ask for help. It seems as though the Brother had little patience for teaching and simply wanted to finish the syllabus. From that time on I gave up study altogether and instead developed ways to cover up the fact. I can still remember learning the mathematics tables. It was quite fun as the whole class repeated the multiplication tables from 1 to 12. I still remember most of them and the ones I don't, I have little tricks for, such as the adding or subtracting of the results of other tables. To this day those tables were probably the most important things I learned in my entire life and the fun of the constant group repetition was probably the best way they were taught. It amazes me to see grown adults in shops using calculators to work out the simplest multiplication or for that matter addition. They have no idea whatsoever of the size of numbers. The other two things we learned as babies were the letters of the alphabet and a rhyme for the number of days in each month of the year. All in all three very useful pieces of information. At least for that I say thanks!

However, learning gave me a physical pain in the head as though it was a reminder of the brutal way we were being forced to learn. My usual trick to avoid being caught out was to calculate the lines I would be asked to say in Gaelic in class based on those who had gone before me. The teacher had a habit of going round the class in a certain order and asking each child to explain a few lines. This I learned to do within the class but no more. I knew no more and was too pained and too bored to bother. A time did come towards the end of national school when I asked for help and Brother Anthony came to my house and had me read from a Gaelic book with my mother present. I read clearly and he said to my mother, "I don't see any problem." He then suggested to my mother that I be sent to the corner class, which is where those with learning difficulties were sent. I didn't like the idea, as I didn't think I had any real learning difficulties. I just couldn't relax enough to study Gaelic. There was too much punishment. I devoted my energies to avoiding the punishment. Gaelic class was an hour of fear every day of my life in National school coupled with regular beatings.

Luckily, there was an escape. My love of comics meant that I read them endlessly. In the beginning I did not understand what they said but, with time, I figured out the meaning of the words with the help of the pictures. The advantage of this is that I could read before my time and as a result had no trouble with English reading or homework. Ironically English was taught with the same gusto if not with more conviction than Gaelic was. However, each day before the class began, the pupils said the "Our Father" in Gaelic, which was written on a large board just inside the door, along with the "Hail Mary." In time I learned both by heart. I preferred the "Hail Mary." It was shorter and easier to learn. Luckily I enjoyed math and saw it as a pastime. I always did my math exercises at home, as I liked to be top of the class in this subject and enjoyed getting the answers right. All in all with my love of math, of comics and my tricks to get by in Gaelic, you could say I practically never studied until the age of 12 when I entered secondary school.

It was towards the end of primary school, around the age of 11, that I was called into the Head Brother's office. Standing there: the local policeman, Brother Anthony and the Head Brother. Another boy sat with a blank, acquiescent face. I was accused, along with this boy, of ringing the fire brigade on a false call, saying someone was stuck on the roof of a house. I was petrified. The more they insisted the less I could recall. In the end I just wanted to get out of that office and repeated word-for-word the statement of my supposed fellow-conspirator, which had been read to me more than once. This seemed to satisfy all present, although the Head Brother seemed very quiet. It is true to say that the more you bully a boy the more he forgets.

Whatever the case and whether I held some guilt or not, I can say this much: What happened in that room was nothing short of pure child abuse, where three fully grown men kept a child captive while he was interrogated and frightened out of his mind into making a forced confession. That was the real crime that afternoon. Even as I struggle with it now, I feel a sense of trauma asking myself what part did I play? After getting a successful confession from me I was returned to class, where Brother Anthony pointed me out and humiliated me, saying, "Now you see what kind of a boy he is," while I sat at the back of the class crying, filled with a sense of isolation and loneliness. He seemed to enjoy this moment. It was as if he needed this to justify himself in some way. It was perhaps a moment he had waited for and it came just before I would finally be out of his control: a parting gift, a final mark of his victory over me. It seemed he wanted to break my spirit for some reason. It didn't stop him however from using me when it came to collections. He knew I had a gift for collecting the most, which I would do to please him as well as to win the prize for the most money collected. He didn't seem to enjoy giving me my prize as much as he enjoyed emptying my collection cans.

One delightful thing did happen though. Once, while eagerly helping Brother Anthony clear a space to put a garage at the Brothers' house for their first car, I found an old copper lantern buried beneath the ground. It was like buried treasure to me and, to my delight, he let me keep it. I took it home and polished it. It was a prize to me.

Brother Anthony loved gardening and, I have to say, he had a very impressive garden. He had lines of cabbages, lines of potatoes, lines of lettuce and so on. All for the Brothers' house. I loved to help him after school. The Brothers' house was only about a hundred meters away and I always volunteered when he asked for help. After, we would sit in the kitchen and have tea and cakes. The housekeeper would make the tea on the old stove and usually another Brother would join us and together we would have a grand time. It seemed that when some of these Brothers entered the school, they somehow went crazy. Maybe they hated the place?

Another event that was to have an impact on my life happened when Brother Anthony wanted the boys to somersault over a table for a show. He let me go first, unaided, as I was enthusiastic to try. As I somersaulted, I hit my lower right back against the edge of the table. This scared me and so I was excused from making further attempts. Brother Anthony then aided the rest of the boys as they began to turn on the table. This event led many years later to numerous unsuccessful attempts to heal this injury, which flared up whenever I pushed myself at sport. I was to learn many valuable lessons in my attempts to deal with this condition. In essence, I learned that I could not trust anyone who supposedly claimed they could help me in the medical profession. It seemed their priority was to get paid and often they did not seem to know what they were doing. Eventually I became disillusioned with the medical profession, but at the same time I gained an interest in healing. It seems God uses all of us in strange ways.

For some reason, I never really understood Brother Anthony's attempts to undermine and belittle me. I was naïve. For years I had sought his friendship, seeing in him a warmth and likeability I was attracted to. I was blind to everything else. Even though I would be hit more times than I can remember by the leg of a chair, suffering this man's uncontrolled anger, I still wanted so much to be liked by him. I was not the only child to be brutalized by this man. It seemed the more I wanted to be liked by him, the less I was. And it seemed this was also understood by those children whom the Brother favored and who never chose me for any of their teams even though I sat and waited until the very end of the team selection, suffering the humiliation of being the runt in the litter, often not being chosen. When I was, I usually waited on the sidelines as a substitute. In the beginning, I had liked it that way, as I didn't much care for staying back after school. But I had a change of heart and now it seems it was too late.

After crying at first I quickly resolved never to cry when hit by this man. In this way, I could maintain my dignity and leave the door open for a dignified friendship. I simply sat while he hit me across the head with the leg of a chair. When things got too much, back home I would retreat to the backyard of my house and cry in the arms of my dog Bell. Afterwards, I would wash out my eyes and put on white powder to cover up the redness. I was not comfortable being seen in this way.

Perhaps my fear of being caught out in Gaelic class was one reason why I learned never to express what I wanted. I did not like to feel exposed. I simply waited and hoped someone would see the effort I was making and pick me for a team or for whatever. I was afraid of ridicule if I put myself forward. Little by little, it seemed to me the world was crushing my spirit. Perhaps my proud spirit had turned people against me? I was not sure. It was the same spirit that refused to be sorry when others would not accept their part, also.

As a boy, I had a recurring dream. I would dream that if I went up the chimney behind the fireplace in the living room, I would come out into the fireplace of another room directly above. This room was very large with a tall ceiling and big, open windows. It seemed well-built but unused, full of empty space waiting to be lived in. This room was a place I could go and hide and get away from everyone else if I wanted to. From time to time I would recognize it in my dreams and go there. For a while I actually believed the room existed, but when I thought about it I realized it couldn't exist and that it was just a dream. Perhaps it was a reflection of a space inside me that was empty or was yet to be filled?

Brother Anthony was a monumental worker and worked tirelessly running football and hurling teams on top of everything else. What his problem was I don't know, but I see that he, in his way, was simply carrying out a greater design. And for that I say thank you, Brother Anthony, that you suffered the guilt of how you treated me, as I know deep down it was not in your nature. Unfortunately, I cannot say the same about Brother Fintan, who was a right bastard.

Apart from anything else I had an inexplicable fear of my father. The mere mention of his name in anger would send tremors through me. I was quite literally afraid for my life. The beatings themselves were easily endured as I was used to them in school where, for some reason, I seemed to endure the most; but the man himself put the fear of death in me and I did not really know why. It was an odd thing and it sometimes worried me, the way I had become immune to a routine round of beatings at home and at school. I hoped it wouldn't desensitize me in some important way, as I seemed to take it all in my stride. Perhaps that is why I received them as it appeared I was unaffected. Whatever the case, the man's intentions were always good. He was a holy man but, like all men, he had his faults. He simply carried much more burden than his share. However, there did come a time in my childhood when he never laid a hand on me again.

There seemed to be many unhappy moments in my childhood, but I could not remember when and how they began. It was as if I woke up one day and was not the boy I was before. It was as if a part of my consciousness had shut down and I grasped to get it back, as if someone had stolen a part of my brain during the night. Even one of my friends boasted to me of a knife that he kept, which I saw, should anyone ever try to hurt him. What he was expecting I did not know, but the thought of it scared me. My friend's willingness to use a large knife intimidated me. Something very strange was going on in my town. I had begun to live in fear and would arrive at school strictly as it started, avoiding any possible confrontation with another boy. I was always the last to get up in the house and would arrive in school alone, the rest already there. School breaks were a source of anxiety until I found my few trusted friends who, like me, were not much liked by Brother Anthony. We would sneak away at break to a local shop where we smoked our cigarettes, bought one at a time from the friendly and loving lady of the shop. They cost about two cents each. When I was younger I used to enjoy these school breaks. Then, I had a host of water pistols that I filled repeatedly and let loose on my fellow pupils. Water pistols were all the rage in the yard at one time. By this stage, I would not consider using them for fear of someone hitting me.

At the same time I noticed changes in my character. For one thing, while looking at my brother's black-and-white film projector, I flew into a rage and destroyed the film before I knew what had happened. This shocked me. Another unsettling pattern started to emerge. I found myself undermining my own happiness. I seemed to find a reason to turn sour and unhappy at times when I should have been happiest. My birthday parties seemed to end up with a fight, as did the Christmas dinners. If someone upset me I would cut myself off from the group and so began a pattern of loneliness and isolation. I was unable to cope with what I perceived as the unfairness of others. I lost my sense of humor. To make matters worse I was accused of being too sensitive. It took all my strength not to be enraged by this ignorance that sought to place the entire problem on my shoulders instead of taking any responsible action to help. Such was the Irish way. Actually, the label sensitive could be applied to the very same people who labeled me. In fact, it could be applied to the vast majority of people I knew. Just because I was honest with my feelings didn't make me any less of a man! I did try to accept the rudeness of others, believing maybe I was silly. But in the end it disgusted me and my own pain was too great to play along with their little sadistic games. I would not respond to stupid, ignorant remarks and for a while this worked. It seems the abuse of the Church had fed its way into every aspect of Irish life, being supported by the submission of a frightened people who were taught to be submissive by being cut off from the source of their power, their sexuality! Perhaps these boys were also training to be religious? It was better to be apart from that even if it meant being viewed as being stuck-up.

It seemed as if I had begun to live my life inside a glass bowl looking out – a little dazed and confused – wanting to put myself right. I did not realize then that, nearly 25 years later, I would learn many things about myself I simply did not know at that time; things that others probably knew and which contributed to a kind of conspiracy of silence in my community. Things that obviously affected others. It's funny how, as a boy, you wonder what is going on and when you do finally realize the truth the whole confusing jigsaw falls into place, bringing with it a sense of freedom and resolution; the wall of the glass bowl melts away. However, in the same way that great heat is required to melt glass, so too an intense energy born from the heart and soul of Africa, imbued with thousands of years of spiritual knowledge and worship, would be required to unseat a mind deeply attached to its own self, revealing a past deeply hidden and repressed.

The primary school did its best to instill a fear of hell and damnation. In one class, the story was told of how a student had tried to win a shilling by putting his hands over a lighted candle and failed. Imagine what hell was like! It was then a simple task to link this to sexuality. Which is, of course, what happened. Each year the Missionary Fathers would come in their robes and preach hell and damnation to all who broke the rules, particularly the sexual and alcoholic ones. The fact that they came from the dark continent where the devil surely lurked, made it all the more riveting. How ironic is it that the very people these missionaries were seeking to save were in fact the guardians of a sacred plant that would one day save me by bringing about an exorcism of biblical proportions within my own soul? An exorcism unlike nothing I had ever encountered, except perhaps in the biblical stories of Jesus. Our little community, it seemed, was "safe" from the darkness these men dedicated their lives to eradicate. Little did we understand the demons lurking within our own selves, hidden by silence, unwittingly reinforced by these very same men. Demons I would one day watch in horror being wrenched from my own soul.

The Missions however gave an interesting, festive feel to this time of year as the stalls arrived, selling everything from luminous Virgin Marys to relics of Padre Pio, crosses from the Holy Land and any other item of religious merchandise you can care to think of. During the Missions I would hide away in the church along with the more adventurous children to hear the Fathers talk about all manner of things. Especially to hear them talk about sex. It was riveting stuff. The townspeople took these missions very seriously. They were an annual cleansing of the soul. A way to confront the serious sins of the year that they might not have admitted to the priest. The people would come out chastened but relieved. Such is the way they were kept subdued: fear, guilt and forgiveness, the Unholy Trinity. The Church thought all it had to do, in return for the right to earthly power in God's name, was to keep everyone cowered down like sheep in a pen. Then, when God would arrive, they could look up and say, "Look! we have them all here." And He in turn would say, "Right, pack them onto that trailer over there and I will take them with me".

In truth the problems still returned as they were never properly dealt with. Ironically this policy probably grew out of a desperation to control sexual abuse among the people, only revealed in the confessional, in the same way as the Church sought to control sexuality. The Church thus created its own vicious circle and was unable to cope with the monster it created.

It was possibly around this time I began to have recurring nightmares where I was being attacked by demons. In my fears and simplicity, I took to drinking holy water and sprinkling it around my bed to keep them away. The missions were probably not the reason for these nightmares, as they were just another form of entertainment to me at the time.

I then began to have a series of accidents, one of which involved being catapulted onto stony ground from my fast-moving wooden bogey cart, banging my head several times. A less serious accident involved teaching my older brother John how to drive our father's car, believing I could instruct him on what I had seen Dad do. Everything went beautifully until John put his foot on the accelerator and, when he asked how to stop, I panicked and could do nothing except open the door thinking to get out. The left-hand side of the car, which I was on, went into the back of the shop wall. Luckily I had opened the door, as it meant the rest of the car was spared the impact. John went straight up to the loft and, in a display not seen since the Virgin Mary appeared in Lourdes, prayed as though enrapt in a vision. I was very amused by this, but, needless to say, our father was not.

Another time, while standing outside the door of a friend who lived next door to a well-known bully, I was suddenly lunged to the ground by the most ferocious attack with cupped fists on my mid-back between the shoulders and not just once. I lay down not wanting to entice the attacker back. Onlookers made one or two remarks in shock but did nothing. The consequence of this is that I suffered long-term pain in that area, the area of the heart. I had my share of childhood injuries to keep me occupied with the healing services in later life and to learn to become disillusioned with most of them.

I remember once, during a school break about the age of 11, I tried to find peace of mind and happiness by focusing on a lilac tree and imagining it shining with life. I had a notion that all life had an essence that could shine brightly. It did seem to glow a little bit. I had the idea that beneath all the shit lay something of beauty worth living for, even if the world around me seemed to be going crazy and each week more and more atrocities were being committed in the name of freedom and religion right on my doorstep. It took years and years of patient reflection to figure out what was going on between the so-called Catholics and Protestants of Northern Ireland. The simple school explanations did not justify this current round of violence, as this was something that was most certainly not romantic. I wondered if it had a direct historical link to the old IRA and therefore some justification – a bit like the pope in Rome and his link to Peter – or whether it basically was what it was, violence and murder? What effect this daily graphic TV display of violence had on me and others like me I cannot be sure. By now we were numb to it. What chance had an outsider to understand? I myself had great difficulty in understanding the difference between UK, GB, NI, Ireland and ROI (UK = GB+NI where UK means United Kingdom, GB means Great Britain = Scotland, England and Wales, NI = Northern Ireland, and Ireland = NI & ROI where ROI means Republic of Ireland.) The confusion comes in when people living in N.I. call themselves British when, in fact, they are technically Northern Irish who hold a British passport. Had I been older, I might have realized it was all simply a cover-up for hatred and anger born out of putrefied and petrified souls. It all seemed such a waste. Once, I composed a letter to Queen Elizabeth asking her if she could do something, but I never sent it. There was a time when my father would drive the 45 minutes to the nearest cross-border town and I would marvel at the wealth of my neighbors compared to the simplicity of the world I came from. Now I would simply stare blankly at the destruction and hatred I saw there. What had gone wrong? It seemed that there was a sickness, not only in my hometown but also in the neighboring cross-border areas. They had become and still are, a police state, an historical throw back. *In his quest Parcival comes to a castle in the middle of a desolate wasteland where no crops grow and darkness has descended on the hearts of the people. At this time the Grail King, also known as the Fisher King, lay wounded in his castle. Because the Grail King was one with the land the land and all in it were sickened as well.*

It was also around this time that I went with a friend of mine into a pub in a small nearby fishing village. Inside I met a tall, well-built man with a beard who started to talk to me about the IRA and made a veiled suggestion I might consider joining it. It was not unusual to meet such people but normally they did not discuss such things with you. They existed, but that was that. After all this was a border county notorious for IRA activity as they slipped to and fro from one side to the other avoiding the reaches of the "Law." As a child I used to fantasize and hope that the troubles would spread across the border so that I could defend my little town from the street corner outside my father's shop, lying flat with an automatic rifle propped by its two legs. But those fantasies were now a thing of the past. In this moment came the realization that I could never support this organization or any other like it. It was brutal and it was evil, even if it was well intentioned. I made my excuses and left. One thing I had learned was not to speak your mind directly in such circumstances. Perhaps the whole IRA thing was taboo in my area, not far from what was called "bandit country" and I did not even realize it. Once, while thinking on the situation, these words came to mind:

> The woman screamed,
> And a child shot forth,
> An Armalite in its hands.

Word Key: Armalite is the manufacture name of a popular IRA rifle.

The English were a fascination to me growing up. A strange bunch, I thought, that loved their monarchy which in truth was only a sad reflection of their once "great" empire. Until the early 70s, we still used what was called the old money. We had pounds, shillings, pennies, halfpennies and, for a time, farthings. We shared our currency with England. What was so wonderful about it was the endless history it contained. I would look at coins coming through my father's till and they would have the imprints of the various English kings and queens of the twentieth century. I was always on the lookout for pennies from the time of Queen Victoria and they did turn up. Some were marked 1897, if I recall correctly. It was an amazing thing. My father also liked to check for these coins and kept a collection of the ones he thought most valuable. I remember half crowns were fashionable at one stage. The Irish coins of course, reflected the change in Ireland's constitutional status and so you had various motifs along with Free State in Gaelic, Republic and other such things. I think I recall seeing an English penny over-stamped with Irish Free State in Gaelic.

However, as I grew up I grew distant from my father who believed in the old ways of discipline, believing that was all I needed to sort me out. His intentions were always good. Unfortunately, in rejecting my father, I unwittingly rejected my own manhood and myself. Years later, I met a Canadian who was visiting Ireland to try to understand why his own father was so cranky and difficult. I wondered if it was an Irish trait, one that I was fast developing: a trait born out of an inability to change things for the better, being under the all-consuming power of a repressed culture which, ironically, in its heart valued freedom immensely. If so, it was because inside lived the frustration of knowing one had been cheated after having done everything one could to follow the dictates that had been handed down. Dictates based on social and religious promises that one would discover in time would never be kept. Instead, one would discover more dictates, wrapped up in pious mutterings, designed to silence the oppressed even further, to hide the rotten underbelly of Irish life that this system had spawned.

But such was the power of this culture. It permitted no easing of restrictions for anybody. I had lost my spirit and with it my voice. Was this not the way this culture was meant to be? It seemed that Br. Anthony had his way in the end, fulfilling his role to break every child to the way of the Church and then cynically placing the Church as the only possibility of salvation from such a sad, sorry situation. The perversity of it is not lost on me. Neither, unfortunately, were the consequences. The Church had an effective game plan to rule the Irish roost.

Naturally with time I became boring, needing everything to be predictable to keep away my hidden fears. It is easy to see how one becomes conservative in such circumstances: the mischievous child too afraid to be mischievous. And what made it worse was that I knew all this. Watching from the sidelines while life passed me by, it took all my energy not to become a delinquent to a society that had created me that way. A woman of my mother's generation once told me how there was great depression in the villages down the west of Ireland. When you consider the fallout of the Great Famine and the way it brutalized the country, a country that was already brutalized by a history of British oppression – coupled with the oppression of sexuality by the Church and State, one can begin to understand why. There is a sickness on the land and people are overwhelmed. *At this time the Grail King, also known as the Fisher King, lay wounded in his castle. Because the Grail King was one with the land, as he lay wasting away in sickness so the land and all in it were sickened as well.*

As a child I became intimidated by kindness, like an abused, abandoned dog. Once, years later, I cried when an English Magistrate of the Peace wished me well in my new life as I set off to go to Australia. I had come before the Magistrate to have documents validated and the magistrate allowed me not to swear on the Bible. His subsequent kindness, despite my rebellious behavior, touched me.

An unfortunate consequence of my fears was that I would not go to concerts, which were at the very heart of my soul, for fear of the unbridled enthusiasm I would find there. Yet I yearned for the spirit embodied on the stage, in the crowd and in the music. Maybe that is why the way of music, or more correctly singing, became an object of bliss for me. If I could transcend my problems and place myself on the podium I would have made it. However, once, Brother Anthony did place me on the stage to entertain the other boys with jokes. I loved the idea of being on a stage. Unfortunately, I froze after one or two jokes and had nothing to say, even though I was known for my humor. The boys heckled me off. After that day my ability to remember jokes declined drastically. This Brother was a clever sadist, clearly experienced with breaking down boys.

There came a time when I realized life was more pain than joy and I was determined not to lose the joy and wonder that life had held for me. I became lonely and did not enjoy the same close friendship I once had with girls. Once I became infatuated with a girl and for days I suffered deeply. I was unable to eat. It was very painful. It seemed as though a part of me I had kept hidden was exposed and I felt something quite awful and sickening. It was puppy love but it was a lot more than that – things which I genuinely did not want to feel. It seemed I could not connect with my whole being to others and enjoy the warmth of closeness. There was a part of me I could not express and it held me back terribly. I simply could not connect with another's love, as I was too threatened by my own feelings. I was also in a constant state of fear of attack. Boys, it seemed, put more emphasis on the pecking order than they did on their friendships. Yet if I was to be accepted I somehow had to fit in.

I was 12 when I had my first kiss. Myself and some other boys went camping to the Gaeltacht area in the west of Ireland. Here Gaelic is the first language. We joined up with some other children who were there studying Gaelic. The girl I kissed left me feeling completely warm and moved. Her kiss was long and passionate. I became embarrassed and laughed, much to her disgust. I had not meant to upset her but this was an experience I was not familiar with. I did not get to kiss her again. Neither did I feel the same way when kissing another girl a few days later who seemed like a wet fish compared to her. Puberty had arrived and I hoped to feel some of the illicit thrill it promised.

While there we stayed in the garden of a beautiful family who had beautiful children. I started to become attached to one girl called Margaret. I have always found the west of Ireland girls to have a special energy. However, an older friend expressed an interest in her so I said nothing. It was our code of honor. Yet I could see she was drawn to me too. She had dark hair and dark eyes, which lit up like candlesticks, along with a beautiful sense of fun – perhaps a touch of the Spanish who had landed there and integrated with the local people many centuries before. For days I could not leave my tent. I was deeply and badly in love with her. I felt sick. Once she went with me alone into the kitchen while the others were in the living room. I remember how she sat against the stove looking quietly at me with her soft, gentle eyes lit up. I looked at her. I did not know what to say. I was entranced by the vision of her gentle simplicity. Her beauty left me in silence. Within minutes my older friend arrived into the kitchen, obviously sensing something afoot.

This was the last time we were alone together. The last I heard of her, she had emigrated to London with a local boy whom she married. If I have one regret in life, it is this: I loved her and I did nothing about it. Still to this day it hurts me to think about what I lost, but I simply had no voice and thought very little of myself when it came to the very essence of who I was. Perhaps it was meant to be my first taste of the Grail? A taste that would repeat itself many years later when I would once more gaze upon the eyes of a girl whose beauty, this time, would inspire me to take a path that would be the most difficult I have ever undertaken; a path that would take me into the darkest parts of my soul, to look at what I had spent my life avoiding. But to do that required a disregard for death, a disregard which comes when all else has failed.

It was around this time that I hit on the idea of self-analysis. I had seen something of Freud and was impressed with the idea that one could resolve problems by simply understanding them. Thus began a life of introspection, collection of facts and possibilities, leading more often than not to incredulity at the difficulty of finding an answer. I had hoped by understanding myself I would snap back into reality as if, by putting all the pieces together, a door would open, linking me back to the real world. I also felt that if I could establish myself among my peers, I could possibly regain those good feelings I had lost in my earlier life. In turn, these might be enough to outweigh and eliminate the bad ones. I realized if I was not growing in good feelings, I would slowly die in the bad. However, to be accepted by my peers seemed to require proving myself as a fighter. This I simply could not bring myself to do in the cold light of day. For one reason, I was unusually scared of being hit. Secondly, I once tried picking on a boy and the boy was scared even though I hardly touched him. This image haunted me and left me with a strong sense of guilt. It was an act of barbarism to pick on an innocent victim. The only possibility was to be really angry. But, try as hard as I could by imagining how I would react, I could not overcome my fear and disgust at the thought of the consequences of such an action.

I realized I had a weak ego, as I was too vulnerable to others. I resolved to strengthen it to lessen the pain as well as help me integrate better. It seemed that, in trying to do so, I was losing a part of myself that I valued and would eventually become like the many adults I saw – distant, unhappy and boring. I had always believed life would be different for me but now it seemed I was being pushed in the same direction like so many others before me, onto some kind of cultural conveyor belt: hands tied, mouth gagged, with the only way out being a life of sanctity and the continuation of a vicious circle of enslavement of others. That was an imposition I was not prepared to accept. It seemed I was programming myself in some way, a program that was not easy to undo and that saddened me. I did not want to forget who I was, lest I lose myself and accept unhappiness as the norm. I resolved not to forget. I resolved to be who I valued the most, the carefree child, even if it took my last, dying breath. Better that than an enforced cultural lobotomy. However, the only way left open to me to recover this lost child was to rise above myself to the light, in order to dispel the dark down below that was simply not negotiable. Unfortunately, that meant the area close to where God lived and the Church had that poisoned.

Another change that took place in my life at this time was my attitude towards my mother. I had rarely obeyed her unless I had to, always doing what I preferred when out of sight. I began to reason that if I did what I was asked then maybe I would feel better about myself. Any possibility was worth a try. So, I developed an unhealthy attachment to my mother, which would take years to overcome. I slowly but surely offered up my freedom. I walked my town in fear and shame. Where once I jumped in the air with delight,

111

I now slinked in the shadows. There was a force at work that I had unwittingly bumped into and it was determined to mold me the same way it had molded the generations before me.

There was a time when I would search out the hidden places in my town and once discovered a tunnel, barely big enough for me to squeeze into, that ran under the road for about 20 feet. Armed with a candle, I made my way in, only to find the other end blocked. I returned there many times. It captivated me. From the farthest end I could see the light of the outside world. It was by keeping my eye on this light, that I found my way out of the dark.

4. The Serpent

What I truly have is inside me.

It was in my first year of secondary school an event took place
that was to set the tone for the rest of my life. One day a
missionary Brother arrived in the school which was also run by
Brothers but with a lot more respect for the children. He was a
funny man who did an early version of the moonwalk dance. He
was looking for boys to join the Hospitaler Order of St. John of God.
They would go to a school far away on the other side of Dublin,
in the Wicklow Mountains. To me, this was like going to another
homeland, as the Wicklow Mountains were a kind of psychological
break in the landscape. I also had a desire to travel and was captured
by the idea. I decided to express an interest. Though how genuine it
was, was very questionable.

It was at this time the Brothers' Secondary school was to merge
with the other second-level schools in the area, including the
Convent. The merging of the schools marked a turning point in the
power of the Church. Its power was beginning to decline, but not its
legacy. That would live on for many more years to come. The loss
of the teaching Brothers and Sisters – not all of whom were bad,
however – was in many ways the loss of the heart and soul of the
community. The baby was thrown out with the bath water. Perhaps
the government felt it was time to overthrow the Church. Although
we rejoiced at the new freedoms, in our heart of hearts we knew
we had lost something very valuable. Worse still, the damage was
already done and the guilty gone into hiding.

The school itself was wonderful. Situated at the foot of the
Wicklow Hills, it was surrounded by the most beautiful country
setting: woods, rivers and fields. It was a gentle place. However,
while I was there, I felt I was losing out on the possibility of living

113

at home and connecting with my peers. I began to feel that this was important if I was ever to come to terms with myself and my fears. I also suffered from homesickness from time to time, feeling cut off and isolated from my family and waited eagerly each week for the local newspaper my mother would send, searching through it for the letter I knew would be there. Before leaving home I had begun to keep my guard up and didn't enjoy the company of my siblings as I once used to. So being away at school was almost a de facto death of my ties to my family. I had kept my thoughts to myself and had, in effect, run away from home. My family was oblivious to my situation.

Once on my return home I looked for my cat Fluffy. My two brothers brought me to her. She was dead, apparently having eaten poison left for the rats. While I looked in shock, they could not control themselves and started to laugh. It seemed that, in some way, at least one of my brothers derived quiet satisfaction in this. Perhaps it had something to do with the car? To me it seemed my world had just gotten smaller. My cat of at least six years dead and the other cats starting to die off. The past was fast disappearing from underneath me and my problems seemed locked into it, out of reach, all conspirators disappeared. To others my world seemed to be growing and indeed it was, but not in my mind. The number of cats steadily dwindled after I left and in time I forgot all about Fluffy. In fact I even made a point of not really liking cats, as that would make Fluffy's death less important. Another time when I returned home, I found my dog Bell was no longer there. It seemed my father had taken him away and dropped him somewhere in the country. He said that he had run away but I thought differently. Perhaps he had. Maybe he was looking for me? He was after all an untamed dog and difficult to master, as he had his own spirit, his own joy of life. My father, at times an impatient man, perhaps felt he could not cope and that there was no need to keep the dog, as the only one who seemed to care about him was gone. All around me the past I had sought to reconcile with was closing its doors and I had no key to open them. Fortunately I had no idea of the years ahead I had to go through in order to finally unlock its secrets. If I had, would I have endured them?

While in this school I and a friend, who shared my adventurous spirit, once tormented a sensitive boy by keeping him cringing under a bed. I enjoyed this moment of sadism because it felt very liberating. But almost immediately I saw it for what it was and backed off. As a result I later became an object of scorn for my co-conspirator, whom I had taken to be my best friend, who it turned out was only interested in indulging his sadistic ways. This was one way to freedom I was not prepared to accept. What goes round comes round, as my mother used to say. However, this it seems was the way of many to deal with the pain of life in this broken society.

One of the strange things in this school was the pairing up of boys, almost like bed friends. It was as if new boys to the school were like fresh, innocent meat waiting to be molded. There was a funny atmosphere to all of this. There was from time to time a sexual tension in the school and I, myself, fantasized about sexual relations with one or two other boys although I never acted on them, even if I tried once or twice to set up a situation. I was too afraid. I suspected my fear was not shared by all. I also did not know what any of it meant about my sexuality. I was completely ignorant and nobody bothered to explain anything. I guess they were completely ignorant too.

It's a strange thing that, in all my years in the primary school, not once was the word "sex" mentioned or anything to do with it. Only once did Brother Anthony mention how God had designed the male sex organs in such a clever way that the scrotum was safely tucked away from harm. This I found very interesting and refreshing. But more is the pity, as nothing more was said. It seems that, when puberty arrived, boys had to struggle to understand what was happening to them. It was taboo. What was that strange discharge during the night? It was taboo. There was a time when boys believed that babies were born through the belly button. Needless to say sex was totally forbidden. As each boy had learned to fear hell, it was a simple equation to link one's emerging sexuality as an invitation to go there and there is not where you wanted to go. Boys however did learn to be brutal long before they learned of hell. A good Irish boy could grow up to be dangerous and brutal without the fear of hell and to be someone who didn't practice sex or know what true sexuality was. Sexuality was a secret garden, especially the sexuality of the female and, like the garden of the soul that the Church sought to protect, it didn't let the people enter there either. For many people, sexuality was about bestiality: do it, savor a quick unspoken thrill, jump off and wipe yourself clean. And don't mention the aroma of the mound of Venus. Every part of the sexual act had the stamp of the Church on it. It was signposted: "This way to guilt and shame. This way to hell." We lived in fortress Ireland and the clerics manned the outposts. Is it any wonder that so many escaped through the only door left open: emigration? Every system needs a way out. Perhaps hell has a way out too?

It was in this school that my love and confidence in mathematics flourished. While we were only 38 pupils, we were blessed to have the most dedicated and astute mathematics teacher I have ever had. I can still remember the moment when my conversion to mathematics took place. I was sitting at the back of the study hall working on some equations. I had a moment of fright, as I was afraid I might not be able to make the transition to this new mathematics. It involved what are called imaginary numbers, i.e., numbers with a coefficient of i where i is the square root of -1. These equations troubled me, as they were not imaginable and therefore not tangible. However, while poring over a problem, in a moment I had a flash of insight and saw the result at some unknown, intuitive level. It gave me a rush to the head and I knew that I had cracked it. From there on, my confidence had been established in the subject. I was not going to suffer the pain to the head other subjects gave me. This subject was going to be my pastime. The other area I enjoyed was the theorems we had to learn for our intermediate examinations – about 15 in all. Each one proved a different mathematical statement and required using insight as well as established mathematical rules. It was powerful stuff and I have no doubt it contributed greatly to my own mental ability to reason my way out of the insurmountable problems I encountered in my life. It established a base of clear reason where one could easily sense the error in a particular way of thinking – and that was vital to me. By coupling this way of thinking with one's intuition, you have a powerful way to find your way through life.

After two years I persuaded my mother to bring me home, making some excuse that the level of math in the upper school would not be sufficient for my abilities. In doing so one could safely say I went from the frying pan into the fire. My mother had other ideas for my education. She worried about my return and sent me to another boarding school for my final two years. The school was based on a hill in the cold, windswept and almost barren countryside of Monaghan, the exact opposite of the idyllic surroundings of my previous school. One could say this school functioned on fear and prayers, coupled with a lot of study. Did it have any other choice? Was not the Church a victim of its own repressed culture, a self-perpetuating organism? Most of the students came from a rural Irish background. Tough men, used to the land and the daily struggle for survival. These were not boys reared on hot milk and biscuits. Left to their own devices they could have launched a rebellion in a small country. Once, while waiting for prayers in the church, some of the boys competed to see how far they could spit up to the altar. This kind of defiance scared me. I also became so sick of the study that, by the last term, I had stopped studying altogether and simply sat my final school exams. Luckily for me, I scraped through, due to my own interest in mathematics and English.

Around this time during the summer break I traveled to Galway in the west of Ireland and met a man in the street giving out leather crosses for free, which I thought was cool. On them was stamped MGSMW vertically and horizontally. I thought he was a nice man and he explained to me what the inscription meant: my greatest strength my weakness. I didn't really understand what that meant, but I pretended I did. I wore that cross for the next few years. At the time I wore a lot of coats of various lengths and grew my sideburns practically down to my neck. I guess I was a bit of a drop-out.

Perhaps now as I write my story I finally understand what the inscription meant. When I was about 12, I had a crush on a girl in my town. She was working for the father of a friend of mine. I told him I was very interested in her. He said that he would ask her to meet me at a dancehall about six miles away. I went, but she did not show up. I was disappointed and, a few days later, returned to my friend's house. When I entered my friend came out beaming. Next to him, clueless perhaps of what happened, was the girl I liked. I was stunned and said almost nothing as I felt deeply ashamed. I never spoke to him about it. In fact, after that, I saw less and less of him. My weakness was to trust people too easily and let them into my confidence. I suffered greatly for that on many occasions. On the other hand, there is also a purity about that and you could say that perhaps it was also my greatest strength. Maybe that is what the guy with the leather crosses was trying to tell me.

At some point or other, I learned how to comfort myself in the way boys do, which led to an endless amount of guilt and fear of damnation. I devised a way to keep the books straight with the Big Man above. Each Friday I would summon up the courage to find guilt for what I had done, count the number of times, promise myself I would behave in future and then, prepared, go to confessions to atone for my sins. Sometimes I was too ashamed to go and would live in fear of damnation. It's interesting the way fear preys on fear. Before entering my new school – called a Junior Seminary from the old days – I visited the penitential island of Lough Derg. It was said that if one made the pilgrimage three times, one was guaranteed entry into the Kingdom of Heaven. The required age for making the pilgrimage was 16. I was 15.

This was no ordinary island. Set in the remote, cloudy, cold, rainy and forgotten parts of Donegal, it contained a basilica, dorms for men and women and 15 Stations of the Cross. Each station had a cross surrounded by stony mounds of earth set in levels. The penitent would spend two days without sleep, praying barefoot at each station, making many passes round each cross. Three times a day they would be called to the hall for toast and black tea. The trick was to get there for the freshly-made toast which was not bad, as it still retained its moisture. Everyone was aware of this. The second night the penitents were allowed to sleep and what a sleep that was!

It was on the island that I sought to purge myself of my sin and make a fresh start. Unfortunately I had forgotten the correct way to make confessions. This was the same problem I had before when having owned up to stealing money from my father, I had sought confessions and was asked to leave until I learned how to make them properly. That had been petrifying, as I had calculated I needed to confess £5 and, with the shock, was only able to admit to a few shillings. I had to repeat this exercise until I had washed away all traces of the £5 I had stolen. Once again I was facing the same problem and, indeed, was verbally thrown out of the confession box. Outside I was too ashamed to ask anyone for help, until eventually I got it right, only to be lambasted for what I had done to pleasure myself. However, the experience I had coming out of the church, confessed, was exhilarating. I was clean and ready for the next life, whatever about this one. It would be fair to say the Church did its best to instill a sense of guilt in me.

Unfortunately it wasn't long after arriving at my new and deeply depressive school that I once more fell into my old ways. Often I would overestimate the number of times I had comforted myself to make sure I had no outstanding debt, as each was a serious sin! I hoped each time the priest would not ask me to quantify my sins, as sometimes I was simply too ashamed and too frightened to say. It depended of course on which priest was on confessional duty. One of them never asked the number of times. So you could, if you were lucky, convince yourself you intended to confess all and get a clean slate while the other always needed to know the exact number of times. What the hell for?

Fortunately, there were other ways to ensure entry into heaven. One of these was to attend Mass and receive confession for nine consecutive first Fridays of the month. This was a little tricky to do, as you could never be sure if you had kept the nine consecutive months. However, it was a good backup plan.

It was while in the junior seminary boarding school I decided to join the priesthood. The annual recruitment drive was on. Another boy I knew, Patrick, was also interested and I spent a lot of time convincing myself through my arguments convincing him. He already had it in his mind, anyway. He later went on to study for the priesthood and, as far as I know, is a priest today. A very nice guy, indeed. Had I been in my right mind, I would never have decided to join, but it seemed that not-so-pleasant forces, which I sought to avoid, dictated my life. The fact was I had become scared and intimidated by life. The priesthood offered the best chance of gathering myself together and, hopefully, heal the bouts of pain, confusion and fear I was living through. I truly considered the possibility that God's grace would help me to feel good. How better to get it than in the priesthood, I reckoned?

I had wanted to return to my hometown more than once, as I was living in constant fear and was unable to begin to address the core of my problems. My parents came one day to speak with the head priest. They had said they would take me away. However, the head priest managed to talk my parents out of the idea. I was defeated! Perhaps it was too late to get a replacement to cover the school budget? Little was I to know that perhaps, in some way, the head priest had acted in my best interests and done me an act of good. Had I returned home, I would simply not have resolved my problems. Left to my own devices, I might possibly have sunk deeper into myself seeing no way out of my difficulties.

Had I returned home, I most likely would not have secured the education I was forced to take onboard, an education that later allowed me to be able to leave this land and travel the world, to taste experiences others could only dream of. An education that offered a way out and a way out I badly needed, as I was unable to cope with the world in which I found myself.

In some unknown way I was being guided, even though I saw this new, barren, windswept school as the worst experience of my childhood and blamed my mother for a long time after. It seems out of the worst comes the best. I had no way of understanding that all is not as it seems and that people do from time to time act in ways they would rather not have to, but in the end they do what they can to make things better. It seems that sometimes the best you can do for someone is to make things worse and hope that one day they will thank you for it.

It was at this time that I took my first voyage outside Ireland. I was 16 and, hitching a ride with the parents of some friends, I made my way by boat across the Irish Sea to Scotland where I was to work for the summer as a kitchen porter. On my return to Ireland I passed through London and disembarked in Victoria train station as it came to life in the early morning. I was amused by the caricature of the English gentleman parading before me. Like a scene from an old Charlie Chaplin movie I watched as the men made their way to work complete with pinstriped suit, bowler hat and umbrella, all in matching black. I was surprised as I watched one man look inside his briefcase revealing an apple and a copy of the days newspaper. Otherwise it was empty.

It was to be 20 years later when I would once more stand in this station and wonder at the changes and the passing of an age. In many ways, not much had changed – the daily commuters still fitting into the accepted norms. Myself in many ways still the same seeker. Yet for me, all of that was about to change. While London might not have changed drastically at its heart, I was about to change irrevocably through my heart.

A "Modern" Grail Quest

The Departure of the Knights (on the Quest for the Grail)
By William Ernest Chapman.

Reproduced with kind permission from The Camelot Project at the
University of Rochester, NY, USA.

5. 33 Eccleston Square

Desperation is the best preparation.

What began as a voyage across the Irish Sea would end with a voyage across the Adriatic 20 years later on my way to Venice in search of Eboga. But first I was to pass through London once more. I guess being Irish one has to pass through this metropolis as it contains the answers to much of our past. It was a symbol of our domination. In coming to terms with it one partly deconstructs centuries of illusion propagated by a medieval notion of master and servant, still embodied in the social milieu that gives London its ambiance.

My travels had taken me through 36 countries: as a student in Canada, a teacher in Africa, an IT engineer in the UK and Europe and a wannabe surfer in Australia. The rest of my travels had been in one form or another a search for the Holy Grail and to this end, once I had saved enough money, I would head off again and make my way through North America, Asia and Europe in the hope of making a connection to a life that I felt did not exist for me due to the work I subjected myself to.

During this time I had explored various forms of healing and applied them to myself but to no avail. By the time I eventually returned to Dublin, after nearly 3 years in Australia, I was clinging to straws and a romantically confused notion of my past. It was a last ditch attempt to face myself and I was scared that it would be my undoing, which ironically it was. However I saw no other choice except to enter the mouth of the dragon. I had come to the conclusion in Australia that I would not find what I was looking for so far away from home.

Dublin, 1997

The turning point in my life began in 1997 when I decided to leave Dublin and move to London for purely financial reasons. In truth, Australia was my watershed and this was the outcome.

I was 36 then, driven by the recurring inspiration that I could turn my life around – an inspiration I had tapped into many times before in my life and which always seemed to give me the energy and drive to carry on to another phase, another place.

I had just returned from Germany with an upbeat sense that I could make things happen for me. I gave up my job there, as I had given up many other jobs before, the moment I had any sense of a way forward to the life I dreamed of. The job, as always, was simply a means to an end. Perhaps I should have paid more heed to the dictate: the end does not always justify the means. Each day I would dream of ways to make that end more real, lapsing from time to time into a state of disillusionment, but eventually always emerging with even greater resolve than before. It meant I was always somewhat enigmatic to my work colleagues. I never really settled into the lifestyle of any contract I undertook. I would remain preoccupied by this burning desire, seeing each day as another day in a life I hated and wanted to be rid of. It pained me that I lived well and yet did not really enjoy it, apart from the times when I took off on one of my travel adventures. But these were a recurring limbo I needed desperately to break out of, as it kept throwing me back into a life I basically despised, yet needed in order to survive the way I did. I drew some sustenance from my moments of freedom coupled with the dreams they inspired. But in the end even this well ran dry. Paulo Coelho talks about this in his book *The Alchemist*. He says that we can live off a source of vital energy for so long, but in the end it runs dry if we are not responding to the call of our soul. It also pained me to waste my life energies working for a system that had no heart, instead of working for a heart to change the system. Deep down I knew that life was a precious gift to be lived and not squandered, but I knew no other way as I was too afraid to try.

So, as in the past, I took an optimistic outlook. First I would sort myself out physically and secondly I would work on my music.

Unfortunately, after three weeks of traveling to London for back therapy I was nowhere near better and became concerned about the costs of continuing treatment. I had to be careful about my funds running low and so I thought London was perhaps a better place to be at that time. After all, the treatment would surely work within three months at most. In that time I could top up my savings and hopefully make some progress with my music. Ironically, the work – which was meant to provide me with the security to advance a music career – was in fact responsible for a worsening back condition. Whether I seriously had any chance of a music career I do not really know. All I know is that it was the fantasy or the dream of such a life that pushed me forward and forced me to face many hurdles and issues in my life. I was, in the words of Joseph Campbell, attempting to "Follow My Bliss."

For a while my work was located near Vauxhall Bridge. Each day, I would take the train from Battersea Park station to Vauxhall Bridge station where I, along with thousands of others, would make my way out of the station via a network of tunnels linking the station to the footpaths that ran into the sprawling streets of South London. These tunnels opened out into the Bullring, a large open area directly under the main road. The traffic above made its way around this circular opening. Branching off in all directions from the Bullring was an open space directly under the road and it was here I witnessed the phenomenon that is the underbelly of London: Cardboard City. I imagine, at nighttime, more than a hundred people slept there, kept warm by the insulation of cardboard boxes. It was peculiar to see all the middle-class office workers making their way to work, mostly oblivious to the scene. However this existence was not to last for long. A new Imax 3-D screen was erected on the site. When I returned two years later, where once were the homeless, now existed a multimillion-dollar Imax 3-D screen, which I attended once with my mother. This clash of cultures in London is not uncommon and requires a strong constitution – one that I am not sure I have.

33 Eccleston Square

I had lived in London before and at that time I vowed I would never live on the outskirts again. So in December 1997 I moved in from the beautiful suburb of Maida Vale to be in the center of London. This is how I came to live in Pimlico, London SW1 and to have an encounter with a man I will never forget and always cherish, James Leigh. I then went on holidays to visit some friends in Canada and officially took up residence at 33 Eccleston Square in January 1998.

33 Eccleston Square, Pimlico, London SW1 was the former home of Sir Winston Churchill, long since refurbished with one apartment on each floor. I had chosen this apartment as it was five minutes' walking distance from Victoria station, ten minutes from St. James Park and ten minutes from the Houses of Parliament. Basically it was as close as I was going to get to the center of London.

There were obviously many advantages to living so close to the center of town. For one it was quite reasonable to hail a taxi to Soho, have coffee, catch a movie and then walk home through St. James Park, past Buckingham Palace and pick up the next day's *Times* newspaper while passing Victoria Train Station just round the corner.

While living at Eccleston Square I arranged to reduce the number of hours I worked at the bank in order to come home and do some work on my music and fitness. Each day I went to swim in the

Queen Mother Center, a very busy sports complex. The routine gave me a sense of achievement.

James Leigh: A Good Man

I shared the apartment with two other very pleasant chaps: Rob, an aspiring actor from Australia and Patrick who worked nearby in IT, not to mention our landlord: James. We were all about the same age. Rob had a gift for laughter and gaiety. I envied him and hoped to be his friend. However, try as hard as I could, I was unable to get past my insecurities and he sensed this. The simple ways of connecting and bonding, such as a shared joke, were beyond me. He intimidated me because, somehow, I became painfully aware of my fear of male bonding, touching a nerve that threatened to expose me to my own secret well of long-held pain. We got along very well though and occasionally shared our frustration about James, who had his idiosyncrasies that sometimes we had to accept without questioning. My own tendency to get a little hot and bothered over such things clearly had its origins somewhere else and this, I suspect, Rob realized. This is perhaps why he was cautious in bonding with me. To his credit, he seemed to genuinely like me and complimented me more than once on my energy and enthusiasm. Maybe he just couldn't figure me out, or maybe it was my own self-doubt that barred me from capitalizing on the connection that was there. He did seem to be astute in his relations with others and I envied him his easy, Australian way with girls tempered by a worldly outlook sometimes missing in that region. In London, you choose your friendships carefully, especially if you live in the same house. It is easier to change friends than to change apartments, especially one as prime as this.

We all made our income from IT, except our landlord James who dabbled in the buying and selling of steel. The flat itself had four bedrooms and a large drawing room with an open fire which was kept blazing most days, even though I believe such fires had been banned from the center of London. That was no impediment to James! One could describe the atmosphere as quaint, somewhat similar to an English country cottage furnished from the earlier part of the century, complete with chaise lounge. The bathroom itself was a joy to use as it contained a large wrought iron bath perched on its own wrought iron feet. This was combined with a heating element that kept the towels warm. In the reading basket you could find an assortment of magazines and one unusual book, filled with Victorian caricatures of less-than-savory poses. Occasionally one could hear strange noises emanating from the bathroom once James was comfortably settled in. This was something I have always found peculiar among the British: their love of sitting on the toilet. Having grown up in a relatively large family, we had no time to waste in the toilet; any stay longer than necessary viewed with deep suspicion.

My landlord, James Leigh (59), the son of an Irish woman apparently with a broad Irish accent, was educated in Oxford and took a liking to me. Unfortunately he suffered from a strong Irish temper. It was probably just a matter of time before we were bound to clash. It was he who read to me, "The Lake Isle of Innisfree," by W.B. Yeats in his managed Irish accent.

The Lake Isle of Innisfree

I will arise and go now and go to Innisfree,
and a small cabin build there, of clay and wattles made:
Nine bean rows will I have there, a hive for the honeybee,
and live alone in the bee-loud glade.

And I shall have some peace there,
for peace comes dropping slow,

dropping from the veils of the morning to where the crickets sing;

There, midnight's all a-glimmer,

and noon a purple glow,

And evening full of the linnet's wings.

I will arise and go now, for always, night and day

I hear lake water lapping with low sounds by the shore;

While I stand by the roadway or on the pavements grey,

I hear it in the deep heart's core.

William Butler Yeats (1865-1939).

Reproduced with kind permission from A.P. Watt Ltd on behalf of Michael B Yeats. Source: Louis Untermeyer, ed. (1885-1977), Modern British Poetry, 1920.

James spoke with the accent of the English middle-class Oxbridge graduate and it was this and his deep fondness of Ireland that endeared him to me. He was most offended when I giggled at his rendition of Yeats, as though I was being most unfair and had not given him sufficient credit for his attempt to speak in the mother tongue. This endeared him to me even more, as I could see the child in him still wrestling with the things of the child. In my initial interview with James for the room I had asked if I could bring a friend home. He dropped his eyes and said in a low voice, "A woman?" I said yes. He replied, "Fine, the more the merrier." I looked at him and we both proceeded to crack up. He later confided in me he could not handle a gay scenario.

To say James was fond of women would be an understatement. He boasted to me of his many conquests. While I was there, I noticed that a painting of a young woman would keep disappearing and reappearing. Rob explained to me that she was an 18-year-old girlfriend he had when he was about 40. What I made of this, I do not know. Whenever his current girlfriend would show up, he made sure to hide the painting. He was certainly an amusing character with a big heart.

Work, Rest & Play

At this time I was working as an IT consultant for Lloyd's TSB, located at Southwark Bridge, facing the city of London. As this was directly along the South Bank of the River Thames, I was able to cycle there each day in about 25 minutes along a pedestrian zone. This took me past the National Film Theatre, The Queen Elizabeth Center, and Lambeth Castle and on the other side, The Houses of Parliament. It was a pleasant and enjoyable morning run on my Raleigh Classic bike I had bought for the job. For a time, my route was diverted by the construction of the Millennium Wheel.

While there I developed an automatic routine of swimming followed by some work on my music. I also worked with two low-budget producers and, for whatever reason, got nowhere. I spent hours and hours trying to instill life and uniqueness into their arrangements and, in the end, gave up. I then tried working on the arrangements myself. I was desperate. I did my best not to think about my age. I decided to keep as many things as automatic as possible and to put whatever spare juices I had into the rest. Location made this possible.

I worked particularly hard on the song, "Set Us Free," which I believed could succeed and get me started. I had written this song in Dublin, having picked up the melody and a few words in my sleep, like most of my songs.

It never saw the light of day, despite thousands of pounds spent on recording along with endless hours in a studio, not to mention the thousands lost in unpaid work time I took to work on it:

Set Us Free

Ship in hand to foreign land,
We sailed that we might be free.
In our hearts and in our hands,
We knew that one day it would be.

For we are sailing, for we are free,
For we are sailing, this land will set us free!

Through blooded hands and sweated palms,
These ships and her lives came to be.
Filled with hope of distant lands,
They sailed that they might be free.

For we are sailing, for we are free,
For we are sailing, this land will set us free!

Now they stand on foreign lands,
No more these ships sail the seas.
But in their hands lay many a man,
Who cried and died on his knees.

For we are sailing, for we are free,
For we are sailing, this land will set us free!

Ship in hand to foreign land,
No more do we have to flee.
But in our hearts we see the land,
We left that we might be free.

For we are sailing, for we are free,
For we are sailing, this land will set us free!

For we are sailing, for we are free,
For we are sailing, this land will set us free!

Words and music by Lee Albert ©1997

Each week I went to salsa classes one or two nights a week in High Street Kensington at Bar Cuba. Unfortunately, the classes were simply too big. One of my more successful dance ventures took place at Easter time, when I attended a five-day intensive flamenco course at King's Cross in London. That was intense and it was good.

London itself, it has to be said, is one of the most expensive and in many ways one of the meanest cities in the world. To eat out costs a fortune, yet the portions are often miserable in size. The overheads are astronomical and the proprietors seem to look for savings in all manner of ways. This is a side of London that really turned me off. Okay, let it be expensive but at least give generously in return. How anyone survives there, I do not know. The cost of housing is astronomical. Entertainment is prohibitively expensive and yet people are not making the money to afford it. The ruin of London for ordinary people is the ability to charge such high amounts because the tourists and high-flyers will pay. The rest just have to put up with it and they, of course, do not want to be left out. Anyway, that's London. From one perspective a large, overpriced tourist business metropolis full of unspoken dreams, dreams that are sometimes misguided by the glittering lights. There are many lonely people who live there, afraid to appear strange by opening their hearts to you or, for that matter, to be cheated by you.

Searching for a "New" Way

Due to the recurring pain I was looking for new and more radical, untried options. I decided that the forms of therapy I had explored before were too costly in time and money and so I began a search for an alternative form of treatment which would cost less and hopefully achieve more, such as MDMA (3,4-methylenedioxy-N-methylamphetamine) therapy, which I had heard about.

Until we know the source of our problems, we do not know and, unfortunately, many a relationship flounders as someone tries to grapple with a past they do not know. Suspicion and paranoia are good bedfellows of doubt and pain and contribute to a world of confusion and guilt. Doubt, because one can never be certain and guilt, because of doubt and the repercussions of those possible erroneous ideas. It was this which made me decide, that no matter what the truth was, it was best to make peace with everyone and not be a victim a second time round, mistakenly persecuting someone for something they had not done. In any case, even if they had, to make peace within oneself is a win-win situation.

At this stage, you could say I was like a human calculator, guarding against fear and any possible threat in my environment. However, I had the capacity for deduction and it was this and a certain reckless abandon that helped me decide what to do.

All through my life I had the belief that there was a key to unlocking my condition, though I was not sure I would have the strength to use it, if I ever found it. My choice of reading was inspired by this. In truth, I could never find a key the "I" could use, as "I" was the ego searching for a way to manage a growing crisis. Later I was to realize that this is something the ego cannot do, i.e., heal the person. It is outside its ability to cope. It knows it needs to do something and uses its box of limited tools to the best of its ability – a bit like holding up a dilapidated house with bandages. However with time, it becomes more and more burdened and, if we are not careful this can lead to a split in the ego or some other mental "disease." The solution is in a realm outside itself: a place it cannot go. The solution is something it is neither equipped nor designed to deal with. It lies outside its frame of reference. It requires the unseating of itself from its center of control. Given that someone in deep pain relies heavily on his or her ego, this is almost impossible to do: a catch-22 situation. Many continue searching using the ego (which, of course, can make useful decisions in this regard), but constantly hit up against a brick wall in the application of what they find, only to be confused and dazed as to why they cannot proceed further. The ego has simply reached its outer limits, an area where it has no power to function or operate: an area reserved for the heart and the soul. But sometimes it is impossible to stop an ego that has taken control unless of course there is something more powerful that knows how to undermine it. This is what I was looking for but I never anticipated the power of what I would find.

In any case, having settled into the apartment, I had arranged for a private telephone line to be installed in my bedroom, where I had set up a small study: my base of operations! Among other things, this gave me Internet access. The room itself was not very large but it suited my needs.

I had heard about MDMA and read a number of books on its usage to deal with marital problems and sexual abuse: it gives an experience of empathy in someone who has become closed off, as it effectively shuts down fear. MDMA has been known to heal personal trauma and also to aid in mending broken relationships. MDMA is a synthesized substance, accidentally discovered in 1912 by the Merck Company. It is commonly referred to as ecstasy. However many substances which are called ecstasy are in fact not MDMA but products with similarities. In the mid 1970s, it was rediscovered by the psychedelic therapy community and began to be used as an adjunct to psychotherapy. One respectable fifty year old user has described it in the following way. "The drug removes all your neuroses. It takes away the fear of response. There is an overwhelming sense of peace, you are at peace with the world. You feel open, clear, tender. I can't imagine that anyone is angry under its influence or selfish or mean or defensive. You have lots of insight into yourself, real insight which you hold on to after the experience is gone. "

So, from my new base of operations I carried out a little research. In my reading and research on the Internet I came across a very respected voluntary organization in the U.S., called MAPS (The Multidisciplinary Association for Psychedelic Studies), dedicated to the study and the dissemination of information regarding MDMA and therapy. MAPS is a membership-based non-profit research and educational organization. It was they who published the book, *The Secret Chief*, about a leader in the psychedelic therapy community and his experiences. So I decided in January to contact MAPS about the possibility of doing personal inner transformation, or simply put, "inner healing" work using MDMA. They told me it was illegal, but I could try ibogaine (the principle alkaloid of the eboga plant) if I wanted, which was still not illegal in a number of countries. MAPS also disseminates information on ibogaine. They warned me it was very heavy, as it delivered a huge emotional punch. They said it was an encounter with one's self!

This sounded a little too daunting, so I did a little research on the Internet to see if I could find any legal use of MDMA instead. Apart from studies being carried out in Israel with trauma victims, I found little else I could connect with. That was not very practical. From the description given to me by the very helpful assistant from MAPS, I was hesitant to try something as overwhelming as ibogaine. However, MDMA did not seem a viable option and I was desperate to try something. Innocently I thought MDMA would achieve the same as ibogaine albeit in a much gentler way. They recommended reading the book *The Secret Chief.* It detailed different sessions held with MDMA and some with ibogaine. I ordered the book from MAPS and supplemented it by researching a number of Web sites on the Internet.

What impressed me about the accounts in this book was the idea that ibogaine was described as a true personal encounter; that it was not possible to avoid the truth. Was this not the key I was looking for to unlock my hidden self? Was it not simply a matter of knowing, supplemented with some emotional release work, in order to reclaim my freedom?

If only it were that simple! Nothing could have prepared me for my encounter with ibogaine, certainly not the accounts in *The Secret Chief.* The amounts used in the book were less than a third of what I would be given and were more similar to what Claudio Naranjo used in the seventies in his therapeutic usage of ibogaine for one-on-one sessions, what I call "mini-sessions."

The Call to Adventure

After my conversation with MAPS I decided to check out some of the ibogaine provider Web sites and decided to e-mail one that appeared accessible to me for information. It was Eric Taub's *www. ibeginagain.org.* I thought nothing more of it and then, suddenly one evening, the phone rang.

I went to my room and picked up the phone. On the other end a soft-spoken American voice sounded. It was a little surreal. Out of nowhere, I was suddenly connected to a world of which I knew little. In some ways it felt discordant, as Eric spoke as though it were all so simple. Yet I was in the throes of my own inner fears and confusion and felt somewhat bowed down by life. Eric, on the other hand, seemed to be living in a carefree world and I was nervous he might have his doubts about me. I was also a little in awe of him and did not want to say anything for which he might think less of me, or for that matter dismiss me. I was nervous.

He made a number of suggestions as to a possible way forward. At that moment I am not sure if I was seriously aiming to move forward or not. All I know is I was caught up in the conversation and did not wish to seem insincere or difficult about my approach. I opted for his suggestion to contact Karl Naeher in Italy, as he was closer to me geographically. Eric then promised to send me some information, which he subsequently did.

After I hung up the phone I felt, *Wow! How real was that?* I guess in that moment, the realization of what might happen to me began to sink in. I am not sure what I would have done if Eric had not made contact with me. Something of this magnitude needs an icebreaker and it is best to come from the therapist. That way the client does not feel he is entering a murky, dangerous underworld.

Having made contact with Eric, I went back to my usual routine. From time to time I would leaf through the literature he had sent me. I never really read it very deeply, as I was hooked and all that mattered was the buzz it gave me to think about it. My decision had been made on some level and I wasn't looking for any reason to unmake it. Like so many times in the past, I latched onto something the minute I thought I had any chance of success. Sometimes this led me into trouble I could easily have avoided and this time might not be an exception. Many times in my life I existed on a wing and a prayer. If I stopped to fathom the situation there was a real danger I might drown. Like crossing a river: if we move quickly and lightly, we can traverse stones that otherwise would not support us. This was to be the way of my life in the year ahead. I wanted to believe that this could work and thus clung to the idea.

In the meantime my problems continued to plague me. My day-to-day life had its routine, but it was characterized by a ducking and diving of situations that threatened me. My life was being propelled by the dictates of my mind and its mental calculations, each calculation designed to give an added boost to carry on; each calculation a way for the ego to draw juice from a hidden reservoir that, ultimately, would run dry. I guess sensing this is what had made me resolve to somehow bring myself, sooner or later, to undergo an Eboga session. All I needed was a final push and I knew many ways to give myself that push!

It had been the force of the events earlier that had prompted my initial contact and for a time I was on the edge of vacillating again. It was possibly the force of events later in the year that gave me the final push I needed. Basically I was scared, looking for an excuse to do something crazy and radical as I felt it was something of that order that I needed. While things were ticking along such an action could not be justified. When things moved to a crisis point, then almost any outcome could be justified. In that sense I welcomed calamity.

I guess a part of me didn't really believe that an option such as ibogaine, with such promise, could exist. In some ways it seemed too easy and I guess I basically believed that there was no such thing as a magic bullet or a free lunch. Now, if I were to believe what I was reading, it seemed I was on the verge of receiving one. All I needed was $2,000. That was the part I couldn't understand. Why, if it was a gift from God, should it be limited to people like me with money? In a perverse kind of way I felt it justified my material gains somehow, as I could access the world at large for all possible solutions. I felt privileged. In that sense, it was not a free lunch. Having said that, the money I earned was based on the scarcity of my skills and not relative to the true value of my work compared to another. How many workers have I seen breaking their backs for a pittance and wondered, *There but for the grace of God go I?* They could not afford to do an Eboga session. Had my own father not worked all his life for a modest income? Could he have afforded one? In any case, armed with my naïveté I was preparing to embark on another adventure. My earlier adventures had been out into the world. This one was to be into my own world, one that would irrevocably change my life forever.

I was to learn a great deal about Eboga and ibogaine, but more importantly, I was to learn a great deal about myself. And I needed either a fool's mentality or a deep faith to go through with what lay ahead. I am not sure I had all that much faith, just hope. However, unknown to myself, the real call I had been waiting for finally came through.

6. Eboga: An "Old" Way

When we deny another's rights we deny our own.

Howard Lotsof, Eric Taub & Karl Naeher

Eric Taub is a well-known American advocate for the use of ibogaine for the treatment of drug addiction. In the early '90s Eric went to Africa in search of eboga. He was selling jewelry when he heard about ibogaine and decided to make it his mission to give ibogaine to one percent of the 140 million drug addicts worldwide. It was he who put me in touch with Karl Naeher, an ibogaine therapist living in Italy who also has his own Web site, *www.ibogainetreatment.com.* Karl also had his own odyssey with eboga. He went to Africa some time after Eric where he obtained a supply of the root eboga (also called Tabernanthe iboga) and shipped it back to Italy. He then hired a chemist to produce a salt of the main alkaloid component, the result being ibogaine, an off-white, grainy powder with a hint of orange.

Eboga, which is at the heart of the Eboga Process, is currently used to treat drug addiction in the West. It has its origins, reportedly, many thousands of years ago in Central Africa among the Pygmies. Ibogaine is the principal alkaloid of the Tabernanthe iboga plant. The Pygmies attribute the discovery of this plant to the warthogs that apparently are very fond of it. These animals dig holes at the foot of the eboga shrubs to chew the bark of the roots. They then go into a state of wild frenzy, leaping and fleeing as though prey to terrifying visions. Porcupines and gorillas also search for these roots.

I did not however come to ibogaine as a drug addict nor as a gorilla—at least not entirely. I came as someone in deep psychological pain. Every addict who takes eboga breaks his or her addiction

145

momentarily, as eboga also operates on a physical level. But this is not the real meaning of eboga. It is only a useful adjunct. The real use of eboga lies in its ability to heal the soul and the deep psychological pain many of us are living through. It clears out the psychological debris after a long and hard path. In the same way that eboga in its most basic function sensitizes the body to drugs and hence is anti-addictive, it also sensitizes the mind, leading us toward a more harmonious relationship with life and oneself; opening us up to the depth and wisdom of the simplistic. Only the prepared can really receive. Anyone who takes eboga does so at their own risk, as there is much to understand apart from the prerequisite health checks that are outlined on *www.ibogaine.org/manual.html.*

Tabernanthe iboga was first reported in 1864 by Giffon du Bellay as a stimulant and aphrodisiac. The bush, which occurs in at least two varieties (T. iboga and T. manii – not always distinguished botanically and apparently of similar, psychotropic qualities), is common in the equatorial underforest. He brought specimens from Gabon and the Congo back to Europe where in 1901 ibogaine, the principal alkaloid, was first isolated by Dybowsky and Landrin. In 1939 an extract of Tabernanthe manii was sold in tablet form under the name Lambarene for the treatment of fatigue and depression. Lambarene disappeared from the market around 1966. The plant itself was officially called Tabernanthe iboga in the late nineteenth century, but is referred to as eboga or eboka by the Bwiti of the Fang. The species name as well as the Bwiti name is taken from the Galwa-Mpongwe or Miene language term, iboga. Eboga contains at least 13 alkaloids that appear to work in a synergistic way with the main alkaloid. However, it is the main alkaloid, ibogaine, which has been identified as delivering the therapeutic results. With ibogaine it is possible to exactly calibrate the amount required based on body weight, thereby enhancing the safety of the client.

Eboga in the Western world is currently taken in two forms. Firstly as ibogaine itself, as described above, and secondly as an extract of the plant called the Indra extract, purportedly containing all the alkaloids present. The science of ibogaine is well studied and quite exact, being used principally for its ability to interrupt chemical addiction. On the other hand the science and action of the Indra extract appear to be unreported: this is why I do not promote its use. It contains a reported 15% total alkaloids by weight of which 8% is ibogaine. As the other alkaloids in the Indra product are active, this material is viewed as having a 15% potency. It is darker and deeper in color than ibogaine and comes as a brittle lump.

The onset of ibogaine is quicker and the pace of the session more intense than the Indra extract, as it appears the other alkaloids in the Indra extract in some way temper this. However, the results are more assured. Numerous studies have been conducted and ibogaine has been shown to be extremely effective as an anti-addictive therapy. It has been described as "an intense, psychoactive drug which causes a mental deconstruction" which allows a person to analyze himself or herself in an intensive therapy session. However, to my mind eboga knocks out and disables the ego, exposing the true state of the mind. In this state one is taken to the problems as opposed to controlling the proceedings. Less is known of its therapeutic abilities, which is what I was seeking. It seemed the most promising option open to me to confront whatever was haunting me, even if it did cost $2,000 a session.

My level of desperation can be measured by how far I was prepared to go in order to find a cure to my problems. Money meant nothing to me. I could not buy the satisfaction of the company of someone I loved, living and working together towards a fulfilling and loving life. I could not buy the joy of a joke shared without shame or intimidation. I could not buy self-respect even if in the world's eyes I was a blazing success, having achieved in many areas, not to mention having traveled through 36 different countries, many of which I had lived in. I could not buy peace of mind. So what good was the money to me anyway or, for that matter, anything I had?

The discovery that ibogaine could block drug withdrawal is usually credited to Howard S. Lotsof, a New York-based former drug user who took ibogaine in 1962. His Web site is called *www.ibogaine.org*. He is sometimes referred to as the "father of ibogaine" within the drug addict community. At the time Lotsof was a heroin user and took ibogaine, believing it to be a new recreational drug. However, 30 hours later, he realized he wasn't experiencing heroin withdrawal and had no desire to seek drugs. He went on to give it to some of his addicted friends and found this effect replicated.

It is worth mentioning here some of the problems associated with the commercial production of ibogaine:

1. Patents are limited for drugs derived from a natural source as opposed to synthetic drugs.
2. Ibogaine's client base is perceived as drug addicts and alcoholics. Drug companies do not see them as sufficiently stable to assure a financially rewarding client base.
3. Drug companies are afraid of the negative image the introduction of a drug such as ibogaine would attract to them, its client base consisting of socially marginalized groups.
4. Corporate entities are worried that ibogaine may lead to a conflict of interest with the alcohol and tobacco market.

Many drugs considered psychoactive were banned in the U.S. in the late '60s. According to the Web site *www.ibogaine.co.uk,* "Ibogaine's current legal status in the UK and much of the rest of the world is that of an unlicensed, experimental medication. It is not therefore an offence to possess the drug, though to act as a distributor may be breaking the law." Also, "Ibogaine is a restricted substance (possession is illegal) in some countries, including the U.S., Switzerland, Sweden and Belgium." Of course, before we become blinded by Western bureaucracy, struggling to understand something beyond its comprehension, let us remember that eboga, from which ibogaine comes, is a very sacred plant in West and Central Africa and its use there utterly outweighs its use here. There it comes under no law and is bound only by God's law.

Eboga's African Context

The Bwiti of West Central Africa use Tabernanthe iboga or Eboga, the plant source of ibogaine. It is integral to their culture and religion. There are approximately 2-3 million Bwiti members scattered in groups throughout the countries of Gabon, the Democratic Republic of Congo (formerly Zaire) and the Cameroon. It is believed that eboga use spread to these local tribes' people over the past couple of centuries, having originated with the Pygmy groups of the Congo basin many thousands of years earlier. There is a legend told of how one Bwiti, while under its influence, was told to dig near a tree, which he subsequently did to find buried treasure there.

The Bwiti religion is commonly called the "religion of Eboga," a religion linked to the ancestors. Eboga gives knowledge of the beyond through the ego death (disablement) that it precipitates. Ritual mastication of eboga permits contact with the ancestors and the gods as well as the confronting and healing of repressed personal traumatic material. It was this last part which brought me to it. At the time I did not realize that personal trauma is a common way to direct one's attention to the spiritual realm.

Within the Bwiti eboga is also used as an aid to concentration and to stimulate recovery from illness. It is used as a sacrament in the

"Bwiti initiation ritual," a complex, three-day "rebirth" ceremony that is a required part of membership of the group. Both sexes (of the Fang Bwiti) are initiated, usually between the eighth and thirteenth birthday – see Nick Sandberg, *An Introduction to Ibogaine*. The overall aim of the ritual is to be emotionally and spiritually reborn, so that the initiate may take his or her place within the group as a true adult. For this a high level of eboga is consumed with the purpose of relieving the initiate of the effects of any trauma in the psyche via the retrieval of repressed memories as well as connecting the initiate to the ancestors.

For these reasons I was interested in trying eboga.

Is Eboga a Bwiti Phenomenon?

In the coming six years I was to become actively involved in eboga/ibogaine usage for my own personal development as well as trying to understand more of its nature. Each experience taught me more and more and my initial ideas changed enormously. Initially I felt – like others – that Eboga was principally a Bwiti phenomenon. This could not be further from the truth. Yes, it has its present known cultural context among the Bwiti. But that is only one face of Eboga dressed up to fit a particular cultural context: the Bwiti themselves have identified various entities, assigning them names, influenced by their exposure to Christian evangelization. To say one is dealing with Bwiti deities is accurate in one sense but entirely wrong in another. Ultimately, it is about connection to yourself, your soul, our ancestry as a species and finally to the spirit, which pervades all of life.

In an African setting an Eboga ceremony has been described as a religious rave. There is singing and dancing while a priest invokes the saints and spirits of the ancestors as the initiate embarks on the Eboga journey.

Eboga: An African Spirituality

Much of the imagery experienced in an Eboga session is African and there is a perfectly good reason for this: our origins as a species are African and this plant has existed for thousands of years in this context. It is not unreasonable to assume that connection with man's origins should indeed put us in contact with Africa. As one experiences connection with the past, the sense of belonging originally to an African world can be very strong, as that is where our ancestral records originate. Eboga is therefore an African spirituality as it draws its energy from the cradle of human life: Africa. In a Western context this spirituality expresses itself in a deepening respect for the Earth, the community, the ancestors, one's parents and, in particular, oneself and one's family: the circle of life.

Eboga Spirituality therefore builds on the natural instincts of a human and, as such, is very natural. The context in which you practice it is not so important. One can dress it up how one likes. However, I am a firm believer in sticking with the essentials and not getting carried away with a lot of dazzling showmanship that creates illusion and confusion in the candidate's mind. It is, in the end, a simple affair, one which brings you directly in contact with your own heart and those you love on all levels. That is what counts.

Description of Ibogaine

Ibogaine has been described by my friend Greta as a "Star Gate." In many ways that is not far from the truth, as it opens a portal to another world.

Ibogaine is a derivative of serotonin but unlike serotonin, it is not very toxic. In fact the toxicity of ibogaine is lower than that of aspirin, i.e., it appears to be a relatively nontoxic alkaloid and can be used in the range of 10 to 50 mg as an antidepressant in humans.

Doses above 300 mg are normally associated with sessions – where dosage is determined by body weight.

For now I would describe ibogaine as an anti-addictive, non-recreational alkaloid of a naturally occurring plant, which initially can cause a massive release of emotionally repressed experiences (when taken in sufficient quantity) causing the emergence of suppressed pain into the body, which eventually will be integrated. The experience is characterized by a deep sensation around the area of the third eye, similar to a sudden realization that one has done something that one should not have done, i.e., the penny has dropped and you are taken (a)back. It can also be described as a serpent which carries a spirit that opens the mind and frees the heart. Otherwise it is just powder: humble and brilliant.

It seems to me now, in layman's terms, after almost six years' personal experience, that ibogaine operates in two ways:

1. It attaches itself to all the body's receptors and eliminates whatever drug is there, providing comfort. Hence its anti-addictive property, as it removes the craving for the drug of choice. Ibogaine itself is not addictive, i.e., if the user craves a drug fix, it will be the drug they crave and not ibogaine.
2. In much the same way it raises the energy or aura field of the person, possibly via its attachment to the body's receptors and thus opens the door to the spiritual realm that oversees the individual's treatment. The treatment involves a mental deconstruction, much like a car engine that is taken apart for reconditioning. If the underlying causes to the addiction are not dealt with, in time the person will be drawn back to their physical addiction. Hence, this second part is vital to successful treatment and generally requires a drug addict to undergo further sessions as the first session appears to be mainly preoccupied with the physical addiction itself.

In its use as an anti-addiction therapy its ultimate goal is for personal happiness resulting from one's independence, personal relationships, love, work and hobbies as opposed to the physiological need for a chemically substituted gratification. Hence, it is possible to temporarily break a drug addiction, but in order for treatment to be successful, the recovering addict needs to deal with the underlying problems or else a relapse is inevitable. This is going to be the case with any form of drug rehabilitation therapy. In this sense I see drug addicts as being one step behind the spiritual seeker. The spiritual seeker does not normally have to take ibogaine for a drug addiction. However, he does sometimes have to take it to make progress along the path, i.e., to face his problems – problems that are often reflected in an emotional addiction such as codependency. Also, the drug addict generally does not have the mentality or discipline (in the beginning, at least) of the spiritual seeker who, invariably, is more successful in his or her experience with ibogaine or, more correctly, the Eboga realm.

I would like to caution anyone considering taking ibogaine not to mix it with any other therapeutic drug. I have heard reports of it being used with MDMA. This, I believe, is a big mistake. In the next part of the book, The Eboga Process, chapters 1 and 3, I detail some of my understanding regarding the deeper meaning of the Eboga Process often overlooked by those who simply have no real personal experience of its whole life cycle. It is in itself a "complete" treatment and to introduce foreign substances into the bloodstream is, I believe, to complicate its task.

As you read the account in this book, it is impossible to escape the conclusion that within the Eboga realm a very intelligent and benign force is operating. It is also true to say that it has a strong sense of humor and does all it can to make the session more palatable. However, there is no escaping the fact that real progress comes at a price and, in the beginning, this can be very demanding. Mental and physical preparation do help to achieve better results.

The Indra Extract

I have taken the Indra extract on a number of occasions using different doses. Once I took it mixed with ibogaine. The first time it worked really well, giving a gentler lead into the session followed by a much gentler experience overall. However in subsequent usage I found it less reliable. It seems that subsequent usage is less predictable than pure ibogaine.

With pure ibogaine I feel we receive most, if not all of the therapeutic benefits of the plant, plus session objectives can be calibrated more easily. For these reasons I prefer to work with pure ibogaine. The traditional way of taking eboga is a reflection of the society it comes from and does not take advantage of the advances of medical science. For these reasons, plus the fact its action is less well known, I do not promote the Indra extract. However it is "possibly" a gentler way to withdraw from physical drug addiction.

Having said that, I believe research should be carried out to explore the production of an eboga extract which incorporates an ideal composition of the total alkaloids of the eboga plant and which can be calibrated exactly, i.e., whose science is properly known. Information on the extract is simply not forthcoming. I believe a scientifically produced ideal extract could have enormous benefits.

I did however find one interesting, positive difference between the Indra extract and ibogaine. The subsequent 24 hours following use of the extract led to a very positive mood elevation, which interestingly, was interrupted when I took marijuana after a difficult and "very" painful session with the extract. (I believe in this case the extract opened healing wounds it did not have sufficient power to close.) Although this mood elevation is also true with ibogaine I found initially it was not always the case and I speculate that one or more of the alkaloids not present in ibogaine may also play a part in this effect – another reason for moving to a more complete compound eventually. It could also be that my first session with ibogaine was dealing with an emergency emotional situation so that the pain still came through afterwards – though it was easily manageable. This however is a minor consideration to the overall success of the session as it is a temporary though welcome, aspect of the treatment. Existing medications can also be used following treatment should they be considered necessary. However, medications in my opinion poison the Eboga energy and for this reason are not attractive. It is best that nothing is taken for at least the first 36 hours after ingesting eboga.

Ibogaine: An Hallucinogen?

What follows is based on the full article cited in appendix 1.

Ibogaine has been found guilty of being an hallucinogen similar to LSD. However, ibogaine produces no drug dependency and has been proved to suppress dependency to opiates, amphetamines, cocaine, LSD and even alcohol and tobacco. In fact the effects of the two drugs appear to be worlds apart. LSD is active at doses of less than a milligram and its activity is difficult to control. The hallucinatory phenomena produced belong to a high and angelic domain of aesthetic sensations. These sensations are far removed from the intimate and personal nature of ibogaine. Also, ibogaine is hallucinogenic only at doses greater than 100 mg and the domain is that of Freud's subterranean world of animal impulse and regression, i.e., one's inner world or inner history. The banning of ibogaine took place as ibogaine was labeled an hallucinogen similar to LSD. Clearly this is not the case. Also, within the Bwiti of the Mitsogho there exists an antidote, i.e., it is controllable.

In my own experience the hallucinogenic role (waking dreams) of ibogaine is simply a reflection of the internal processes one is going through and as such it is not principally an hallucinogenic drug. You could say it produces a waking sleep or indeed, opens one's faculties at a paranormal level. This is quite different to a purely hallucinogenic experience. The label of hallucinogen is somewhat misleading as paranormal visions result from our own innate processes which can be opened via a catalyst. Angelic experiences do occur with ibogaine but I believe they occur through the medium of the soul and are not a direct result of ibogaine itself.

MDMA on the other hand may bring about a temporary opening or change, or catalyze a new state of mind. However, in the end, the underlying problems always return and this newfound state of well-being gives way to them as we naturally resort once more, as we did when we were a child, to hide behind the ego's protective mechanisms. Sometime after my experience with ibogaine I was to have the opportunity for three therapeutic sessions with MDMA and these I recount in my next book along with another three ibogaine sessions. My MDMA sessions were very valuable and useful and led on one occasion to physical healing – a miracle if you like. I believe there is a reason MDMA can work in this way and I explain it in the next book. However, I prefer to work with naturally occurring substances, as I believe these exist for a reason and help rather than hinder the body. I am not comfortable with synthetic, non-naturally occurring drugs in general.

There is little recorded evidence of ibogaine on the illegal drug market as its appearance and disappearance has been both swift and non-eventful. It seems the drug dealers rapidly became aware that its use would deprive them of a large part of their clientele.

Eboga: A Mind-Splitting Agent

Based on my own experience I would also describe eboga (at the correct dose) as a mind-splitting agent which disables the ego by placing the ego's complete attention in two places at once, thereby disabling the ego from controlling the mind. This causes the ego to disconnect, momentarily opening the door to the truth of what lies beneath, which the ego seeks to mask through its manipulations. Eboga keeps this door open. Hence, if one has a very active controlling ego mind, it loses control and the underlying exposed true self (soul mind) is taken over by the power of the Eboga spirit. This works in conjunction with the liberated soul, temporarily freed from the prison imposed by the ego, i.e., the state of the soul can be fully expressed within the Seat of the Mind – see The Eboga Process, chapter 1. In this state an intense healing journey takes place.

It does seem that a strong soul and a strong ego go hand-in-hand, the one the complement of the other. A strong ego is possibly one part of a spiritual path with a useful role to play, indicating the strength and determination of the soul. I believe the ego has higher and lower functions, the higher functions being influenced by soul or inner child choices which ultimately feed down into the lower functions which are closer to animal instinct. How else does one cope with the pain of one's path, except through developing a strong ego? The ego acts as a mental manipulator, redirecting our true responses to more acceptable responses thus hiding the pain. A strong ego is not the problem. It is what one does with a strong ego that counts; intention is everything. Without good intention one becomes seduced by the strong ego and moves away from the soul to the selfish animal. With a strong ego one can achieve much good as well as effect change for the self. A strong ego also contains the force of the pain we suffer until its power is eventually transferred to the soul. That's a useful ego!

However, the developed soul has a deep storehouse of strength derived from its path and this is where right action ultimately comes from and should come from, inspired as it is by the pure heart, pure intention. It is perhaps the development of a strong ego that simultaneously develops a strong soul and so, on our path, the development of a strong ego may be a step along the way. Unfortunately too many become infatuated with their egos, preferring to forget their soul (inner child) and hide from what lies there and troubles them: their past. They believe that their ego, having served them well dealing with past trauma, is best held onto, i.e., kept at the seat of the mind.

The purpose of Eboga is to bring an end to the domination of the ego and to release the soul which has grown from it. It is, if you like, an important stage in the evolution of "Cosmic Man."

An Eboga Session

It might be helpful to view a session using the analogy of a 36-hour plane journey. We arrive at the airport somewhat flustered, lugging our baggage behind us. With a little relief and a little trepidation we settle into our seat on the plane. We sit and wait; nothing much happens. Then the engines begin to fire up and we start to move slowly. Before we know it we are taking off, a little perturbed, at the speed of sound. Once in the air, we encounter a number of air pockets leading to turbulence. Occasionally this is too much and we throw up. But after about five to seven hours the plane settles down and we sit back and watch a very fast, educational movie which we don't seem to be able to avoid. After this we are worn out and simply want to be left to ourselves to ride out the rest of the journey. Towards the end of our 36-hour journey we fall asleep and wake up on the ground parked or we have a few hours' sleep and encounter a very soft landing. We go to the luggage collection to discover half our bags are missing. We don't give a damn because we are so relieved to be alive and well and, anyway, most of what was lost was just a lot of rubbish we didn't need. The next day we relax and simply enjoy our good fortune to be alive soaking up the sun in the five-star hotel we have been booked into by the airline right on the beachfront in lieu of our very demanding journey and loss of luggage. The following days we may be wondering about our lost luggage. However, all in all we are doing pretty damn okay!

The full session itself (as opposed to the mini-session) lasts between 15 and 36 hours. Thirty six hours is the norm. A period of one to three days is recommended for recovery after a session and this applies to long-term drug addicts as well. It seems that the more one prepares for the session, leaving open a period of time afterward, the more likely it is the session will succeed. Methadone users are advised to leave at least a week for recovery. The session can be physically demanding, with an inability to coordinate voluntary body movements for up to 24 hours. Insomnia can occur for up to one week. However, in my own experience one usually remains awake the first 24 hours, followed by a short period of deep restorative sleep. The following weeks can see one's need for sleep lessened. In some cases perhaps increased, when a person may have been too disturbed to sleep properly before. Everyone's experience is different but there are certain similarities between different groups such as drug addicts, spiritual seekers or victims of psychological abuse.

The full Eboga session can be divided into three phases. The session normally ends by entering a fourth phase. This fourth phase is characterized as a 24-hour relaxation period. It is like a divine "pick me up" where one feels great, as though one does not have a problem in the world. It is not a time to pass judgment on the success of a session. It is a time to enjoy what has been achieved. I once made the mistake of giving an interview during this period in which I raved about how successful the session had been. The session had achieved miraculous things. However, there was still more to be done and I only realized this later. A therapist can sometimes latch onto this period as proof of the success of the session and the advancement of the client. However, the client needs to wait a while before he or she can properly calibrate his or her progress.

The first phase can be described as a waking dream state. Within 15 to 20 minutes a numbing of the skin, along with an auditory buzzing and an oscillatory sound, can occur. After about an hour, one undergoes a mental crisis followed by the commencement of the session proper where images begin to appear as if in a television. It is here that the most difficult work is done. It is here where our emotional psychological framework is opened and worked upon. Like dreams that act on the events of the day, Eboga appears to use a dreamlike state to act on the events of the past and thus reduces the stresses and traumas of early life experiences. The scenes that appear are often short and for a reason. They are long enough to catch the sense of the scene and they are short enough not to get caught up in the content of the scene, which is an ego-orientated reaction.

The first part of the session is the most demanding as it involves the visuals and direct encounters with oneself and the spirits. It can also involve awareness enhancement and behavioral modification. It is interesting to note that initially (i.e., in early sessions) much of the visuals appear on a TV screen, which I believe is a reference to our addiction in the West to TV. Apart from the intervals of grace which Eboga gives to help us along, this phase is all business. Normally one cannot move without being overcome by nausea, as though one is disturbing a large body of mercury finely balanced within oneself. For this reason one should lie perfectly still. In subsequent sessions this sensation lessens and quite possibly disappears. Once past this phase the remainder is quite "straightforward."

The second part of the session is like an intense rerun of the first part without the emotional and cathartic content, where you are taken step by step through many different lessons derived from the first phase, as well as many other lessons. It is like sitting in a classroom in the seat of your mind with a teacher standing at a blackboard going through all kinds of things for you to know and learn. This is described in the words of Howard Lotsof as "Massive Thinking," which best describes the sense of huge thinking which goes on hour after hour. It is overwhelming and unimaginable, the vast amount of material one needs to deal with and process. It left me with little interest for conventional therapy. A parallel can be drawn with an over wound traditional watch which needs its spring released, an "Ego Unwinding." This results in resetting the ego mind to a more natural state. It is as if the material in one's mind that has not been processed in one's life, due to the resistance caused by the underlying trauma's exposed in the first phase of the session, is being dealt with. This still leaves the need for the retraining of one's emotional intelligence and one's automatic ego reactions. This takes place through a period of integration, which is most noticeable in the first year after a session.

I think the success of a session depends on how honest you want to be with yourself and how greedy and ego-centered you wish to be deep down. Many want the benefits of change, but do not want to give up the ego desires that underpin their unhealed state. Even with a repaired subconscious you are faced with the unlearning of the patterns you have adapted to in dealing with your earlier pain. This comes about in part by your subsequent rediscovery (integration) of the world around you, made easier by a sense of inner knowing and guidance.

The third phase is a little more difficult to describe. There is a definite sense that one is in the Eboga energy but "it does not appear" to be carrying out any specific function. Of course at some level a function is being carried out and it is wise to rest during this time. You could call it "The Coming Down." It is normal to experience a short deep restorative sleep during this period and to wake feeling quite refreshed. During this third phase I usually reflect on things in general.

In my own experience a major session usually lasts 36 hours and ends like the switching off of a light bulb. A person's experience may be such that the effects have worn off quickly. They may feel no reason to lie around and prefer to get up and chat or do some things. There is no reason why this should not be a valid thing to do. I would caution that, if abuse has been uncovered and the identity of the person is known, it is probably best to remain away from that person for at least a few days to allow the ego to regain its composure.

There are of course two other phases to the Process: before and after the session itself. I discuss these, along with my own ideas regarding the phases mentioned, later in The Eboga Process, chapter 1. For now I hope this helps to clarify what is actually going on. Once you have read the account of what happened to me, it will be easier to appreciate my later description. For now I will leave things as they stand. In time I hope to deepen my understanding further and amend accordingly.

Eboga, to my mind, operates before and after the event, i.e., the session does not begin at the point of ingestion of the eboga. It also operates best when it wants to operate. If it is meant to be then it will flow. It is rarely easy, by all accounts, until most of the healing sessions are completed. Then it becomes a tool for refined inner work and a vehicle for the divine to work its miracles through us and only requires a small dose. These sessions can be very joyous occasions.

It is somewhat sad that ibogaine is viewed as a medicine and not as a sacrament. We live in a world where everything is secularized. Man is too proud to bow his head. He seeks riches in this life so he can always hold his head up high. He forgets that the soul, which inhabits his body, wants to be respectful as a husband might want to be when in awe at the knowledge that his wife embodies: the great mother goddess.

A Note on the Eboga Spiritual Realm

There are definitely three presences at work in a session. Firstly, there is the Eboga spirit or energy which makes it all possible. It is like the medium through which the spirit entities operate and affect their work. It is carried by a serpent.

Secondly, there are the entities directly connected with the healing work of the Eboga spirit. I believe that the entities associated with the Eboga spirit are human souls that have transcended. That is why the Bwiti is a religion linked to the ancestors. Thirdly, there are the onlookers, souls who are connected to us in our life who appear due to the opening of our own psychic faculties under the influence of the Eboga spirit. These can be friends or friends to be and they are present for a reason. Their link to us in this life possibly reflects their link to us before this life. They can and do offer advice but they are not directly carrying out the healing and can appear out-of-sync with the Eboga entities. This does, however, give a more realistic feel to the experience, where the person being healed can develop a reality check of sorts.

The Eboga spirit working in you, under the guidance of the entities in conjunction with you, carries out the actual healing. Further, there are moments when under the guidance of the Eboga entities one experiences a higher presence, which for now I will refer to as God in the classical sense. Later in my writings I go on to examine the nature of this presence. Why this presence should make itself known at certain times and not others I suspect has something to do with the workings of one's soul during a session which one is not aware of.

Apart from these three presences there is also our personal guide or guardian angel. (In the second book I will explain its role and why I believe in its existence.) One can call it the witness or guide. It sometimes prompts us in a session but mostly remains quietly observant. It is possible that it participates in some way as yet unspecified.

For me Eboga is not and should not become an orthodox religion. We have enough orthodox religions. What we need are new ways that work and don't cloud the issues. The Eboga spirit is such a way. The whole point of Eboga is self-knowledge. Thus its appearance in the Western world at the dawn of the Age of Aquarius is wholly appropriate. The whole point of orthodox religion is adaptation to another's viewpoint, a straitjacket to change. An Eboga religion is inherently contradictory unless it acts as a vehicle to bring others to self-knowledge. Unless you discover for yourself, you have not yet discovered. In that sense Eboga is a spirituality, an African spirituality. What counts is change. Eboga is a way to change.

Why Choose Eboga?

Why go through this? Well, personally, I knew how strong my ego had become in my own self-defense and at times I felt a good kick in the arse was needed, but while as a child I might have suffered it, as an adult I was not prepared to be humiliated in that way. I needn't have worried; Eboga was about to give me a big kick in the arse and break the stranglehold of someone who has become overly reliant on his ego. Much like a clock that has been over-wound and stops working, thus exposing a frightened and confused child. Gradually, with time and integration, the child is released and the grip of the ego lessened until one reaches the point whereby one is relating more from the inspiration and astuteness of the child rather than the deductions and calculations of the ego. Here one can rediscover what one has lost in life and, like a child, appreciate life as the gift it is, placing needless worries and guilt where they belong: in the garbage. The intelligence of the child is divine. The intelligence of the ego is simply functional, as it is in every animal.

So with the promise of so much, was I going to back down from something that was difficult when I knew it was something difficult I needed? I was too clever for conventional healing and, frankly, fed up with the way it never seemed to uncover anything of great significance. Yes, Primal Therapy is great in its own way, but it is handicapped by the hold of an ego which becomes stronger the deeper the problems go. Imagine, if you will, someone who has been abused as a very young child, although nobody knows this. In time that person may blank out this memory and, with it, a very deep charge is placed in the psyche to act as guard. For that matter, imagine any other trauma you can care to think of. If this person enters therapy with a strong repression in place, how likely is it that he will by pass his ego and voluntarily choose to remember, if by remembering he is going to feel devastated?

It was after my first session with Eboga (which I describe in the chapter "The Crossing of The First Threshold") that I became captivated by its potential. My mind was full of conjecture and I wondered how on Earth I would get to grips with the knowledge that lay behind it. Karl told me that to truly learn its secrets, one needed to do five sessions. I asked what happens then. He replied, "One then has the knowledge." I didn't really understand how this was supposed to happen. He told me of one woman who went into a dream state of sorts and was out of it for days. When she returned, she was a healer. I imagined that to become a healer you were taken away and taught by the guides one encounters in an Eboga experience. Unknown to myself then, I was to learn the ways of Eboga at first through sheer, terrifying experience and later through subtle beneficence, the key being an openness to consider the divine possibilities. All the questions I brought with me to each session ultimately were answered by the events that unfolded until I reached a point where I felt I was connected to its spirit and could appreciate its subtlety.

The moment of truth, in my understanding of Eboga, was to have a high point in Brazil (the climax of the second book), 33 months "exactly" to the day of my first session. However, I did not reach a fuller understanding until a few years later. My session date in Brazil had been completely accidental, based on an invitation I received to go there and the schedule of availability. However, after my session I began to realize that there was a connection in the various session dates involved. The most obvious item being: I had just left 33 Eccleston Square before my very first session.

You might be forgiven for thinking I was brave to face my problems in this way. The truth is I had no other choice. The alternatives were not very palatable. It is not possible to escape life. Wherever you go, it is there. The only option is to change it. With Eboga, one can feel like a child, afraid to confront a situation. However, like a loving parent, it takes you by the hand to look at what it is you are avoiding. And like a loving parent it does not force you to look at what you cannot deal with. It presents to you what you can deal with and your own persistence allows you to face it. As you heal and become stronger, Eboga brings you deeper and deeper to your core. In pain, we spend most of our time avoiding ourselves.

With Eboga, we more and more encounter our true self and we know it is a moment of truth; i.e., Eboga brings us more and more into the truth of ourselves and of life. The many emotions we encounter are varied, but it would be fair to say that at times it can feel along the lines of: you have just lost your lover and life is a horrible and lonely experience. That all passes.

A Universal Language

The gods speak through symbols, so it is said. This was to be my experience also. Perhaps, like a painting, symbols speak a thousand words and are more effective than language with its limitations. Whatever the case, I found that my ability to interpret the symbols presented to me was heightened, as though some hidden faculty within me had opened. It made me realize how much untapped potential lies dormant within us. These symbols were used to answer questions I had and to show me things about my past life I was not aware of. It seemed as if the entities from the Eboga realm worked through symbols, while my soul companions worked through voice – perhaps because they exist on the same plane as myself. The use of symbols is very important as it bypasses the ability of the ego to interfere as we often only see what we want to see. The interpretation of the symbol comes after the symbol has been presented, i.e., the symbol is unadulterated.

In a full session, as one experiences connection with the past, the sense of belonging originally to an African world can be very strong. This, as you soon will see, was to be my experience.

7. Windsurfing: A Psychic Opening

If you look for the voice within,
You will hear it before you know it.

A Place in Spain

While I was grappling to come to terms with my problems and investigating the possible use of eboga, I arranged to participate in a windsurfing instructor's course in Greece. You could say this was a time of happenings. I was determined to move forward. On one level I was working on my music and pursuing a long-held interest in surfing, albeit windsurfing. On another level in trying to do what I wanted, I was painfully aware of the personal problems I needed to deal with if I was ever to be free.

I remained in contact with Karl and set off on the first part of the four-week program, two weeks' training on the island of Lefkas, Greece, at Club Vass in June. Before I left, I decided that whatever happened, I would secure my place in Spain by buying an apartment there. It had always been a dream of mine to live there, or at least to have a strong contact with the country. I should have realized that it is not possible to "buy one's place" in another country. However, at the time, I was afraid that the weight of events in my life would later on make it impossible for me to do this, as I might not feel free enough to decide my own future or indeed be emotionally strong enough to do so.

While in Greece I completed the purchase of a small two-bedroom, nicely furnished apartment in Spain. It was cozy, well made and well positioned; set in Alcocebre, a beautiful area on the east coast about 1½ hours north of Alicante. While it was a little difficult to get to, I had visions of going there with friends and using it as a retreat. I was determined to have my own place, as I saw

Spain as a country I would happily go to if I decided to throw in the towel on my efforts to achieve my goals. I was drawn to the warmth of the people and in particular the warmth of the women. I also felt a strong pull to the rich, almost mercurial nature of the flamenco spirit and the Mediterranean love of food. It spoke of life.

A Mirror on Life

During my time in Greece I had the most amazing experiences and returned home a different man than when I left. I had decided to go there because I seriously wanted to make changes in my life and surfing was something I had always dreamed about. I saw the ad in the paper and decided to give it a go. It wasn't surfing but it was windsurfing and I had the chance to become an instructor. I felt that this was probably the best way to learn, instead of taking a regular course. I had never windsurfed before and in two weeks I made remarkable strides. I came back from Greece a very happy man.

While in Greece I was lucky to be under the instruction of two amazing teachers Andy and Russell. Andy had a penchant for changing his hairstyle. He had his own sense of right and wrong and he stuck to it, believing in a code of honor which he studiously applied in his day-to-day affairs. You could say he was a little eccentric, but you could not say he didn't know what he was talking about. His windsurfing was superb and at times awesome as he attempted and often succeeded in doing a somersault. The fact that it would take place in full view of the club was, of course, accidental. Occasionally Andy's view on things could seem a little strange and with the bit between his teeth somewhat frustrating. However, he was a good man and I felt lucky and honored to have him as a teacher.

Russell on the other hand was a different kind of character. About the same age as me, he had entered windsurfing not many years before, being disillusioned with the world of graphic design and seeking to get away from the pointless stress that it entailed. His approach to windsurfing was much like my own. What he did he did well and to say he was not a diplomat in his dealings would be doing him a great disservice. He showed extraordinary ability at diplomacy, giving someone every opportunity to see the error of his ways. But, he was not afraid, if necessary, to show where he stood, which could come as a fright to someone who had underestimated him. He was also very patient and went the extra mile, only coming out in his diplomatic way to nudge you on when he felt perhaps the time for babysitting was over. It was this quality that made working with him such a pleasure. We hit it off on his upside and I was glad and relieved that I had not placed him in my little theatre of people I did not somehow like, as I felt the distinct possibility of projecting one of my phantoms onto him. These things sometimes are touch-and-go. The fact that he took a liking to me made the difference. Both took my interest completely seriously and worked continuously to help me through. Given that I was coming to the sport at the age of 37 with no previous experience, they responded to the efforts I made and I progressed onwards and upwards. I was both amazed and gratified.

During those two weeks I drew endless parallels between the art of windsurfing and life itself. For me, learning to perfect a tack or a gibe, i.e., turning the board around in different ways, was an opportunity to perform graceful movements on water. This fed into my own inner love of movement and form. I was delighted. All of me was involved and I knew that the longer I tried, the more I would learn to become holistic in my approach, i.e., mind, body, board and nature working together. I knew this had to be a good thing and just what I needed. Each day I went out and tried endlessly to master each movement. I was constantly battling with nervousness, imbalance and body movements I simply had no experience with. A seldom-acknowledged fear of drowning, which was later to emerge in a session, played a part in this nervousness. However, I was delighted, as I knew I was learning to use my upper body to work the sail while, at the same time, almost independently, using my lower body to balance the board. This I found quite appealing. It was a way to break the rigid holding patterns of my body and mind and to bring me closer to the art of movement.

I remember Russell telling me not to struggle with the board when attempting to do a beach start. A beach start involves catching the wind under your sail as you stand up by the winds power onto the board. In the beginning, with each failed attempt, the temptation is to struggle to bring the kit back into place instead of letting go and starting all over again. It has after all taken a great deal of effort just to arrange the kit. It took me some time before I eventually learned to work with the elements and to see how much easier and exciting that was. It was a parallel for life, i.e., let go and with a small amount of effort reorder the situation, working with the elements. (Sometimes we work with the elements, but the elements don't want to work with us – like people! This we have to accept.) Or put another way, don't try to control what you cannot control; instead, work with it. In the end there is no such thing as a perfect situation, but there is a perfect way to deal with every situation.

Once I mastered the handling of the kit I felt as though I had tamed a wild horse on the water. This was an aspect of windsurfing I found really appealing, as it tied into my own propensity to draw parallels for life from things around me, seeing in everything an inter-relationship, a common thread, a common law.

During my first week in Greece I had this dream:

> I meet this guy and he shows me by example that by simply just touching somebody I catalyze in him or her the ability to somehow heal themselves.

Why it should come at that time I do not know but it left a lasting impression on me – it was like a form of education. The previous year, I had begun to have recurring dreams which involved a girl with dark hair who appeared to be teasing or innocently playing with me in some way. I had begun to describe her as the love of my life. At this time I also had another dream about her. As it was not long before that she had appeared in another dream, I was surprised that she should reappear so soon. It seems she was trying to make her presence known to me somehow. In some of the dreams I am being tempted sexually by her, but resist, as I feel threatened. I feel it might expose my sexuality and leave me vulnerable to rejection because of it. I am also confused in the dreams, as I confuse feeling dirty and impure with the open expression of my desires.

The course itself was relentless. Each day began around 9:30 a.m. with a talk followed by tuition and practice on the water. This meant hauling boards and sails to the water's edge. On the water endless energy was expended in trying to keep the sail positioned, invariably leading to lower back pain. Some mornings we started earlier, taking mountain bikes into the hills and returning exhausted to begin the rest of the morning's training. The afternoons were physically more demanding, as the winds increased dramatically due to the rise in air temperature, causing the winds to be sucked down from the mountains. In my own case the evenings were no easier, as I developed the habit of staying out most nights until 3 or 4 a.m., drinking in a variety of bars. In particular, I hung out at one very comfortable bar called The Tunnel. It was run by Miltos and Makis, two very cool individuals who had a great selection of world music.

In spite of everything I eventually learned to water start, but only after realizing that it was fear that was holding me back. On the evening of the ninth day Russell said to me, "You can have all the tuition you want in the world, but there comes a point where you have to put it into practice." This was Russell's diplomatic way of telling me to go for it and face the fear. I realized then that either I would make the grade or drop out under the pretense that it was not for me.

I was not about to throw away something that I had worked so hard to reach, especially surrounded by some of the finest teachers the industry could provide. I knew I was in a privileged position. I knew if I gave up I would feel like shit, knowing that life was getting the better of me in the end. Each day I had fallen off my board a hundred times as I had struggled to master my balance. I had gone through moments of feeling completely useless and demoralized. It was tough and in relatively high afternoon winds a little scary. Having mastered my balance more or less, what was left was to allow myself to be carried by the winds and let go of the pointless desire to control the elements. That is what was frightening me.

The next afternoon, with steely determination and winds picking up, I walked my board to the practice area. I felt it was my last chance. The water took on a new look for me, filled with an energy I hadn't noticed before. Russell passed by and asked how I was. I said fine and that is how I actually felt. Clearly, at some level I had made a decision to let go. I had also resolved to tame this beast and, as the winds rose and I got into position, I threw off my fear and went for it. My whole heart, my whole mind was committed; my intention was pure. The next moment I was standing on the board and whooping away, cracking out to sea. I couldn't believe what I had just done as I had been very scared of flying out the front of the board. In an instant a great load had been taken from my shoulders and I felt that a deep fear I had been carrying around with me for a long time had just lifted. I had shaken the monkey off my back. I was exhilarated. It was truly incredible. I had been pushed to my physical emotional and psychological limits and suddenly I felt great. For the rest of the day I related with perfect ease to those around me.

I had entered the course determined to do my best and let nothing get me down or make me feel or behave negatively. Each day, I was determined not to let my old ways prevent me from succeeding on any level. I realized everyone had something to teach me. All I had to do was ask myself, *What has this person got to teach me?* I would learn it, take it on board and carry forward. During my time on the course I turned a blind eye to every negative act I perceived around me. I carried onwards and upwards. It was a blessed two weeks. I learned a lot about myself and my relationship to others. I felt renewed. I called it my "Dude Conversion."

I can see now that the intensity of the course, along with my steely determination coupled with pure intention, was an excellent preparation for what lay ahead of me. My ego, unable to cope, threw me back onto my inner self, my soul, which by the power of intention became engaged. These two weeks kick-started my soul.

Once I had begun to master the art of windsurfing, I was constantly delighted by the way the water changed and challenged me. In the mornings the waters were calm, with light winds allowing practice of basic maneuvers. However, in the afternoon, when the winds picked up to three knots and little white horses appeared, it was as if the masculine spirit of a Greek god had come down from the mountains and was making its presence known. Gone were the gentle waters, to be replaced by an unknown presence – a presence that filled the air with mist and a sense of energy. It was as if the real master of the waters had awoken and wanted some serious engagement. Not only this, but the seascape changed constantly and one could become transfixed by it.

The water constantly challenged me to act properly to master the art, as if somehow egging me on to become a part of it, to run and play on its slopes, to dance on its shoulders, to play with God. Unlike life, where one is easily buffered by money from proper action, i.e., you can easily run roughshod over most things and get away with it if you have the money and are not too worried to be eventually isolated, the waters hold back no secrets and it is impossible to fool yourself in this way. If you are struggling to make a certain movement on a certain piece of water, unless you adjust to the changing circumstances and go with the flow, you will always struggle and not find the enjoyment it has to offer. In this way a part of you dies and suddenly you discover a more forgiving terrain, kept hidden by stubbornness, much like a little child who has no choice but to adapt constantly to a changing environment it knows little of.

Andy pushed me at the end of the first two weeks to complete my level two tests in windsurfing and powerboat skills and I knew behind his feigned sternness he had a heart of gold and was doing his best for me. His own skills were superb and his instruction top-class. I really felt very lucky to have two such great guys watching over me.

To become an instructor it is necessary to reach level three personal skills and it was my intention to return for the second half of the course later in the summer. Going from level two to level three is no mean feat though. It involves planing the board over the waters, much like a powerboat does, with both feet in the foot straps holding on for dear life. However, with everything completed to date along with my level two skills, I could safely say I did bloody well!

Is Reality an Awareness of Suffering?

On the day of my level two tests with Andy I swam in the water beforehand to feel comfortable for later and to overcome any fear I might have of the water. While practicing, suddenly all tension dropped out of my body and I felt perfectly at ease with the board. I was relaxed and in position and simply sailed out. My test went really well. Later I stayed out in the sun and became dehydrated, which was a little scary. However, I was content and delighted to have made the grade to this stage.

I felt I had come of age by facing my fears on the water. I felt more alive than I ever had. I felt I had gone through an initiation of some sort. It was like a shift into reality and it came with some physical discomfort. Two weeks after the level two tests I was getting ready to board a plane and had to ask for medical assistance, as I was suddenly gripped by nausea and a sense of disorientation. I wondered then if, in regaining our normal mind, we go through some kind of organic change as well. Do our minds shift in such a way as to leave us feeling sick momentarily? Or was the answer a lot simpler? Had someone spiked my drink two weeks before?

I had not had such a period of happiness for years. This resulted from two weeks of intense physical, psychological and personal effort, which seemed to snap something inside me and left me smiling with intense pleasure. There was a downside to this though. The night before returning home, I was filled with intense happiness at being alive. While talking to people I felt happy and at the same time, I seemed to be picking up on their sadness. It felt very hard to endure both together and I wondered if being happy meant you had to live with other people's unhappiness as well. I began to see the advantages of being closed down to happiness, as most of us are and maybe that is one of the reasons why. Unfortunately it wasn't long before I was complicating my life sufficiently to bring an end to that happiness. Perhaps those few weeks of happiness were deliberately meant to show me what was possible if I only tried.

I speculated, in the end, that someone must have spiked my drink on the morning of the test with something similar to MDMA, but this feeling of happiness lasted for some weeks after I got back. Perhaps the MDMA opened the door that the course had loosened, working as a final push? Perhaps having had my soul kick-started, the MDMA catalyst, or whatever I was given, broke down the remaining barriers to my soul and exposed its inner joy in spite of the pain the ego sought to mask.

After returning to London I found myself seeing right through people. I found this disturbing. I could feel how they felt about themselves and me. For the most part they liked me and that I found unsettling. I found myself seeking to close down my mind and to shut out the sense of extra perception I had somehow acquired or tapped into. I just did not want to see these things, much like someone who has lived without a hearing aid and then finds improved hearing quite disturbing. It was only a matter of time before I would reengage my ego in its old manner of self-protection and return to my old self.

Adjusting to life back in London was difficult.

An Angel at my Table

Around this time (early July) back in London I met Greta, who was working in a wine bar in Kensington run by a young couple. I met Greta by accident. At the time I had a date with an English artist and wanted to bring her somewhere nice. I had walked around Kensington and came by chance upon this wine bar nestled down a back street. I knew such places existed in this area and had gone scouting. On the pre-arranged night I turned up and my date was late. Greta was serving me. She was in very high spirits. We spoke in Spanish and English and I enjoyed the rapport. During our little repartee we talked about sports and she mentioned something about not needing them when you have a boyfriend! I was taken aback, as I think was she. She later confided in me she did not know where that came from.

Eventually my date arrived and lounged in her seat, as though about to fall asleep. We ordered and Greta served us, but this time there was not a peep out of her. She was very quiet. The evening went okay, but I felt my date was somewhat a little distant. I had enjoyed talking with Greta as I had a lot of links to Spain and simply enjoyed the warmth of the Spanish. Warmth was no small thing to have in a city like London, which could be very cold and isolating. It seemed people there practiced the art of isolation and I was getting pretty good at it myself.

The next day, while sitting at my computer terminal, I told my colleague I was going to go back and ask Greta out. She accepted.

I still remember how she arrived on our first date dressed in red shorts, bobbed red hair and a big grin. I fell in love with her right there. We had coffee together and so began a long and lasting friendship. She was the first angel I was to meet on my odyssey.

There are few words that do justice to describe Greta. A pure soul, full of integrity is the first thing that springs to mind, along with the guts and spirit of an Andalusian. Nothing would stand in her way. She was determined and invariably in high spirits. Yes, there were things that she did not like to face, but she was no coward, always willing to learn and try. I enjoyed immensely having someone to talk to who shared a lot of my offbeat views, as well as supporting me fully in my adventures with Eboga. She was a blessing in my life and yet, deep down, I knew we would not always remain lovers, but I hoped we would remain friends. Our time together was not without its clashes, given that we both had fiery, sometimes untamed souls.

It was this realization that later made me understand that there are times when love is simply not enough. For the time that was in it, we were right for each other. We both needed security and love and this we gave each other in a city that could be merciless to the lonely. At the time I did not realize how important she would become, as I am not sure I could have survived what lay ahead without her love and support. She was a perfect companion and partner to me and I hope I to her. However, there was something I was still seeking and I had not found it and knew I would never be happy unless I did. There was a connection I had yet to make with someone, someone I had not yet met. For this, I had to change and so, for now, I was not ready for that connection, regardless of how badly I wanted it.

I learned something very important from Greta. The person who loves, grows as they receive the most beautiful part of another by witnessing it and appreciating it. In doing so, it becomes a part of them also. Greta's beauty and warmth was to become a part of me. So much so that, years later, as I expressed my newfound ability to love, I wondered where I had learned some of my ways and remembered: Greta. She renewed my capacity for love and lifted the years of loneliness I was carrying around with me.

It was no accident that she later assumed the role of warden in a Chelsea home for the aged, being absolutely marvelous with the people there, sometimes coming home at night to cry with sadness for what she felt. I could see Greta as a flamenco dancer, as she had the talent to do much more than she thought of. I was in awe of her way to handle people, as opposed to my own, which tended to be much too blunt. I was also in awe of her openness and the kind of values that come from inner knowledge, not from an acceptance of the rules and roles laid down by society. We met shortly before I was due to return to Greece.

A Sad Parting: One Door Closes, another Opens

Towards the end of July I gave a dinner party for some English friends. James had been away for the weekend and when he returned blew his top that I had not asked permission to have the party. I was surprised he even knew, as I had put everything back meticulously, including his pen, papers, etc., which were on the table I had used in the drawing room. He had noticed something, some small detail. I don't remember what. That was all I could bear and so after an argument I informed him I would be leaving.

In a way this incident summed it all up. No matter how good a situation I would find myself in, there came a point where I gave it all up simply because I could not accept the outcome of some action on the part of another. My own expectations of people and myself were altogether too demanding and unrealistic. Pride was both my weakness and my strength. I knew this, but I could not bring myself to accept the humiliation without feeling hurt and unfairly treated. Time and again this happened. Just as I would feel I was getting on my feet I would just throw it all away. It was pure lunacy.

Rob on the other hand would have managed this situation perfectly well, putting everything into perspective and laughing on cue if necessary. Me, I could not and this saddened me deeply. When was I ever going to learn to deal with people? How could anyone possibly live up to my expectations? It seemed I created an idealistic image of someone I liked on the basis they would never do anything to hurt me. Such a person, I am afraid, does not exist. How, with such unreal expectations, could I accept insult and injury and still be able to smile? As a child I also tried to accept such situations, but it seemed things only got worse with my feeling undervalued and abused. As an adult, I did not have the confidence to believe that I could still feel good about myself while accepting the ways of others. I felt that, once they treated me badly and I accepted it, a pattern would emerge. Perhaps I needed to learn how to stand up for myself and express myself properly but somehow that was a very threatening thing and I never felt quite able.

I needn't have worried about James. He had a heart of gold and, if anything, was more scared of me than I of him. Stupidly, I was throwing away a lifeline I needed like so many other lifelines before. Yet in my naïveté and lack of self-worth, this is how I saw things. The old saying, to chop off your nose to spite your face, was one I knew only too well. It was perhaps this knowledge that contributed to my desperation and desire to seek help via the use of Eboga. I could not go on losing the people I loved and feeling anger for those I wanted to feel love for. It was too sad and too pathetic. My situation had been perfect. I now had a nice apartment in Spain along with my home in Dublin. I was financially comfortable in London and yet I blew it all away!

That, it seems, was to be my path.

Around the same time as my run-in with James, I had this dream:

> I am watching a bird in a cage. Suddenly the door on the cage opens and it takes off flying around the kitchen in my mother's house. It is white with colored markings, medium sized. I think I should get it back in the cage, as I am afraid my mother will be upset. As I am putting the cover on the cage, other little blackbirds escape and I then realize it is futile trying to get them back in. I know it is meant to be that these birds should be free.

This dream seemed to be telling me that I was about to break free of my cage. Perhaps it was a dream in which my forthcoming Eboga odyssey and its meaning were being hinted at. Odd that it should come at a time when I was separating from James.

James passed away around New Year's, at the age of 60. He suffered from cancer of the colon. Yet, while walking around with a morphine pump, he still found time to laugh and to eat a platter of cheeses, which he loved. They were exactly what he was not meant to eat. This, along with drinking one of his favorite, though competitively priced, wines. He was a phenomenon.

I was sad we had parted without making up properly, as I truly loved him and miss him. He had no wish to see me leave and had retracted his statement. However, events had already been put into motion that were by now unstoppable. They say death begins in the colon, the storehouse of the residue of all our negative emotions. There was more to James than met the eye. I am grateful to have had the opportunity to know him. In our last conversation by telephone (he rang me), we talked about him coming over to my new apartment for drinks. We did actually make up one day before I left, standing at the kitchen door where I told him that I thought he was a good man regardless of our differences. He was moved by that and thanked me. He had the heart of a child. Yet I still, at some level, felt hurt and did not feel well enough to bond so soon again with him. I hoped that would change with a little time. Unfortunately, time ran out. With hindsight, I can see that he was an important influence on my life even if our encounter was sadly short-lived.

Self-Created Turmoil

Before leaving for Greece at the end of August to complete my course in windsurfing instruction, I moved my belongings into storage and left 33 Eccleston Square. I also impulsively purchased a small apartment nearby in Chapter Street in need of complete refurbishment, as I did not want to wither my money away on high rent.

On reflection it was possibly the biggest mistake of my life. I had a nice apartment in Dublin and a small apartment in Spain. Everything was perfect. I can remember walking outside my apartment feeling I had the world in my hands.

Why the sudden upheaval coupled with a reckless abandon on my part to try it all? I had everything I needed to carry through on the dreams I had identified for myself. Now I put all those dreams in jeopardy simply because I could not relate properly to those around me. I seriously complicated my life and seemed to make a 180-degree U-turn away from what I had discovered. Perhaps I had come too close.

My state of mind was disturbed and confused.

All my life I had put my dreams ahead of material gain on balance, but now a part of me was afraid that maybe I was meant to take this added opportunity by purchasing a London apartment to complete my material needs. Clearly, I did not understand the ways of the universe.

I was confused and it wasn't long before my happiness turned to stress and desperation. I did not understand the path of least resistance. I also did not realize that, once I had begun the process of liberating the soul, events would be such as to continue to challenge and undermine the ego. How else could the soul make its escape good?

Supernatural Aid?

I arranged for my first Eboga session with Karl to take place during my second trip to Greece. The sudden turn in events after my previous return to London from Greece made me realize I had not dealt with my problems and, if anything, I was more determined than ever to try Eboga (ibogaine) to help recapture some of what I had uncovered the first time round in Greece. I had two further official weeks of training left to complete my course. I arranged to take six to seven weeks of unpaid leave from my consultancy role in Lloyds TSB Bank in the city area of London to try to capture some of that earlier joy. I was lucky to have had such a gentle and understanding boss who assisted me in this request. I was also lucky to be seated next to a beautiful and switched-on English Indian woman called Sam, who radiated warmth and was a good conversationalist. Sometimes good company is hard to find in the computing business.

It was not really a time to be leaving my work, as I was just getting on top of things financially and had taken on new financial commitments. Had I realized my earlier joy was perhaps due to more than nature I might not have taken so much time off. On the other hand, I was determined to be happy and this was a way I saw open to me. Usually I grabbed any possibility to get my life straightened and this one was as good as any. I was also painfully conscious I was not getting any younger for what I wanted to do and was becoming depressed by a sense of being stuck in my life and myself.

Before leaving for Greece while lying in bed half-asleep in 33 Eccleston Square, I had a waking vision.

> I can see a girl who is sitting patiently in the lotus position. I know her but I can't figure out how. I just know I know her. It is as though she is waiting for me.

I was intrigued by this and wondered what it could mean. Perhaps I had had an encounter with a benevolent spirit guide? It seemed that somewhere someone was waiting patiently for me.

I returned to Greece amidst the most disappointing wind conditions for that time of year. I was unable to get the practice necessary to lift my skills to the required level due to the poor wind conditions. I completed my last two official weeks of training before heading by boat to Venice for my first Eboga session.

I took a 3½ hour taxi ride about three in the morning on 8 September 1998 to arrive at the port of departure somewhat innocent of what lay ahead of me. For me it was another task to undertake and with that I sat on deck waiting to arrive, wondering what lay ahead for me; as I had done 21 years earlier on my first trip outside Ireland, crossing the Irish Sea to spend a summer working in Scotland.

What was I Expecting?

It was indeed a new chapter in my life, as I had just left 33 Eccleston Square in August and was now embarking on an adventure which in truth came with a one-way ticket; an adventure that would reach its climax exactly 33 months to the day of this, my very first ibogaine session, my very first entry into the realm of Eboga.

I am not sure what I was expecting. I knew that I had effectively forgotten and lost touch with my past, a past I found more and more painful to recall. In doing so I was more and more losing touch with myself and my dreams. Could such a situation be turned around? Did I have the strength to go through that? Well, I certainly couldn't do it on my own and deep down I hoped I had found something unbelievably powerful, a kind of Holy Grail. You could say that, in a way, I was desperate and I was clinging to straws.

In a way, I did realize it might amount to a personal death and an awakening to a world and a mind completely different from what I was used to. What else would work? Was it not what I was really looking for? Was I not seeking to bring an end to a part of me that had outlived its use, but which at the same time had served me well, a part of me whose dictates I followed? Perhaps its time had come to end?

I did feel a little hesitation about that, as there was a tinge of sadness in me to lose the person who had come through so much and survived, the person who had struggled to protect and maintain me against the world's domination. Did I really want to lose that part of me? Did I have any choice, if I wanted an end to the needless waste my problems were causing my life? I wanted my dreams and I wanted them badly. My situation was impossible and it wasn't getting any better. There was no point to keep fighting a cause that led nowhere. I was not James Dean. I needed a good kick up the rear end and a clear sharp look at reality to see what was going on.

And that is what I got!

8. Journal: Voyage 1977-1984

When one is not able to be a boy,
The best one can do is try and be a man.

While at the school on the hill I began to fantasize that I could find a place of comfort among strangers, blaming my problems on the environment I was in and the lack of opportunity it gave me to build up my confidence. I believed that maybe what lay at the heart of my problem was that I was basically a coward.

So, at the end of my first year in my new school I took my first trip outside Ireland and worked for a summer in Scotland at McTavish's Kitchens in Oban, lying about my age, claiming to be 17 when in fact I was just 16 at the time. My sister had worked there the year before. I traveled by boat. This journey to Scotland was my first major adventure away from my homeland and reflected a deep desire to find something outside myself. Something I could not describe at 16 years of age but could only sense. It was a beckon of hope that, for a time, lifted my spirits.

The two major departures of my life were to be signified by such a journey. Without realizing my first journey was the beginning of a quest for the Holy Grail. It was to begin a repeating pattern of travel that would continue for the next 21 years culminating in a journey to Venice by boat in search of eboga, which instead of being a journey away from home, was a journey toward home, albeit a spiritual one. There, unknown to myself, I would find the key to the Grail I sought and finally begin to understand what I had not even considered: the divine feminine: the goddess.

My summer in Scotland was a welcome respite from my past. All in all it was a happy time amidst a beautiful summer. It also reinforced my taste for travel and escape. However as I returned to Ireland I duly forgot about my summer, as my mind became completely focused on what I saw as my true reality – the school on the hill and the fears that I faced there.

There were of course some good moments in this school on the hill. Once Clannad, a famous Irish group from Donegal, came to the school and played. It was a piece of heaven. I can still hear the notes from the huge bass being plucked and the gentle, loving, Irish voices singing. At least somewhere in Ireland lives a faith in the heart, I thought. Another time we were shown a film called *Tommy,* which was completely outrageous for a Catholic school as it touched on drugs and rock and roll. I was fascinated by it and enjoyed every moment. How it got into the school I do not know.

I was still struggling with inner pain and turmoil and in desperation I convinced myself that I could be a priest, as the idea of a loving God looking after me filled me with a sense of well-being which I longed for. I even toyed with the idea of being a saint, as this conjured up images of inner tranquility. The only problem being it seemed too much like a copout from the real issues at the center of my life, namely my inability to fit in and be myself. Whatever about fooling others, I didn't like to fool myself and didn't try, as that seemed a more relevant and grounded way to be. In the end it also seemed the best way to perhaps one day recover my lost self. However, in my heart I hoped that a few years of seminary life in contact with God would help solve my problems and leave me with the courage to return to the real world. Who knows? Maybe I would even stay on and become a priest. I managed to rationalize my decision, even though deep down I felt I was possibly playing a part in a charade.

The seminary in Maynooth, St. Patrick's College, was a much more civilized place than the school I had left and with time I settled down to a comfortable and manageable existence free from the constant fear I had felt. When I first arrived there, my room was two doors down from what was called the ghost room. As a child, I would sit around the fire with my siblings telling ghost stories. Now I was confronted with one of those stories. The story went that a number of students living in this room had thrown themselves to their death and so the room was turned into a shrine with the entrance opened. There was even a stain on the floor which could not be erased and was purported to be the blood of one of the victims. The first night I was there I heard sounds that unnerved me. As it turned out, they were simply due to the waterworks of this old building. Soon the fear of the ghost room was forgotten. However, another event took place which was far more interesting. One night, sitting up in my bed, I imagined what it might be like to invite Christ into my life. Everybody was talking about it. So I decided to give it a go and see what would happen. I focused on this idea and the room seemed to get brighter and brighter. At first, I thought that maybe it was my imagination, but suddenly I believed something was really happening and I panicked. I sat up with a fright and it went away. I tried to repeat the experience but nothing happened.

The first days in the seminary went well and I made friends with a boy who appeared to be a little timid but in fact had a wonderful sense of humor. We hit it off and I felt very happy to have his friendship. I was in a safe environment and, for the first time in years had a real friend. I felt myself and I enjoyed myself deeply. I thought finally I would be able to open up and restore myself. As we settled in, another boy took a great liking to my new friend and, before I knew it, he was swiped from under my feet. In the beginning he tried to include me, but I never felt properly included. I didn't want to compete and, as time went by, I lost him. I felt deeply hurt, as I was not prepared to appeal on any level to our friendship, as that would bring about the very thing I sought to avoid: humiliation. A normal boy would have easily adapted but I was not normal and when pained I became disabled. Once more, even here in God's heartland, I returned to the shadows. I kept to myself, ashamed by how I did not fit in – particularly as my friend was a competent football player. Perhaps it was then that I realized my past was a serious problem and I was burdened by it. Going home was a constant reminder of the pain and hopelessness of my situation. As time went by, I became more irritable out of frustration with my life. It seemed I was being molded into an Irishman, like someone protesting as a straitjacket is put onto him.

One of the ways I tried to overcome my problems was to endlessly repeat a little prayer, which I had been told brought miracles. I had hoped this would lead to God's healing. I managed to keep this up for days, but soon tired of it.

While in Maynooth I had my record player, now six or seven years old at least and still as good as new. My favorite music had become Leonard Cohen and I found great comfort listening to him. It seemed he somehow shared my world and that made things okay!

Ironically I decided not to join the seminary choir as I wanted to be part of the football fraternity and become more integrated with my peers. It seemed I was still trying to reconcile my past and had in fact become its prisoner, compromising what I really wanted to do under a cloud of low self-esteem. To this end I joined the athletic club, rose to become its chairman, won an award for the improvements I made, but never did manage to make the transition into football – as a player.

Once, while in the seminary, I did try to involve myself in the spirit of renewal that the Church seemed to be promoting at the time. I was one of the many seminarians who stood in the Phoenix Park in black robe, white collar and white satin as the pope, John Paul II, arrived in his helicopter. There were more than 1.3 million people in attendance for the Papal Mass, the largest gathering of Irish people ever. It was hard not to be caught up in the enthusiasm of the occasion, even if one had one's doubts about the philosophy of the man. The oddest thing was this. One of the pope's private secretaries, an Irish priest, gave a talk to explain the circumstances around the death of Pope John Paul I to a group of seminarians, including myself. I found this baffling, as I listened to the secretary explain the events leading up to and after the death of the pope. The talk left me with more questions than answers and I wondered what on Earth was this man doing spending his time convincing us of a death that was not meant to be a murder? It was definitely one of the more intriguing moments of my life. It led me to wonder if the pope had not, in fact, been murdered. What was going on at the heart of the Vatican anyway?

It was not long after that a conference of renewal for young Christians from all over Ireland took place. Unfortunately, it turned into a conference seeking to reaffirm the power of the hierarchy, as well as celebrate a past that had failed us. Naïvely I thought it was about liberating the Spirit. Afterwards I got together with my fellow seminarians from my diocese and planned to organize an event for the youth of the archdiocese of Armagh – hoping to succeed where others had failed. Armagh is a diocese that had seen its share of the troubles of Northern Ireland and could do with a little of the comfort of the Spirit. The diocese straddled both sides of the border and as such had two very different experiences of life – one strewn by the troubles, the other preoccupied with the seasons and the cultivation of the land – the part I came from. The constituency of the Irish Church is based on the whole geographical area of Ireland, while the political map is divided between the Irish government in Dublin and the British government in London. This, no doubt, adds to the confusion for non-Irish to understand the situation and also feeds the idea that Irish nationhood would eventually come through the Irish Catholic Church. In any case, with optimism I went along to a meeting of diocesan priests to discuss how the event should be handled. They sat there staring, as though clueless of what was being said to them, only revealing any intelligence when it came to making decisions or halting anything that was too risky for them. What in hell's name were this lot about, I thought? Is it any surprise the Church subsequently imploded when its underbelly became exposed? I soon decided it was all a waste of time and went back to my day-to-day life in the seminary.

In the seminary, I still wanted to prove my abilities on the field, but I couldn't get past the basics. No one took me seriously in this. By the end of my second year I was facing a dilemma. My degree would finish either the following year or the year after, if I stayed on for honors. I did not wish to be seen to leave just as it suited me and so I had to make my mind up soon. The other factor weighing on my decision was the anointing at the beginning of third-year equivalent to becoming part of a Brotherhood, a nominal stage on the path to full priesthood. I decided I wanted to be part of this, as it was a special bond to my fellow classmates as well as being something special with God and life – a form of initiation. I resolved my dilemma by deciding to stay on for the anointing and postponing my decision until afterwards. Finally, one day, soon after the anointing, I formalized it within myself. I entered the little church where my classmates and I prayed daily. I knelt before the altar alone and spoke with God. I reasoned if God were a just God, he would want me to find him for myself in real life and not to stay sheltered under the auspices of a Church I had not properly questioned. I had things to do and, unless I was true to myself, how could I be true to God? This seemed to do the trick and so I left this little house of prayer where I had knelt many times before, as well as fallen asleep after late-night, unsanctioned escapades climbing over the wall to get back in time for early morning service. The fact that I had not been entirely honest in my motives for entering the priesthood, I hoped

God would overlook. I didn't mention it though! Now I had the daunting task of informing the dean of my decision. It was not long after that I left the seminary side of the university and became a lay student. It was a transition to the real world.

You could say I was a lost soul not knowing which way to turn. I had little real sense of connection to others. You could say I was disturbed and soon found reason to isolate myself. Ironically, I was quite popular, able to put out but intimidated to receive. This baffled those who genuinely liked me but could not get close as I pushed them away, often misreading their ways. My only dream was to be a singer and possibly a dancer, inspired by such heroes as Michael Jackson. It was the dream that kept me going. Whether or not it was real or just the fantasy of a schoolboy did not matter. It was a ray of light in an otherwise dark world. However, my faith in the dream was waning and I feared for my own future and livelihood. I also wanted the dignity a degree would confer, feeling somewhat worthless in myself, with little to distinguish me from the boys in the street who had shunned me and whom I imagined would be only too happy to laugh at me if I amounted to nothing. Whether I realized it or not, I had shunned them and, in a sense, was saying I am better than all this. I finished my third year and was given the opportunity to study honors. I took it. My subjects were math and chemistry. The truth was I had little interest or liking for chemistry, but was afraid of the alternatives. I felt an outsider in my own country and lived in fear of being in its society, which I saw as broken and potentially cruel. Fortunately, the professor of the department was a charismatic and flamboyant individual called Charles Martin Quinn. His love for theoretical chemistry, with its emphasis on mathematics and quantum mechanics, drew me in to the subject.

Around this time my classmates were making applications to various schools in North America. I decided to follow suit, hoping the opportunity would present me with another chance to sort myself out – I wondered if part of my inability to get back on my feet was not related to the Irish culture itself. I would have preferred to study in the U.S., but that appeared too daunting and potentially fearful. I settled for a small, well-established university, Queen's at Kingston, Ontario, Canada. Here I enrolled in the School of Graduate Studies in Theoretical Chemistry. I was 21 going on 22. Queen's is proud of its strong Scottish Protestant links. So a Southern Irish Catholic is liked, but treated with certain suspicion by some. It is a very conservative Ivy League Canadian university where the cream of Canadian society sends their children. Probably not the place where I was going to feel very comfortable.

Although I was glad to get away from Ireland, I lived with a pain in my heart for the life I had left behind, which remained unresolved. I was cut off from a part of myself I loved deeply. I felt lonely, frightened and disorientated. I was in pain.

Before I left I wrote this poem on the back of a paper bag I later found among my things:

> The myths of worlds beyond,
> Broken by a single plane.
> The wonders of a boy at home,
> Thinking of places like Spain.

When I left Ireland, I was determined to make a fresh start. I wanted to leave behind the "Bleeding Jesuses," as we called them, who moaned about the past and how the present was no better. I wanted to cut loose and create a joyful future, like the one I saw on the TV growing up with the Beach Boys and the Monkees. I had no more time for Irish suffering and I had no more time for my own suffering. I wanted to be free of all that.

So I studiously avoided being involved in Irish organizations wrapped up in nostalgia. I wanted to integrate into the new world and move forward, not to have one foot stuck in the grave and the other in the past. I felt many were hiding behind our history instead of facing their own lives. I wanted to put its atrocities behind me. I did not want to become one of its victims, as our educational system seemed intent on making me. I wanted to reconcile with the English and I wanted to succeed. I had no interest in being a loser.

At this time I felt I was drifting along in a sea of change of which I was not fully aware. I didn't seem to have any other choice. I had not been prepared for life. Going to boarding school had been a way to contain me and the seminary had been a way to try to heal me. I was still as I had been throughout my adolescence: lost, pained and confused, simply taking whatever avenue opened itself that I felt safe enough to follow.

The night before I left my cousin and her husband in New York, to make my way up to Kingston, Canada, I had a conscious dream where I felt I was desperately searching for a part of myself I had lost. I was looking everywhere, as though trying to lift a heavy load from my mind. Frantically I felt as though this was one of the few chances I would get before the veil of confusion descended once more. I eventually found the place at the end of a long path somewhere deep within myself. This came with a huge sense of relief and a kind of "eureka." I had once known this place long ago and almost forgotten it. Yet it still existed. I woke the next day feeling a lot better in myself, with a sense that I was still connected to a part within I valued greatly. This was the part my whole life was dedicated to restoring: my secret life.

As far as my romantic life was concerned Canada didn't turn out to be any improvement on Ireland. It was a painful reminder of my predicament and the problems I brought with me. And so in searching for myself, I sought to live alone, hoping to unravel my inner world. I didn't. Instead I simply discovered the loneliness of being alone.

With hindsight, every girl I have truly loved in my life I have given everything I had until I had no more to give. It seems that was the only way I was able to express my love. I gave until there was no more they could want and thus it seems they wanted no more. Which meant I always ended up alone; certainly not with the girl I had sought. I would wonder what I was doing wrong, as this happened to me time and time again. And I would wonder why they would go with someone else who treated them badly. Perhaps now I have the answers, but then all I had was a bewildering bafflement as to why I could not get off first base. I guess I was too insecure and timid in their presence. The capture of the eyes was too much of a threat for me to venture there. The truth is, I was clueless about girls and had no idea that one could build a relationship around the mutual joy and affection that the childlike love of one person for another can bring about. Women were a foreign species. I could not start a relationship, as I had no idea where a relationship started or what it meant. I was literally blinded by my broken sexuality.

I chose to study theoretical chemistry, as I actually had some liking for the subject. It drew together a number of disciplines I had found fascinating, namely mathematics and quantum mechanics. However, even though I had a love for such things, my greatest love of all was singing, which in many ways is the pure sound of mathematics, its soul.

The studying was tedious, as was the research. My peers were not particularly inspiring either. Outside of class I spent most of my time preoccupied with trying to live an independent life to prove to myself I could cope. For the most part, I lived a lonely and baffling existence, filled with mental anguish, uncertain and afraid of what to do. It was fortunate that I had chosen one of the least interesting areas of work, as it brought about my departure.

I decided it was absurd for me to try to complete a Ph.D. Which is why, supported by my Brazilian post-doctoral supervisor Alfredo, who said I should look for work with people, I completed my master's and left. However, an amazing thing happened while I was preparing my thesis. My work had involved making computer calculations based on existing formulas for the elastic component of the cross-section resulting from the scattering of high-energy electrons onto an atomic system. In my own calculations, I uncovered a further formula, which could use these results to calculate what is called the inelastic component based on the existing formula for the elastic component, which up to then was the only part that was calculated. It was a stroke of luck and exactly what I needed to convince my dissertation committee to grant me my thesis. Like so many times before in my life, I managed to pull the rabbit out of the hat when it came to the crunch. It seemed, amidst all my problems someone somewhere was looking out for me.

In my dissertation I wrote an inscription in Gaelic: "Through understanding we gain our freedom." One of the examiners, a surly man who never had much time for me, asked if it was some kind of IRA slogan. I think he reckoned I was a bit of a republican freeloader. Perhaps I was.

I had hoped my time in Canada in a secure environment would sort out my insecurities and put me on the road to my own life. This was not to be. My problems did not budge. They continued to torment me and I continued to be tormented. Friendship was very difficult and I seemed to live in my own world, not the world of others.

It was to be some time later before I fully understood the mechanisms at work in my relationships, being genuinely caught up in my distrust or dislike of one or another person. When I did, I chose solitude rather than form part of a circus that I had the presence of mind to know was going nowhere. Solitude was a halfway house between sickness and health, until I was able to deal with my problems. Real friendship on the level I longed for threatened to expose all the hurt of separation I had suffered. Knowingly or not I avoided the pain and knowledge of this tragedy which was never far from the surface, preferring elusive dreams. My pain was too deep to allow me the luxury of self-deprecation, which is a useful aid in forming close friendships. As a result, I often reacted negatively to another's comments, becoming cold and distant. There was a party going on in this world and I was not a part of it. There is a poignant tale told by Jean-Paul Sartre called *No Exit*, where the protagonists end up in a room together that symbolizes hell and are at odds with one another. Their differences are irreconcilable and they are fixated on them. In the final act the door swings open showing an azure void. Then the door swings shut and they are locked forever in their chosen hell.

In the end it seems I was more like my father than I realized, as my father always seemed more relaxed and delightful in the company of women. But I didn't look for similarities between my father and myself. It was only many years later that I was grateful that the similarities did exist.

It was while in Canada I met one of the few friends I would feel close to: Liyanda, a Rhodes Scholar student from Botswana. I never felt her equal, as she came from a dignified world I only dreamed about, while I felt as though I carried a hidden mark of shame. So, while we were good friends, I remained a little in awe of her. It was through her I accidentally bumped into Bishop Desmond Tutu in Soweto a few years later when he answered his doorbell while I was looking for his son Trevor, a friend of Liyanda's. Through her, I also learned a number of Southern African dance moves which moved the whole body, as if a serpent were passing through it, moving this way and that. The same serpent whose energy passes through all of us but is for the most part dormant; a serpent that I would one day grow to understand and love, but first I would have to travel through the wasteland of my inner world and it would be the spirit in a serpent that would guide me. Liyanda, like most in Southern Africa, liked to dance. And Liyanda embodied the spirit of freedom. She did not accept less than she was entitled to and she expected the same for everyone else. This was the time of Apartheid and once, a few years later, I witnessed her practically hit a white South African on the border post for insulting her. That was Liyanda.

When I first arrived in Kingston I attended a small Catholic gathering on Sundays, which was a source of comfort to me. The students and staff who attended were very nice to me. However, I was searching for answers and freedom from my pain. As none of this seemed to make much difference, I decided to attend a meditation course. As it turned out, the teacher had a keen interest in Krisnamurti, a philosopher who had renounced his title as the new World Teacher, The Matreya, given him by the Theosophical Society. Seeing some films where he talked eloquently of the beauty surrounding us and how no book or teacher could replace the personal search for truth, I decided to read some of his writings. I was impressed with the way he had walked away from everything in favor of a personal and simple encounter with truth. He taught that everyone should find their own truth, questioning everything. Ironically, he taught that nobody can teach you the truth; you have to find it for yourself. Krisnamurti explored at great lengths the many ways in which we keep ourselves in ignorance and cut off from true beauty.

This way of thinking greatly appealed to me. Although I did not fare too successfully with the meditation course, I decided to explore Krisnamurti further. Ironically, his book, *The Awakening of Intelligence* became my new bible. It was a source of comfort. In a way his teaching was quite simple. Once we create tension between ourselves (the subject) and the object we perceive, we are out of relationship and thus are not experiencing the truth. Because of this I wanted to attend one of his talks where he resided at Brockwood Park in England, a school modeled on his ideas. I only managed to get there after he had passed away, but while walking in the small garden where Krisnamurti used to meditate, I had a strong sense of his presence with me. Brockwood Park was a place of tranquility and comfort I visited from time to time while living in London. In time, I was to realize that the way to break the tension between the subject and the object is through an open and loving heart. At the time, though, that never occurred to me.

With Krisnamurti's thoughts in mind, I decided I had to give up all belief and start again from scratch. I was too laden with guilt and confusion to be able to make my religion work for me. Further, the comfort I received from my religion was a trap, as it maintained many erroneous beliefs and fears.

It was around this time I had my first experience of sexual intercourse. It was an experience filled with fear and foreboding, as I strove to ride roughshod over my fears of hell and damnation, having decided to lose this belief some time before. This didn't make it any easier though. I wanted to have a fulfilling sex life as I believed it would be a sign that I was whole and had arrived. But sexuality and woman were a foreign land I had yet to know. Sexuality and relationships did not sit well with me. I had never really started a proper relationship, as my sexuality had me completely confused. There was something sickening about it. Worst of all, it blinded me from the simple germination of affection between a boy and a girl.

I needed a fresh start. I realized the cancerous effect my religion had on me, being imbued in the ceremonies and customs of the church. This meant losing my connection to the church, which I missed. Giving it up would make my life even lonelier. In the church I had found consolation from time to time. But I reasoned it was necessary to break from it if I was ever to find the truth and free myself from a pain I could not understand. A further unfortunate consequence of this break with the church was a break with the only connection I had with my community, as it was through the church that I maintained my links with my friends and acquaintances when at home.

Life was becoming more and more difficult on one level and a lot simpler on another. The way I squared myself up with God and overcame my fear of punishment was simple. If God was a loving and caring God, then he would be sympathetic to someone who wished to find Him for himself or herself. In this way I could begin to let go of everything and begin again.

Krisnamurti was a source of comfort. I could not understand a lot, but I could sense I was close to something good. It was a few years later that I realized I did understand. In the meantime I hoped that when I did, my life would improve. Basically, I wanted to break through the grip on my being that these unexplained fears exerted on me. Krisnamurti talked about connecting with what is and allowing everything else to melt away. I guess it depends on your definition of "what is." It was around this time that I started to document my thoughts and dreams, looking for clues to help explain my condition. I decided that the only way to find the truth was to eliminate that which was not true!

It was through my friend Liyanda that the opportunity came to teach and work in Africa. I had decided to go, as deep down I hoped the spirit of Africa would somehow heal me in the same way my own land had once nurtured me. In truth, I was running away from the world of plot and intrigue which hurt me deeply, in search of a simpler, gentler way.

Just before I was about to leave I got engaged to Francesca, a French-Canadian girl from Toronto studying fine art. She had shown me kindness and allowed me to share in a gentler and happier life than the one I had been living. With her I felt safe and connected to a more passive and safe way of being. I needed this badly. I reasoned that I would fall in love with her in time and that I had what I needed. I thought that, given my condition, it was difficult for me to be in love straight away. With time, that would come. She probably was a substitute for my mother's protection, even if I didn't realize it at the time.

The decision to marry Francesca was a desperate one. As a boy, I had resolved to wait for the right person. The problem was, I didn't know who that was or how to tell, as I seemed to become easily infatuated and clearly I could not marry everyone. I was afraid to end up like the many couples who seemed locked into their own private hell with someone they did not love, living out their days together. My wish had been to have at least one relationship that ultimately blossomed into friendship before committing to marriage. In that way, I could have more confidence in my decision. I wanted to end my life with someone I truly loved and would grow with, not to repeat the mistake of so many others I saw as unhappy in marriage. More than once, I had suffered lovesickness and I knew how, in that state, the wisdom of the heart is often overlooked and eventually one falls to pieces. So I decided as a teenager to keep my guard against falling in love and thus not find myself married by the age of 18. It was this guard which unwittingly protected me from falling in love again and which, in some ways, stunted my natural growth. However, I don't regret it one bit, as I was not whole and thus not ready for a full relationship, as love is not enough.

I had heard of the idea of soul mates and wanted to believe in that, but wasn't sure what it meant. At this time, though, it seemed that all of these good intentions were forgotten and I latched onto Francesca. I needed support and most of all, I needed love. In her way, she had taken me in off the street, much like a dog without a home. It was only years later that I realized that true love lives in the soul and grows in the soul and is unmistakable, coming as it does with an ache and a longing. Everything else seems shallow in comparison. It is only when you enter the soul that you recognize it. In truth, true love is the love of "soul mates" as all true lovers mate with their souls.

Having arranged a post through Liyanda in Botswana on the border with South Africa teaching A and O levels in the chemistry and math department prior to getting engaged, I decided to proceed with the idea, as it was something I wanted and felt I needed to do. I hoped it would help me. I had the idea that the simplicity of life in Africa and the energy of the place might in some way heal me. Eventually it would, but not in the manner I anticipated and not while I was living in Africa.

Surprisingly, I was to re-experience Africa's healing energy some 14 years later whilst surrounded by the antithesis of rural African life: the grandeur and learning of old Europe, Venice. My journey to Venice would mark the second major turning point in my life. The first being a moment in my childhood yet to be uncovered by Eboga. Was the choice of Venice, a city of romance, a sign of what was yet to come?

Approaching The Grail Castle

Launcelot Beholds the Towers of Castle Carbonek.
By Edmund H. Garrett.

Reproduced with kind permission from The Camelot Project at the
University of Rochester, NY, USA.

9. The Naked Self

You have to lose your mind in order to find it.

Venice: A Place of Mystery

It is difficult to describe the experience of entering Venice by sea. The majesty of Venice is something to be experienced and entering by sea is one way to be captivated and transported back in time by its beauty.

As I entered, all around the spires of churches and stately buildings dotted the skyline. Gondolas side-by-side with water ferries traversed the waterways, bringing tourists and natives to their respective destinations. It was rush hour in Venice. Even here, modernity had cast its hand while the past struggled to keep pace. I watched with envy the moorings to private homes and imagined what it must be like to live there. Unfortunately, fewer and fewer people do, as the city becomes less hospitable due to the rising waters and the damage they inflict. Venice echoes its glorious past, stripped of its power and now somewhat impotent to protect itself. One can't help but wonder if it is a symbol for what is yet to come for many more centers of government dotted around Europe, as the march towards power in the hands of the few gathers pace in Brussels – power corrupts and absolute power corrupts absolutely. However, a place of wonder it remains and I unsuspectingly entered its arms to receive something of its mystery.

The journey lasted about 24 hours and I arrived early Wednesday morning, 9 September, 1998 around 9:30 a.m. My plan was to return to Greece to continue with the windsurfing afterwards. Karl was meant to meet me at the Port of Venice. Nervously I disembarked, discreetly glancing in all directions, but nobody appeared to be looking for me. I waited at the port side and then decided to ring him from the nearby café. When I rang him, he told me he had gone to the airport. I do not know how he got it wrong. Not long after he arrived. I felt he was not happy and his quiet deportment made me feel very uneasy. I could not decide if he was upset with himself or me. You could say there was a slight cultural gap between us. We made conversation on the journey back but I felt uneasy with him.

Leonard Cohen: The Chelsea Hotel

Before arriving at Karl's apartment we visited a doctor friend of his who checked the blood and ECG tests I brought with me.

As far as I was concerned everything was agreed upon and I was holding my nerve together to get started. It therefore came as a shock when Karl's friend started to quiz me about the wisdom of my choices. Karl watched and said nothing. I could not believe what was happening. I was very angry, as I needed support, not undermining. On top of the cool reception I had received on arrival I was really quite pissed off. I was also fed up with all the needless complications when my intention was clear and I had come this far, having paid a lot of money. The whole situation was descending into farce, as I needed my willpower for myself at this time, and not for others.

I wanted to focus on what I was about to do and not waste my energy on trivial matters. I certainly wasn't going to express my fears and doubts and open up a discussion which would lead nowhere, as in the end the decision was still going to be mine and no one else's. While keeping my inner fears to myself and wishing to bring the matter to an end, I said, "I am prepared to take a risk that could kill me, as it is preferable to the hell I have been living through." That brought the conversation to a close.

We left the home of the doctor and arrived at Karl's, where we set about trying to get organized. Karl collected his things, measured out the ibogaine and together we headed off to find a place for the session.

We attempted to book into a hotel. They gave us a small, dingy, uninviting room. The kind of room reserved for the lonely and impoverished. I said I didn't think it would be suitable. It was like something from a Leonard Cohen song and I had visions of myself as a broken-down addict. The managers didn't seem to want to help and so we decided to leave and go to Karl's home instead. I was relieved. I think they may have had some idea that he was working with drug addicts and so were not too keen on his further business. So by about midday after a great deal of frustration, we arrived once more at Karl's apartment and set about the task of carrying out the session. I was doing my best not to fall into the trap of expressing my frustrations, preferring to focus on the important task at hand. The room we chose was a small spare room. The apartment itself was on a noisy thoroughfare but was typically Italian and had a certain charm to it. The room, however, was quite interesting. On the walls Karl had many African masks from the Cameroon, which, along with the dark colors, gave the room a special kind of feeling. It had the somber sense of being in the African forest. Yet the daily sounds of city life intruded from the noisy street below. Karl pointed out that many sessions had been held there. As the session itself got underway I felt I was in a very special and holy place. I could sense the energy and presence of Africa. I had the desire to be reverential, as I felt I was on holy ground. Later I thought to myself the scientist may see this experience as a way to cure addiction or unmask childhood trauma, but it is, in fact, much more and deserves respect and reverence. What's more, to fully participate and benefit from a session, it can be no other way. It is an inner cleansing, a spiritual rite of passage.

As the session progressed, Karl proved himself a very capable and patient therapist. He waited quietly on hand and attended to my every need.

Crossing the First Threshold: Life & Death

Waiting to receive the ibogaine I was afraid that perhaps Karl would decide against the session for whatever reason, given all that had gone before. I was in awe of what he stood for, unable to grasp the full implications of the situation. Before I knew it he had measured out the ibogaine in a matter-of-fact way and handed it to me in some water, as though I was about to take something for a cough and he had another 50 patients to see. His apparently aloof manner intimidated me and seemed peculiar considering the power of the substance I was about to take. Given my abused state of mind, it took very little for me to be intimidated. Our cultural differences certainly didn't help either. He had seen it all before, I guess. I was another client heading for the chopping block. The sooner we got started the better.

I had been fasting from the day before. I suggested to him that he heat the mixture first, as the ibogaine had not dissolved very well. Half in a state of panic, while waiting, I tried to clear my mind and "psych" myself up. I realized that I didn't know what I was about to do but I had decided to do it and that was that. In a way it amused me that I had reached the point where I would risk my own life. I found that comforting in some strange way. There was always a final refuge from the pain. At least it meant I wasn't going to spend the rest of my life cowering in the corner, but actually do something about it.

Before taking the ibogaine I took a moment and thought to myself, *I have done some crazy things, but this has got to be the craziest of them all. For all I know, I could die today.* I then ingested

21 mg/Kg by body weight of ibogaine on 9 September 1998 at 14:45. I was simply not prepared for the taste. It was disgusting. The foulest-tasting salt I had ever tasted. Karl seemed to think I was making a fuss over nothing. I thought to myself, *He is not the one taking it.* I do not have the German taste for strong coffee and I imagine that would certainly have helped. Psychologically, nothing can prepare you for the first time you take it, nothing! And no one can appreciate what you are going through in those first moments. Anyone who seeks to help another in this should undergo at least one full session to properly understand the needs of the situation. It is not a recreational experience! However, to be fair to Karl, he was not to know the depth of my fear and he certainly did not know the depth of my pain. Perhaps my controlled manner belied my true feelings to him and he was simply trying to help me relax.

It may be that the circumstances surrounding my session contributed to its success, as they brought me to a level of crisis I had never before experienced in my life. Crises are a wonderful adjunct to change. I was to discover that once a date has been made with destiny, events unfurl exactly as they are meant to.

Shortly after, I went to lie down and began with a prayer in which I asked for all my spirit guides and guardians to be present. I was scared. To be honest, it seems strange to me now to have made such a request without properly understanding the makeup of the angelic realms. Do we have guides? If so, what form do they take? Do we have guardians? If so, what role do they play? And finally, are there other beings, which surround us and take an interest in us? If any of these beings were attached to us, why would we even need to ask for them to be present? Anyway, I was covering all my bases just in case, as I was entering a world I knew little of. I did not want to be left exposed to anything I couldn't handle if help was at hand that could be called upon. I was also confused in what to expect from the angelic realms due to the few new age commentaries I had read from time to time describing angels, etc. I have never really found the readings very interesting as they do sound a bit like vivid imagination.

Karl in the meantime took precautions to block out whatever light he could and set up a small lamp covered by a scarf to allow him a minimal amount of light to take notes and observe. He said nothing, simply watched and acted when necessary. Low light was essential to enable me to be able to see the images, which would form on the ceiling and in the room before me – a room, which more and more seemed like it was in Africa.

The ibogaine took about 40 minutes to take hold of me. I gradually was unable to move and each movement sent a wave of moving liquid through my body as if I had become a mercury thermometer. This was unpleasant, so I strove not to move at all. I felt it in my body like a serpent moving slowly, waiting to pounce. I was in its respect. Eventually it felt like a ball of fire in my stomach. While the ibogaine had been taking effect, I could hear the sound of drumbeats. Initially I thought it was Karl fiddling with my tape recorder I had taken along for making notes. In fact he was doing nothing and so I had dismissed the sound as being irrelevant. This caused it to go away, but once I realized it was coming from the effects of the eboga I encouraged myself to be receptive to it again. It returned. Slowly, it seems, my soul was being transported to Africa. You could say that Karl's room was becoming an urban jungle with the sounds of cars and occasional flashing lights blending in with the beats of African drums – a surreal sense filling the atmosphere as the walls of time and space began to merge with another plane; a plane where one could be transported through time and space.

Shortly after I had ingested the ibogaine and before I became immobilized I started to go to the toilet and by the time I was under its full influence my insides were completely empty except for this strong, disgusting salt taste in my system. An empty system was very important, as the powerful movements in my body could not have retained anything and given I could not leave the bed, would have presented a big problem, a problem I know Karl was prepared for. These movements were like waves of descending force through my body, contracting and expanding my insides right down to my anus.

During the initial effects I became very self-conscious and felt myself in a way I had never felt before. I felt extremely goofy, closed and awkward as though I were hiding behind a mask. This was very depressing and, frankly, I felt I could not live with myself if I was like this. I felt like shit. I disliked myself intensely.

Self-Disintegration: The Rise of the Eboga Serpent

Then I felt as though my mind were splitting in two. This scared me, as I thought maybe I was going mad, having a psychosis. A part of me tried to hold it together, but I felt pulled in two directions at once. My mental calculations were rising rapidly in an attempt to rationalize and control what was happening to me, but I could not keep up. It was then I felt as though my mind were melting, being split in my crown. Some force was coming at me from both sides at once, dragging my mentality to both sides of my brain, lost and confused, my mind trying to remain in control from two opposing points of view simultaneously. All it took was a moment's lapse of control, as my mind appeared to rapidly jump from one end of the mental spectrum to the other trying to pacify both sets of thoughts at once, to concede somehow that the battle had been lost to this new, unknown power that had entered its domain. I could not hold on and felt my thoughts give way, melt.

It was as if this opposing force was required to arrest and depose my ego-thinking mind from the seat of the mind, like a mental tug of war where my thoughts were being pulled in two directions at once. I was terrified of the impending annihilation; my only weapon, rational thought, de-empowered. I felt my center of consciousness disintegrate as if it was being melted away, leading to a splitting, a pouring out from the area near the third eye. It was an awakening perhaps of my imprisoned higher faculties, a part of my soul, frightened and bowed under to the power of a controlling ego. These higher faculties were to aid me during the session.

It is only now I can see that my ego had to be knocked out and disabled to allow my unhealed soul to properly emerge from behind its guarded doors. For the rest of the session, there ensued a struggle between my now-weakened and unseated ego and the Eboga spirit to keep these doors sufficiently opened, as the strong animal ego, out of years of force of habit, sought to pick itself back up to regain control after life had once more knocked it down. It would, out of pure animal instinct, work tirelessly to regain control of the mind and thus shut those doors on the broken soul once more. How else does a herd maintain its solidarity unless it achieves a common mind driven by its own pecking order? It has no use for a liberated soul. It does however have a great need for a controlling ego.

The way to a person's soul is to bypass and unseat the ego. The ego is guarding the broken mind and thus the true expression of the manifestation of the soul. It lets nothing out. Conversely and unfortunately, it lets nothing in. In a session the ego becomes involved as the Eboga energy struggles to hold onto the link created in the first moments of ego-unseating or, as some like to call it, destruction. In truth the ego is never destroyed, only bypassed. We only think it is destroyed because we are so "attached" to it. The deep problems of the person bring about the ego's attempt to regain control (apart from its own wish to regain its seat within the mind) and so the session is paced to take into account the strength of the

Eboga energy and the opposing strength of the ego that wants the soul back in its box, out of harm's way. The ego itself has been formed through years of choices made with free will by the soul. In time, the soul loses its power to control it and we are imprisoned in a world that, to some extent, is of our own making. The road to hell is a slippery slope and each wrong choice closes a door behind us. We believe we can open it again but it is not that easy once closed, as it becomes fused into our ego apparatus and benefits from the strength of all the other wrong decisions made, often to protect underlying trauma – the sum of the parts being greater than the whole.

That is not to say the ego is bad or malicious. It simply is working under orders. Unfortunately those orders in time over-empower it. Hence issues will alternate in depth to maintain a balanced situation, depending on how the entities choose to proceed in our own best interest, so that the ego does not regain control.

I keep referring to the ego, but in truth I did not really understand the nature of the ego at that time. By the end of the second book, 33 months later, this situation was to change, as my consciousness became much more clarified due to a further three sessions I was to undertake. My ego would only eventually give up the strength of its mission of control once it had been reprogrammed in time, after the healing of the soul allowed it to re-exert it's influence. The ego would learn that it no longer needed to protect the mind from so many phantoms and so many fears because they no longer posed as great a threat as they had. The soul was re-empowered.

You may wonder what exactly is the ego and what part of you still remains once it has been disabled and weakened? Well, you remain as always. In this case somewhat horrified and terrified, but the real you nonetheless. I define "you" in the unhealed state as a reduced part of your own soul, i.e., reduced because of the blocking effect to the totality of yourself due to your unhealed soul and its complementary over-empowered ego. The ego is a natural part of the animal with important roles to play. Roles that in time I would learn to respect. However, it also has a blocking effect with an unhealed soul. Before the session you are under the influence of a controlling ego, a guarded fortress if you like that derives your sense of well-being from your animal mind by manipulating everything you do and think. In this way it circumvents your true, connected feelings and gives you at least some sense of comfort, i.e., you don't derive your sense of well-being from your soul. Your actions are completely compromised by the ego, hesitation being a natural part of your existence instead of the freedom, knowing and spontaneity of the soul. One example of the ego operating: you might derive vain pleasure from some good deed you have performed instead of the sense of well-being which is natural that comes from your soul when you have carried out some good deed. In other words, you are disconnected from your soul, your heart, your full self and derive your pleasure from the manufactured responses of your mind. You are wrapped up in the manipulations of the ego, which is using the animal mind and its responses to make your unhealed state bearable. Thus you are not truly connected to your full self. In this state the ego can be happy, knowing it has all it thinks it should have. But if anything goes wrong, it cannot fix itself, as it is not a healer. That is why we must look outside the ego to find healing. The ego's maintenance engineer has to be brought in from outside. The ego in the end realizes this. That is why it agrees to submit to the session even though it is still subject to its own impulses.

So you are always there and the unseating of the ego simply exposes you to your true state of mind without its mental addictions to cling to. Imagine if you like, the ego as a wild person being held back by two strong men. Occasionally it will manage to break free of their grip, but they will subdue him again. All it can do really is wait to be freed. At the same time, by the power of intention it has agreed in part to submit but at times it simply cannot help its own instinct to rebel. Thus we still have a perspective on the situation as we look at the proceedings while experiencing our true self without too much ego interference – the ego being a mentality manipulator. In this case its ability to manipulate disabled – its prejudices however, in part, still affecting our understanding and thoughts. Which is why the session still involves behavioral modification and awareness enhancement.

Hence, healing is not about fighting with the ego. It is about healing your soul and your emotions that, in time, reprogram the ego. It is only when the soul and emotions are healed that we have the power to release the ego from this role, leading to greater awareness and fewer sources of pain. Put conversely, the power of pain does not invoke the power of the ego as the pain has been removed. The ego becomes much more passive. However, for a time, we may still react to situations negatively and the ego may appear to manufacture the same responses, but through integration we realize we have nothing further to fear from these once-entrenched phantoms.

That is why any healing is going to take time and cannot be instantaneous. It takes time for the mental, emotional body to catch up with the healing of the soul in a period of integration and relearning, a gradual movement to a new, trusting state of mind. This I would eventually learn, but for now, I was truly ignorant of what was happening to me.

And so, here we see the true role of the Eboga spirit: the healing of the soul and the temple in which it resides and through which it is expressed: the inner child or the naked self. Once the soul is properly restored and healed, I was to discover, it is then given the opportunity to align itself to a higher power. You can call this salvation if you like. This comes before complete psychological and emotional healing, which comes before significant personal transformation or metamorphosis – the belly of the whale. But that was to be much later. For now my soul needed healing and it needed it badly!

Now that the soul was out, the energy of the Eboga spirit wafted it along a tunnel of reclamation, much to the ineffective protest of my terrified ego. Eboga quickly unearthed the hidden and protected material necessary to carry out the healing work. It needed the high dosage of ibogaine to give it sufficient power. Without it the ego could not have been unseated; the level of work needed could not have been done. I lay in horror at what I perceived as happening to me, as I was truly exposed to what I felt deep down. My soul was undergoing liberation. One it had long waited for. One which conventional psychology could never and would never be able to achieve, as it lay in the power of the highly protective ego to control and prevent anything truly disturbing to be revealed.

Writing now with the hindsight of experience, I believe it is fair to say that the Eboga spirit wrenches the dark forces keeping the soul in a state of pain by unhinging them through a process of self-examination, leading to a realization of the truth. It is as if it is the lie that keeps them in place, a lie that is supported by the hapless ego simply doing its job the best way it can. The ego, however, does not act totally independently. We have free will in our soul (child) and this free will elects which path to take in the face of this suffering. In that sense, the ego (a much-maligned entity) is innocent, simply being a function of the animal body, the mind. It is the child (the soul) in us who ultimately chooses what course it takes. Many of us can remember life decisions made as a child which later became programmed into our makeup (egos) and which we were unable to alter later on. However, once the lie is exposed through our good intention, and faced with the help of the Eboga spirit, the program can be made obsolete. The force, which holds the program in place, can be described as a demon that thrives on the darkness of broken emotions. The Eboga spirit wraps itself around these parasitic "demons" and wrenches them out of the body and soul, whereupon they disintegrate in the cold light of day leaving the broken emotions to be healed. In much the same way that debris is burnt up upon entry into the Earth's atmosphere. It leaves behind a somewhat emotionally bruised individual, but in time, nature and nurture take care of that. It is the over-conditioned ego (which is now open to change due to the weakening of its power via the healing of the sources of pain and denial) that is the last to change and this it does much in the same way a newborn child learns its new environment: through trial and error with an open mind and an open heart.

As I lay in complete panic begging for help and unable to calm myself in any way there appeared before me two rows of young angelic female beings caressing my aura, which started to make me feel very relaxed. They knelt to both sides of my outstretched body. Their appearance was ethereal, calm and deeply focused. They caressed the beads on my body trying to relax me. They were preparing me for what was to take place. I did relax but once more lost my nerve and started to panic again.

I have never, to my mind, experienced such panic before. Then, while in this state, I saw small, soft, pastel-colored bubbles oozing from the ceiling, falling down on me. I thought at first I was hallucinating an image of rats or something horrible. When I was a child we had many rats in an old storehouse, which I did not like. Soon this panic subsided as I realized I was looking at small gentle and soft, pastel-colored bubbles falling down on me and I felt the presence of powerful and helpful forces. I also realized that any image I saw was not physically real and so was not too worried if

I would see rats or not. It was a delightful and relaxing experience. I knew now I was in safe hands and began to identify with its company. I felt safe. I had arrived and the session was underway. I was delighted as I realized I had at last found the real thing: the source of the Grail. Knowing that, I was prepared to take whatever was thrown at me. Prior to this it was anybody's guess as to what was going on.

Then an unusual thing happened. I was offered the type of session I wanted! I recall three types were offered to me and the one I immediately plumbed for was an image of children on a merry-go-round in a small park where I was looking in from outside the gate. The taste of the ibogaine, though, was still disgusting. I felt my insides and sinuses overrun by its presence.

With my psychic faculties opened up before me, I could see a guy to my right hand side dressed like a compeer with black tails and hat. It was as though he was in the pit of a theatre – the master of ceremonies. He immediately started to rubbish someone I knew. I really didn't bargain on that and I didn't like him being negative with me about someone I knew and felt sorry for. So I said, "I don't want to listen to that, please." He didn't say any more on the subject.

There then followed an opening scene that was simply amazing. I saw before my eyes two tigers (even though I am told there are no tigers in Africa) one on either side, jump into the center of my vision and behind them the savanna of Africa, beautiful Africa. Before me I could see the African terrain – the bush, the red earth and the sparsely clouded blue sky. It was as if my released soul was being taken to a faraway place of healing, a place, perhaps, it had once called home.

Meeting the Audience

I then seemed to be in a theatre where the stage was set and on it was a screen. To the front were curtains like any stage and in the pit the compeer giving me advice. To my side I could hear what I took to be perhaps three angel guides chatting away. They were all happy and I thought that was because I was with them. I believed it was because the person they cared about cared about them. That was what I felt at the time and that was a nice feeling. The truth was, I was clueless about the makeup of the spiritual realms and so had a lot of misconceptions about what I was dealing with.

One soul was very talkative and chatted away with me. Then the other started talking to me and, while I was talking to her, the first seemed to become impatient. I asked the second soul what she was doing and she seemed to be working on a tune. I thought perhaps they were responsible for my creative inspiration, music in particular. She broke from her companion, as they seemed to be arguing, but she seemed to be fine with me while the other was upset for some reason. I tried to talk to the first soul to make things better, but she went completely quiet. During the session however they all shouted advice to me on certain happenings. I felt, how could you go through life ignoring such beautiful beings whose existence was geared to helping you? Had I known whom I was dealing with, I would have understood their purpose differently.

One little soul was incredibly beautiful and I spent a lot of time talking to her on her own. She was not involved with the argument between the other two and seemed to be apart from them in some way. We seemed to go to a very quiet and private place where nothing existed but the two of us and I was nervous. I could not keep the conversation going, as all I wanted was to be in her presence. She told me her name and I remember thinking how beautiful it was. I could not remember it later though and that bothered me. I spent a lot of time talking to her and it was a beautiful, blissful experience. She was completely open to me in a very sweet and gentle, innocent way, as though her true self that normally hides connected to me because it trusted me. I was very touched. Eventually she flew off and I felt it was because the destructive force in me that seeks to destroy good things came out in some small way and scared her. All I knew was that she was simply the sweetest, gentlest being I had ever met and she was clearly a little insecure.

Then the musical soul companion asked if I could be her teacher. I agreed but frankly was unsure how that was meant to work. I thought maybe she would just hang around me somehow, observing and learning as I carried on with my life.

I can now say, almost 6 years later, that I am quite certain I know each of these souls in real life. I realize now these guides were actually the souls of friends I was yet to make. So, in that sense, they were not really guides but a foretaste of my life to come. More correctly, they were soul companions. I know this as I have met their counterparts in real life, each with the same personality as I experienced it. They have each played a role in my recovery. The little angel has been my inspiration to heal. Only now can I see the full meaning of all I have encountered. It has taken me almost five years to understand the difference between the souls of others in this life, who become companions for a while at least and the souls and spirits of those in the heavenly realm.

But more importantly, the purpose of meeting these soul companions was more significant than this. I reached a stage four years after this session where I entered a very dark night of the soul where my whole inner world was raw, exposed and incredibly painful – the belly of the whale. It was then that I met my two companions. I subsequently came out of a very dark place and knew it was meant to be, as it was there that I had met them.

After this encounter with my spirit companions the session got fully under way.

Preliminary Healings & Lessons

One of the first things I was shown was worry spirits that flitter around and sit on people's ears and these worry spirits prompt you to think about something you are worried about or afraid of. I was told I could keep them if I was attached to them, if I was fond of them, or I could get rid of them. At the beginning I thought I wanted to keep them as they were cute (can you imagine I thought that?) and then, on second thoughts, I decided they were a pain in the ass and had been bugging me for a long time and said okay, let's get rid of them and consign them to the base of the brain where all primitive parts of man reside.

At the time I was worried I had missed my chance to be rid of them as I dilly-dallied and didn't strike while the iron was hot; but on second thoughts, that could simply have been a worry spirit trying to trick me! In any case I was concerned about wholeness and felt somehow everything had its place. Was that naïveté? I did not realize it was not just a simple matter of getting rid of worry spirits. In fact this worry-free state could only fully come about when I consciously took back my life and detached myself from each choice that gave rise to worry and hence, a worry spirit. With the benefit of hindsight the question of whether to keep them or not was somewhat rhetorical and showed how square I had become, unable to see the hidden humor in the question, becoming instead obsessed with the answer.

My soul companions, led by the compeer, then shouted at me to simplify my life. How true! I was entering into one of the most complicated periods of my life. I had engaged myself in a whole assortment of business transactions I had never before taken on, simply because I thought, *why not?* I felt I had the abilities, but had always shied away from using them, as I had ideals of a life based on things, which I believed in. In the year leading up to my session I had grown disillusioned and wanted to see if the materialist way had benefits I had overlooked: in for a penny, in for a pound! I needn't have bothered. The materialist way was not my way and never would be my way. But I had to learn, like so many others, the hard way. Maybe that was my final baptism into life, which I had studiously avoided until then and once it came, it came with a vengeance followed by the source of my salvation. This period I was entering was indeed a dark, depressive period. Ironically to the eyes of the world I was riding high. Inside I was beginning a downward descent. Only I didn't realize that at the time. In a sense I brought this upon myself in an attempt to shake up my life and to force myself to confront deeper, darker issues. They told me to sell my apartments. I said, "Even the one in Dublin?" (My home.) And they said, "No, keep that one." At this stage I was completing the purchase of a third apartment, a small apartment in London after just having bought an apartment in Spain. The life genie was most definitely out of the bottle.

Messages started to come and they came in the form of symbolic clues. I would somehow have to work out the answer. I was surprised at my ability to do so. For example, I asked where my heart was and a fish came into full view. As I had given a fish broach previously to my new girlfriend Greta, I knew it referred to her. My ability to read the clues seemed heightened and on reflection I believe it was because some inner psychic functions had come to the fore. The purpose of this question had been to uncover the identity of the woman of my life (the one who kept appearing in my dreams) and the answer showed how clever were the forces I was dealing with. They gave a straight answer to a straight question and carefully concealed the answer I wanted, as now was not the time to receive it. After many unsuccessful relationships based on living out unresolved childhood issues, I was hungry for a true and rewarding relationship, one of my own true choice. But this would take some time before I was ready. For now a lot of personal inner work had to be done.

There appeared to be three things taking place at once. Firstly I had the theatre show, which seemed to frame the events and offered encouragement and support after each event was gone through. Two beautiful young girls would appear like the assistants of a magician, walking across the stage, throwing balloons at me as a prize for getting something right, i.e., making the right connection to the event played before my eyes on what appeared to be a home movie screen. I kept telling them how beautiful they were and they seemed to like that a lot. Then, in concert with the beautiful stage girls, in the orchestra pit, I had the compeer, who was giving advice all the time to my comments on what I saw and what I thought I should do. Meanwhile behind me to my left side I had my three soul companions chatting away, often trying to give me messages and seemingly arguing among themselves. I could not see them directly but could hear them to the edge of my left ear where a light glowed around their presence.

One of the first visions to appear grew from what appeared to be a small anthill whose grains bubbled up from a point in the sand into a small mound. It was like watching a light grainy image of a home movie on a cloth screen. A scorpion appeared on the screen and I thought how beautiful it was. It had long furry legs that seemed soft and cuddly. I saw myself as a young child crawling toward it to play. I then realized that the scorpion represented someone I knew from my past and the message behind the scene was: even though they can look playful, I should beware, as they can sting quite easily. I had been looking with the mind of a child and the feelings of a gentle heart that innocently trusts everything. This same innocent state of looking would figure right throughout the session and indeed would be the source of many of my original childhood problems. It seems we come into this world innocent, not understanding the dark ways we need to learn and overcome.

I then went through a period of self-hatred, asking, "Who wants me?" I felt alone and helpless.

I encountered my father who had passed away some years before. This was to happen at a number of points throughout. He appeared to be a little distant, slightly turned away from me. It was as though he knew I was angry with him. I was and a part of me was avoiding him in the session. I didn't realize until my fourth session in Brazil that he was not to blame for what I thought he was to blame for. In fact my father had loved me very much but for different reasons had difficulty in showing it. He was a good and hard-working man and I hope he is now reaping his reward. I later realized how much we do not know or understand and how important it is to heal the past to put an end to misdirected anger and hurt. I was to understand this in my fourth session. In the meantime, I felt he was looking for my forgiveness. I said, "I forgive you, but it is up to the others to forgive you themselves." I felt he was happy with this. Obviously there were issues between us, but not what I thought they were!

A number of lessons followed and were delivered with a fine sense of slapstick humor. I realized a sense of humor certainly helped. Scenes appeared where I gained insight into a number of very deep and personal issues. I was shown things from my childhood that I simply could not have known about. Apart from the healing in those areas this gave me a peace of mind, afterwards understanding what before had been very confusing.

To be honest, at this time I really did not know what was proper behavior in relating with this spiritual realm and it seemed I was being educated not to be so serious about it and to simply be myself.

We clearly have many misconceptions born out of our religious practices.

At this time I felt as though I were working on things to the front of my mind, while a lot of things were being worked out to the back, i.e., in the background. So it seemed to me they were keeping me occupied in the foreground with the show and, in the background, they were doing a lot of real work and perhaps getting the two to coincide so that it would all seem coherent. There was a kind of super intelligence at work.

An African Exorcism: Humility First!

After a number of the preliminary healings the screen opened up again and I saw the African savanna once more. I saw a happy, well-fed and not-too-tall middle-aged man dressed in tribal wear, carrying a staff and waiting under a shady tree in the bush as one does in Africa. He appeared, to my recollection, to be wearing a hat made of furs in a circular fashion and loin skins round his waist. At first I thought he was an Aboriginal man with a didgeridoo (in fact it was some kind of walking stick) and I was quite delighted by this scene and started to joke with him. "It's the didgeridoo man," I said. I was being condescending, even if I had not meant to be. That clearly did not impress him. That was not the way you greet a tribal elder, no matter how friendly and jovial he is. However, he was sitting there welcoming me, coming out from time to time from his shady seat to grab my hand, trying to get me to go with him. I felt very warm towards him. He exuded warmth like a favorite, though switched-on, uncle. The scene before my eyes was like an image reflected from a burning white light – the detail all in bright radiant colors.

I called him the didgeridoo man in part because the presence of the Eboga serpent in my body sounded a little like a low-level didgeridoo playing. It also felt like a serpent moving very slowly in me, whom from time to time became agitated and moved slightly, but sharply like a snake, if something very difficult was being dealt with.

I then realized that I had little chance of advancing until I learned my place and humbly asked for permission to progress forward. I realized that I was being disrespectful, as I had a deep sense of the reverence that was required and deserved by this man. I realized how much we take these things for granted, hiding our condescension through "well-meaning" laughter. The time had come for me to realize my place in all this and joking was not going to be a part of it at this time. I was an initiate about to be initiated and had to come to that state of mind, a mind completely focused on arriving in a new place. I gave him the name Mr. Ebogaman. I kept knocking on that proverbial door, asking to be let in. I actually was not sure how this was going to work, as I imagined that I would lose my mind if suddenly I were in the scene and out of my body. I was scared that I might not be able to return if I found myself wholly and completely in another world. I didn't realize I would always have one foot in the world I came from.

At this time, though, I was confused and wondered how to make that jump onto the screen with Mr. Ebogaman from my position lying on the bed. At the very beginning I actually thought I was going to be dancing in the village – it just opened up. I did not realize that the observer in me would stay in the body and watch me on the screen. This delayed my progress, as I was quite scared at the thought of leaving this world for another. However, I was very keen to progress, knowing how important that was for my healing. After all the years of trying to heal myself I was not now going to miss this opportunity. It had simply been too hard to get this far.

I asked many times for entry. I said, "Please take me, Mr. Ebogaman." In waiting and pleading for entry, I was to have my first very important lesson about the spiritual world. Humility is paramount and I very quickly realized I was in the presence of something that would not tolerate anything less than complete respect. This was just as important for me as it opened the door to my truer self. It was like being a seven-year-old child, truly attentive and respectful to an adult and it seemed I had to rediscover this state of being before I was ready to progress further. Most of us lose the ability to be in this state as it has been abused out of us and we are too angry to return. But once in this state, we feel more real and authentic than we have felt since being a child. It is a truly wonderful state of being. For those who have the initiation experience this is the point of regression or submission to one's true self.

I begged Mr. Ebogaman to excuse my arrogance and to please permit me to go with him. I was genuinely afraid that, if I screwed up, I would lose my chance for healing that I had searched all my life for. This was indeed a good motivation factor. I also asked the soul companions, whoever they were, to be with me. I said, "I want to be humble."

Next I seemed to leave Mr. Ebogaman and began dealing with some other issues. Issues came up, most notably issues with sexuality. I was shown an image of the phallus and it held no interest for me. At one point I wanted to cut off my dick, as it angered me. Here I encountered a classic dilemma. Unsure of one's manhood, one is unsure of one's sexuality. When one's sexuality has not fully ripened or has been interfered with in some way, it is simply impossible to understand it or one's manhood properly. A rite of passage is clearly needed; one that teaches what it is to be a man who can enjoy a full, rewarding sexuality! This the Eboga spirit facilitates as the healing of one's sexuality is a very deep process and, quite frankly, conventional methods are ill equipped to do this for those whose sexuality has been damaged. I then went through some other childhood scenes and saw present-day images involving members of my family.

I returned to Mr. Ebogaman. He continued to beckon to me to join him and I tried my best to be with him. At this point, I was afraid that I might lose my opportunity and was very relieved to see him again. The more I tried to be with him, the deeper my sense of humility and respect grew. Eventually I was brought to a real humility, not a humility where I was ashamed of myself but one where I felt good about myself. Next thing I knew, I saw him grab my hand and then saw myself, white-bodied in simple tribal wear which covered my waist, going along a path through the bush with him: I watched all this from my bed. The path lay about 20 feet to the other side of the dry grass and was sheltered by some bush and low-lying trees. I appeared to be part of a small group returning to the village.

Clearly I had unlocked the door through my inner descent into self. I had succeeded in connecting with him out of a deep desire to do so and a deep respect for him and what I was about to be a part of. My approach from that point on was one of humility, respect and dignity. This set the tone for what was to come, whereby I remained humble and respectful throughout, eager to do my best.

A Spiritual Homecoming

I then headed off towards the village along the bush path with Mr. Ebogaman. As we were approaching I could hear the drums and the sounds the African women make when they are joyful or about to celebrate. Their mouths become like echo chambers as they holler and scream their delight. I also had a moment where I saw myself playing drums in Africa.

We arrived and were greeted very warmly by the women of the village. I seemed to be standing in a shaded area with a thatched roof, open to the outside – like a communal meeting area. It was very informal and I seemed to be surrounded, in no particular way, by a small group of woman as though in a social gathering. They wanted to give me a name and the name they gave me turned out to be a joke, as they all laughed and I was a little confused. They called me Money-Pants, a reference, I imagine, to my obsession at the time of building material security. Later on I was given a proper initiation name.

I then became conscious that I was a white man in a black world and someone said to me I should be black. Suddenly I felt the need to be black and then I saw my white body turn to a golden brown. I thought, *This is great. I am a European in a black world.* I felt I had one up on my European counterparts and then I realized that I needed to drop that attitude, as it was a form of social superiority. I lost the attitude and then felt that I really belonged here: that these were my people, that I was one of them. I felt I had found the original home of my soul which had reincarnated over the centuries to where it was now. Here I felt more awake and more alive than ever. Here my spirit was at home. Here the pretensions and hang-ups of my acquired race no longer mattered. Here I was among my true brothers and sisters.

For a while I met and joked with the village people. One woman jokingly said I should marry a black woman. On reflection it was as if the choice of who I was to marry had already been made. There was a great festive mood in the village and everybody seemed to have been waiting for this day with great joy and anticipation. I had a sense of the joy of returning to Africa where I had first traveled some 14 years earlier as a young teacher.

Journal: Africa 1984 – 1992

The energy of Africa can have a disturbing effect as it opens you up in an almost sensual way. The controlled nature of life in northern Europe seems less real when confronted by its raw earth. Perhaps it was this that prompted me to go to Africa directly after Canada – a strong sense of spiritual freedom. I did not want to return to the confines of my life in Ireland and hoped in some way to open a healing door within myself. Hence I arrived in Botswana.

Botswana is a landlocked, desert country about the size of France and in 1984 was one of the most stable and content countries in Africa. It gained its independence from Britain in 1966 and soon after diamonds were discovered, which meant it became a wealthy country and the people were, by and large, cared for. Had diamonds been discovered earlier, who knows what would have happened? When I was there, the population was 1 million. In 2000 it was 1.6 million.

The school itself was originally a bush school opened after independence. By the time I had arrived, it was beginning to feel the city descend upon it, even though the population of the city at that time was not large. By now, I imagine it has doubled or tripled. The school itself still had a lot of natural bush as part of its grounds, which gave it a special African feel. It had a mixture of classrooms, from the early bush style to the more modern. The first classes had been taught under the trees. When I arrived, AIDS was unheard of. One year later, in 1985, the first case was recorded. Today 330,000 (2001 estimate) carry the HIV virus, i.e., there is a 39% prevalence rate in Botswana. It is the highest in the world. The average life expectancy has dropped from 72 years to 39 years of age.

Botswana is home to the Bushmen of the Kalahari, also known as the San, a spiritual people who have lived there and practiced their earthbound traditions for more than 20,000 years. They are the oldest inhabitants of southern Africa. Sadly and ironically, the present government, that was part of the original movement for independence, seeks to displace the Bushmen from their natural habitats in the Kalahari to make way for further exploration. In so doing, they are effectively practicing the same policies that whites used to gain control of South Africa. It is interesting to note that the time difference of arrival to the Kalahari region of the Bushmen and the general black population is much greater than the time difference of arrival to South Africa between white and black South Africans. There is a chilling similarity.

In an area originally set aside in the Central Kalahari for indigenous Kalahari inhabitants, the Botswana government trucked more than 2,000 San out of this area and put them into dysfunctional camps on the fringes when it wanted to free the area of people to promote diamond mining and high-end tourism. Forced removals began in 1997. In some areas, water deliveries have been discontinued. In October 2001, a Botswana governmental statement in the local press read, "We all aspire to Cadillacs," said Lt. Col. M. Marafhe (now a minister).... (The San) can no longer be allowed to commune with the flora and fauna...."

Botswana is famed for the Okavango Delta. The River Okavango, which rises in the highlands of Angola, never reaches the sea. Instead, its mighty waters flow into the sands of the Kalahari. This gives rise to a 6,000-square-mile network of channels, lagoons and islands drenched in a blue-green wilderness of fresh water, emerald reed beds and towering trees. It is an oasis in the desert for the larger animals of the Kalahari. Unlike the rest of the desert population, there is a large variety and abundance of wildlife, of which fish, crocodiles and hippopotamuses are but a few. In the same area lies the Chobe Game Park, where herds of wild elephant roam freely. Not a world away on the borders of Zimbabwe, Zambia and Botswana, lie the great Victoria Falls, known locally among Zimbabweans as "Musi-oa-Tunya," *The Smoke that Thunders.* Five separate falls plunge more than 100 meters into a sheer-sided chasm to the gorge below. They hail from the Zambezi River that meanders for more than 2,700 km. of African countryside. To stand at the top of the falls among the tropical trees and to be embedded in a soft mist of warm air is an experience you will never forget.

Traditionally the people of Botswana relied on farming and not much else. Vegetables were not well thought of. Meat was the staple diet. When I arrived in 1984, it was the time of Apartheid, Nelson Mandela and Robert Mugabe. Mugabe was considered the hope of Southern Africa. If ever an example of the devastating consequences of not facing one's shadow was needed, Mugabe, in time, offered it. On the other hand, as if the light was complementing the dark, Mandela was a shining example of the spirit of man and what it could achieve under adversity.

I was 23 years of age then and knew very little about A-level chemistry, which was equivalent to the first year in university. In my first year there I worked day and night to prepare my material, afraid I might be caught out.

I had visualized a private, well-run boarding school and this image was one I felt I could live with for a time until I felt better about myself. In a way, I was seeking a return to the security of the seminary. I also had a notion I might find my soul in Africa, where I would be free from all the stresses and strains of modern life, protected from a harsh world. The irony is that, in going to Canada and later to Africa, I was more and more cutting myself off from the world I had longed to reconcile with. However, I felt I simply had to get away from it all, as I could not come to terms with it. I wanted to empty my mind and excise the cancer left behind. Luckily for me the headmaster, David Matthews, was a good man and in many ways was like a father to me, somehow perhaps understanding my pain even if I myself did not realize it at the time.

The very first class I taught was considered to be the worst class in the school, 4C Chemistry, in the final term before their public exams. I was nervous. My plan was simple. I prepared a large number of chemical equation questions whereby one balances the equation based on the mass and the molecular weight of the compounds. I reasoned that I would be able to capture their interest, as these equations led to a lot of marks on the exam and this class had been written off as failures. In the first five minutes of the class I thought I was witnessing a street riot. I looked straight down the class and roared at the top of my voice to shut up or get out of the class immediately. Silence followed. I knew I had my one chance and immediately began writing the rules for solving equations on the board, followed by the issuing of examples and questions to answer. I singled out children at random, particularly anyone who had opened their mouth. I bombarded them with questions and I made them repeat my reasoning. I blinded them before they could figure out what I was up to. There was one black boy, as big as a tree trunk and quite intimidating, even though he was only 15. Within half an hour I had rows of children quietly coming up to my desk with their answers for me to check, including the big boy as mute as a mouse, looking into his work, wondering if he at last had managed to get something right in this subject. I never had another problem in that class and most passed, when they had been earmarked for failure. The trick was to play the exam game and focus on the questions that required the least memory work. I made many friends among the students and one boy later came up to me and thanked me personally. The same boy is now the chief of one of the main tribes in Botswana. It was an interesting school with more than 38 nationalities, mostly from other African states, Europe and North America.

Soon after I arrived my fiancée came out for a visit. Things did not work out and she refused to return. In my youthful logic, I reasoned that I could not marry someone who was unwilling to return to discuss matters when I had a job to take care of. So that was the end of that. I refused to go back to Canada. In a gesture of bravado I threw the silver ring, which signified our union, into the bush at the back of the house. On repenting I looked for it but never saw it again, lost somewhere between the snake holes and the red earth. One consequence of my intended marriage meant I benefited from having my own living quarters; a small bungalow nestled in the bush. Here for a time, I experienced peace and relaxation, having at my disposal a small supply of marijuana and a collection of Reggae tapes. I managed to have this bungalow on the expectation that my wife-to-be would be joining me. I also inherited a somewhat fierce, but loyal and loving dog called Arthur.

On the other side of the school fence, just beyond the untouched African bush which surrounded the school and formed part of my garden, a small shanty town existed called SHAH (Self Help Housing), where every night the sounds of ordinary African people would rise in the air, filling it with the sounds and beats of the African heart. For two years I enjoyed their companionship. Under cover of darkness I would, from time to time, visit them to obtain a supply of marijuana wrapped in newspaper for about 25 cents. At this time, I also developed a love of fusion music as typified by such artists as Herb Alpert and Bob James. One particular album stood out at the time, *Brothers in Arms* by Dire Straits. I heard this while spending a blissful weekend deep in the outback with some South African friends turned refugees. It seemed Africa had soul and it certainly had none of the inhibitions of the body that seemed to cast a plague of leprosy over my homeland. Here sexuality was celebrated and enjoyed as one of life's greatest gifts, God's finest prize. What a relief that was!

One of the more interesting and touching customs I adopted from my time in Botswana is to say sorry when someone hurts himself or herself. In the beginning, not understanding the custom, I used to say, "Don't worry, it is not your fault."

Once I invited some fellow teachers to my home for evening drinks, which coincided with the night of a huge electrical storm. We turned out the lights, opened the glass doors which merged the veranda with the living room and watched in our armchairs as the storm gathered in strength and anger. Never had I seen anything like it. Across the sky, the fury of the storm gathered pace, everywhere a cluster of electrical strikes appeared, reaching a sustained climax totally obliterating the sky. This was Africa and this was the sun-baked monsoon season when the atmosphere could swiftly change, turning the ground from a dry, red earth to a flood-filled mud bath. The smell of the rain-drenched earth, a tonic for the body.

There were times when I socialized in the community. Occasionally I went to a jazz club called the Blue Note. Here I would see Hugh Masakela, the Lion of Africa, play jazz and play it well, wiping his forehead from time to time with the handkerchief he kept in his pocket. I did not know the man, but he was renowned. He ended up in Botswana like so many South Africans before him, as a refugee. He once came to my house for a party I hosted for a group of musicians. It was an open invitation. I was taken aback when he came up to me surrounded by two minders, looked me in the eye, (he was shorter than me) and said thanks. I was taken aback as I took him to be a man who had been around and I suppose I didn't expect such consideration. I still remember that moment vividly to this day.

One day however, this cycle of life was violently interrupted when during the night a contingent of South African troops crossed the border and sought out known refugees living in the area, which was the capital and close to the border. They entered their homes and shot them. They were acting on intelligence gathered through informers and also, no doubt, with the collusion of some members of the Botswana government. Overnight South African refugees were not very welcome. It was not long after that Apartheid fell. In the meantime, however, pressure was placed on the Botswana government to make life difficult for refugees whom South Africa saw as a potential threat, as South Africa was feeling very threatened at that time.

The first I knew of the incursion was when my dog Arthur jumped up on the bed in a whimper. We both sat still listening to the sound of automatic gunfire. Later that day I went with my friend Tembe, a fellow teacher my own age, to survey some of the damage in the SHAH across the road. It was unmerciful, walls splattered in blood and the indents of bullets. It was not the last raid, either. In fact, for a time Tembe, along with his new wife and baby, stayed at night with me in my bungalow for fear the South African forces might put him on their list of targets. He himself was a South African refugee, but mostly by choice it seemed. So I did not feel in any great danger. He came from a well-placed family in the Transkei and for whatever reason had decided to go into exile. One didn't really need much of a reason in those days.

Earlier I myself had had a closer look at life in South Africa when I went with some friends to visit people they knew who ran a club in Soweto (South West Townships). On entering Soweto we had to hide under the seats of the car in order not to be noticed by the security forces or anyone who might inform on us. A very odd thing I saw there was when I paid a visit to the neighboring colored township nicknamed El Dorado, I believe. Everyone was the same off-white color! I thought I had undergone some kind of strange 3-D dimensional shift where I was in some kind of parallel universe. It was the weirdest experience I have ever had. This was the sickness of Apartheid where it conveniently locked people it did not want to know into ghettos and I felt it in my gut.

One friendly and likeable acquaintance I made in Soweto, a Portuguese Mozambican who gave me a lift back to Botswana, was later shot dead during a holdup at the nightclub I had stayed at during my visit. He was a partner in the club. Arthur also met an untimely end while guarding the house of his new owners in Swaziland. He was a fierce dog and would not let the intruders into the house. They killed him with a knife. This left a sad mark on me, as I had left him one day without him really knowing what was happening. My last memory was of Arthur looking up at me, wondering what was going on. He, who had been so brave and faithful to me, didn't know he would never see me again. How sad life can be for man's best friend and how sad it is to have to sometimes leave him behind.

During my time in Botswana I took a trip home stopping over in Israel in 1984-85, where I visited my sister who was teaching in a Palestinian university in the West Bank town of Bethlehem. Israel was a country I loved, as the land seemed to have a gentle, spiritual air, a beautiful sense of wholeness. Before I arrived Zionism and Judaism were somehow interlocked in my mind and not separate entities as, in truth, they are. Liyanda and I had discussed many things, including the manipulation of facts by governments intent on rewriting history and the suffering of the people of South Africa and Palestine. I had great respect for the writings of Noam Chomsky, a renowned intellectual who analyzed the workings of the Israeli state and highlighted its criminal activities against the Palestinian people, but I had to see it for myself. (In fact, I once sat in on a small group at Queens University listening to Noam Chomsky talk on the subject.) I brought with me a list of facts I had gathered regarding Palestinian land seizures and descriptions of what used to exist on these lands. But the truth was, when push came to shove, I could not bring myself to believe that governments would lie blatantly, in particular the Israeli government. Perhaps my upbringing of patriotism for the Irish State had somehow transferred itself to sympathy for the Jewish State?

I went to the Zionist information center in Jerusalem and, to my amazement, discovered the history of Israel as told by the Zionist information center had been rewritten to conveniently overlook the displacements of the Palestinian people. Excited with my discovery I made notes to take with me. When I returned, I discovered all my notes were missing from my luggage. Had I forgotten them? Or had they been seized during a customary search of luggage at Tel Aviv airport? This I would never know, but one thing was for sure – the days of my political naïveté were over.

Speaking with a young Muslim Palestinian man called Mahmoud, a friend of my sister's, I was made aware of the depth of depression among the men. They arose every morning to make the long journey to work in Israel doing menial tasks, earning only a small amount and being subject to the rules and regulations of the Israeli State. In the Gaza Strip where I stayed at night I was shocked to see open sewers and rubbish strewn everywhere. If ever I needed to see a mirror of the relentlessness of what I myself was enduring in my own life, I found it here in the ordinary lives of Palestinian people. However, in Mahmoud's house where I stayed, I was touched by the gentleness of the people, their hospitality and the care and attention they gave to their homes. We all slept on the floor and, when it came to eating, we crossed our feet and ate with our hands from the bowls placed in the center. The whole extended family ate together from the same bowls. The food was delicious. Just like in Southern Africa, I was also struck by the care young Palestinian men took in their appearance.

At this time I reached a crisis point. I was turning 25 and felt with an incredible force that I was a loser. I felt finished and over the hill.

I had failed to turn in the direction I had wanted to go, even though I had achieved in worldly terms: I had an M.Sc. and had been made head of the chemistry department. My class results were impressive. I was on a merry-go-round of existence, spending all my efforts keeping body and soul together, fighting the demons that seemed to haunt me and thwart my every effort for real change. In desperation I turned to the services of a black American educational psychologist who suggested to me to try LSD to gain a better perspective on my life.

As luck would have it, an acquaintance of mine had a friend visiting from Holland who actually carried LSD with him, aptly named Superman, with a logo of Superman on the front. It was quite bizarre, really. The psychologist said my life was just beginning, although to me, I felt I had missed the best part and was depressed by my inability to break through the barriers that seemed to wall me in from my true and abundant self. I was not living my own life.

I had an LSD session with the psychologist and later had a second session with an acquaintance using a higher dose. This was held in the Kalahari Desert. The second session was the more profound, giving me a vision of the world I had not yet realized. Perhaps the first had failed in order to guard me from having my mind manipulated by an errant viewpoint. In the first I was amused by the fact that my psychologist looked like a leprechaun. In the second everything seemed real and alive. The world appeared a very different place. I was surrounded by great beauty and life, although I was a little paranoid at the dog present in case it took on a strange form based on stories I had heard. In fact, nothing like that happened. It was a perfectly calm experience. While driving back in the car, I watched as the exterior passed by like the brush strokes of a Van Gogh masterpiece. I resolved to find this view of life for myself. If I needed a vision to carry me forward, I had found it here. Soon after I became a vegetarian but had to give up due to the natural lack of vegetables on the dinner table. However, for the next 15 years, I refused to eat red meat. I never took LSD again.

One of the sad consequences of my time with the counselor was the advice I received. He suggested that one way to put the past behind me was to destroy the possessions I had that reminded me of the past and to wipe the slate clean. This I did, but it didn't change anything. To my regret I burned letters, photos of my childhood and journals of my writings and poems, among other things, in one big bonfire. It was a desperate attempt to overcome the pain and insecurities that still plagued me. Did it help in any way? Who knows? Probably not. I continued to be tormented. My counselor also suggested the way we deal with the past is to compartmentalize it and forget it, i.e., repress it. This view shocked me and I realized the counselor was not as enlightened as I first had thought. It was completely foreign to my way of thinking.

However, the psychologist did say one thing that stuck: I was brainwashed! I wasn't sure what to make of that and I wondered if I could figure out the actual brainwash itself. This thought probably reinforced my decision to abandon all belief in the search for self-awareness and personal freedom. It's an odd thing to have someone tell you are brainwashed and to wonder what form it takes. The mind that is thinking is the brainwashed mind. How can "it" work "it" out? Once two young teachers interrogated me as to why I cut myself off and I sat for over an hour answering their questions, thinking that maybe I would learn from it. All I learned was the selfishness and arrogance of others.

While teaching at the school, I had progressively cut myself off from the staff, seeing their ways as ultimately limiting as they turned in on themselves, being as they were cut off from their natural habitat, left with only themselves to project their problems onto. It shocked me how some felt very personally about certain students whereas I felt they were the ones who needed help. I felt sorry for the students. Once more, like many times before, I had succeeded in an area I did not seek, being promoted to head of my department after the first year. And once more I found myself alone, but it was a loneliness filled with the spirit of Africa and that made it easier.

I decided to leave Africa, forced into action by a burning desire, once again, to make my way in singing and possibly dance. It seemed when times hit their worst I would turn to the one light I had left in my life: my bliss! I concluded I was missing the satisfaction and reward of doing something I truly loved and, as long as I avoided these, I was contributing to my own pain and cutting myself off from a well of goodness that could replenish and nurture me. During my time in Africa my home country seemed like a little piece of land somewhere in the northern hemisphere. I had disconnected from it and did not want to return there for fear I would sink back down into my problems again. Meanwhile my recurring inner desire would not leave me alone and I felt compelled to follow it. I knew I was someone with lots of natural ability but felt I was living my life in chains. Perhaps if I had an average amount of ability and could subject myself to other people's ways, I could have found contentment. But I could not. Perhaps if I had not been gifted with reasonable intelligence, I would have had no other choice and ended up like so many who lived out their lives in a mental prison, sometimes committing suicide to find peace. I don't think we properly understand suicide. I don't believe anybody wants to commit suicide as though out of extreme self-hate. I believe when the human animal has reached a point where it is unable to bear the pain, a suicide button is switched and suicide is viewed like taking a pill, just another way to stop the pain, "a task to do." We are all capable of suicide.

In the end however, it is a suicide that is required, but not a suicide of the body. Instead what is needed is a suicide of the ego, which, some twelve years later, I would find. In the same way that desperation can lead to suicide, it can also lead to undergoing a process that nobody in their right mind would choose. Perhaps that was a reflection of how desperate I was to become as it is only in this state of desperation that we can see past the terror of Eboga to the hidden beauty beneath, only revealed once the demons which imprison us are confronted and released. They would not find a home within us unless we were too afraid to ask them to leave. It is not Eboga that we should be afraid of, it is the demons that it wrenches from our being; beings that cling to our soul, where like parasites they suck us dry until eventually life becomes nothing but a burden. Eboga poses no fear. It is what it exposes that frightens us and equally, once these fears are exposed and the demons destroyed, Eboga shows us a world pregnant with beauty.

I wanted to be free. Leaving Africa was, in my opinion, the only way to maintain whatever freedom I had left. Such was the strength of the force within me. I decided I had to leave the school and return to find my way. I had saved $1,000 along with a free return ticket and, after working another term, I left and was on my way to the U.S.A. I had had many girlfriends while in Botswana and had become reasonably comfortable, but still was always fearful around strange men or men I was not sure of. At this point I had no real clue what was going to happen to me. I was afraid to share my desire for a life of song and dance with anyone, for fear of being ridiculed.

One of my lasting memories of Botswana was a camping trip I took to the Chobe Game Park with my girlfriend Godisang. We had camped on the edge of the perimeter near the campfire. During the night I heard a lion roar as clearly as if it were outside my tent. It scared the hell out of me. You'd think it wouldn't bother you because supposedly you are safe, being part of the circle of encampments around the fire, presumably with guards on duty. But when you hear the clear, crisp sound of a lion roar into the clear, open African night sky, it is all too real for what you think.

It was while in Botswana I received a piece of advice I never forgot. I asked the lady who managed the kitchen, Ma Ferie from Zimbabwe, when would I know I had met the right person to marry? She replied, "Don't get married if there is any doubt in your heart." With the benefit of hindsight she could just have easily said, "Wait until your soul tells you."

Before leaving for the U.S., I fantasized about riding the trains with the hobos crossing the plains of America. I reckoned that if I could live a simple life, free of all worldly concerns, I might break through my torments – little did I understand my problems.

After an unsuccessful attempt to settle in the US, which included moving between 13 different homes between Boston and Baltimore in a 3 month period; followed by a trip to Spain, where I had to bluff my way across the border as I was penniless; I ended up in Peckham, a run down suburb of South London.

I learned one very valuable lesson during my time in Peckham. Given that I had little more than those who surrounded me, I began to understand how alienated they felt from society and how the laws of society meant little or nothing to them. Laws are there to create a level playing field and to safeguard individual property rights. However, when you have no property and are completely outside the system, these laws serve no personal purpose and thus mean very little. These people had no personal investment in society and thus had no reason to support it. That was quite an illuminating insight for me. Personally, in this environment, I felt little interest in the law and saw it as belonging to a different world. Those who broke the law were simply responding to their environment and were no more criminal than most ordinary folk who lived out their daily life untroubled by it. One size does not fit all.

During an interview for a job with EDS, as a trainee Systems Engineer in Information Technology, I told the lady interviewer that I had made the choice for good in my life instead of bad. Everyone at some time or other has to make this choice and I had made it. Impressed, she left the office and returned a short time later to inform me I had the job. I had good reason for saying this. Many times in my life I had to unquestioningly choose the positive and the good. There was clearly no relief to be found by going in the other direction. For one thing it would only be a matter of time before someone bigger and meaner knocked me down and I would simply suffer more pain and humiliation. That I could not cope with. Basically, the other way led nowhere. I had no choice in the midst of my deepest pain except to choose the right road, even if it meant further humiliation.

I needed this job. I simply could not survive in the world pursuing my interests. I was much too lonely and vulnerable. At least with a job I had the security of an institution until I felt strong enough to try again. In an institution, no one can hit you. Ironically, people saw my gregarious nature and wondered why I would make such a choice to be there, not realizing that outside I was intimidated to be myself.

While in London I had a strange experience. One night I woke and felt as though two strong hands were holding onto my hands, lifting me up out of myself. I panicked and it stopped. Perhaps there were forces unknown to me always ready to give me the strength to carry on and not drown within myself.

Another time I was clearing out the flower beds at my home, raking my hands through the soil and was transported to a world of calm, inner collection. Everything seemed very real, very independent and yet all connected. When my friends (who had visitors) called me into the house I just waved and indicated I would come shortly. When I did appear, they were miffed as they felt I had been ignoring them. Nothing could have been further from my mind, even if it was the truth.

It was while in London that I began reading books on primal therapy as developed by Arthur Janov. I was very impressed by its reasoning. In my mind there was very little to fault. Every event was hardwired into the mind and carried with it a charge. By accessing the event the charge could be released and the mind restored to normal function. It seemed to me that this was a more advanced way of thinking than Freud. To achieve this, you usually worked with a therapist who guided you into your past in order to access the emotions surrounding the events. This led to much crying, weeping and anger. But the anger never seemed real to me. Perhaps I was afraid to access it. After working one-to-one for an initial period, the client would then work in group. It was in one of these groups I finally did manage to touch my anger after listening to what another client had done. I had been quietly and calmly listening when, from nowhere, my anger suddenly hit me. I did not even know why. Ironically, the therapist ended the session just as I was entering what was possibly my first and perhaps last real connection with my buried anger from the past. This lack of insight on the part of the therapist disillusioned me. It seemed the therapist did not really know what he was dealing with. Either that or, as is often the case, he was afraid of his own emotions and thus unable to explore others. Or worse still: he just wanted to go home.

There were other odd aspects to this therapy. If anyone should have been cured, I reckon it was I. I went most nights of the week, as well as having individual weekly and twice-weekly sessions, along with working privately in pairs in what is called "buddying." I had left my more lucrative life in London to be in Brighton, where

I stayed for a number of years vigorously pursuing a cure to my mental health. All the time, I refused to be sucked into the property market or any other possible business venture. I did not want to succeed financially, as I was afraid of becoming impotent, thus losing the hunger of the search. I preferred to be on the ground with the other seekers. I invested my time and money in therapy, giving up the opportunity to earn lucrative deals in the IT world. My credo was simple. The job was a means to an end. If I were ever to acquire wealth, it would be as a result of doing something I loved, hopefully as a singer. In that sense you could say I flitted my money away on therapy and travel. I reasoned I would be happier for it and, in the end, do quite well anyway. Had I lived my life on a financial basis I would have soon led a materially comfortable life, but I refused to be defeated and that felt like an option for defeat leading to a life in a gilded cage. In this state nobody would take my ambitions seriously, least of all myself.

I did have one interesting experience around this time though. While making love I could feel an electric charge pass through my spine as if sparks were going off. You could say I learned one thing from my huge efforts to make this therapy work: you can have all the therapy in the world, but if the time is not right, the issues will not emerge. In that sense, maybe I got all I was meant to get at that time? Perhaps I just didn't realize I had reached my limit for now. Patience is definitely a virtue. However, in another sense it was like an elaborate sales trick where you keep convincing yourself that you can get there with just a little more effort. But you never quite do. Fortunately, the universe had its own plans for my healing and ironically it was to be the energy of Africa, which I left in search of my soul, that eventually would give me the healing I craved.

While living in Brighton I saved what I could and using my credit cards, I planned my first major trip hoping it would somehow free me. While sitting in a taxi on my way to the train station, I listened to the news announcing war had been declared on Iraq. It was 1991. I was 30. Arriving in Heathrow, the army was out in force and there were few travelers. In the next three to four months I traveled from London to Botswana, where I visited my old school. I hitchhiked from there up through Botswana, into Zimbabwe and on into the beautiful Eastern Highlands. Staying there was blissful, as the Highlands were green and beautiful with mountain landscapes visible from my bedroom window. From there I hitched a lift to Harare.

One of the interesting parts of my visit was a trip I made to the Great Zimbabwe ruins that are a work of engineering triumph. The word "Zimbabwe" is a local word that means "stone dwelling." The old white government attempted to deny the site's African genesis as they wanted to maintain that the land was empty of people and culture before they came. Hence the reason why, after becoming independent, Zimbabwe was chosen as the new name for what was formerly known as Rhodesia. The site dates from around 1200 AD and the ruins are the remains of an extensive town.

The Karanga people who lived here ruled an inland empire from around 1000 AD until 1600 AD. They were traders who smelted gold and traded on the Indian Ocean for glass beads and porcelain from China. The city of Great Zimbabwe, which at one time covered more than 1,000 square miles, developed into the center of an empire known as the Munhumutapa Empire (also called Monomotapa Empire) covering the modern states of Zimbabwe and Mozambique. Ming Dynasty (1384-1644) pottery has been found at the site. It is an Iron Age site with stone walls up to 20 feet thick and 36 feet high, built of granite blocks without the use of mortar. The Great Enclosure is the largest single ancient structure south of the Sahara.

I then flew to Western Australia, landing in Perth, a different world altogether. It felt like I had escaped a war zone and was on board with the refugees. Once airborne the shift to the luxury of a first world existence was quite remarkable. As we approached Australia, I looked down and could see little lines of white wave breaks where the seawater encountered low-lying islands, submerged under the sea. It was a beautiful sight amidst the deep blue sea and the clear-blue sky.

After 6 weeks of travelling and hitchhiking around Australia, I went to Hawaii via New Zealand. While on the north island of Hawaii, I hitched a lift with a man returning from a day out surfing. I was very impressed with his almost spiritual air when he talked about his surfing. I decided then I wanted to try it at some point, as it looked like one way to find the peace of mind I craved. I witnessed one surfer on the North Shore making huge waves. In fact they became so threatening that everyone came in off the water. Apparently, the waves make their way up from New Zealand and they alternate from good to massive – the largest I had ever seen. He showed me a photo of one wave he had surfed, a fifty-footer! These guys, it seems, are so addicted to their sport they almost court death itself. It is phenomenally addictive for some as well as being totally spiritual.

After a short tour of the US I arrived back in the UK. I was offered a position in Frankfurt, Germany. The money was good enough to warrant coming home to Brighton to continue with the therapy on weekends. It seemed a reasonable option to take. I wanted to maintain a sense of home, pay my bills and continue with my healing. Unfortunately, I did not fit in with my Brighton housemates, who could not quite figure me out. Who in their right mind pays rent for a second home and flies there on weekends? It was also around this time I developed a neurotic interest in vitamin supplements, believing that they would compensate for the lack of red meat in my diet and further believing that they would offset the stresses and strains of the life I was living. It was also around this time I had a strange experience on a trip to visit my brother in Madrid. While standing and watching a large hall full of dancers surrounded by TV screens showing soft porn in a plush Madrid nightclub, I suddenly felt connected to everyone there. It was a wonderful and beautiful experience. I felt whole and connected to everyone around me. *The hall filled with music and flowery perfume and their hearts overflowed with a feeling of love and unity for each other and all of Creation.* What brought this on I do not know. Indeed, I found it odd that it should happen in such a way, tied as it was to the sexual energy in the place. It was an experience I hoped I would one day experience again. *It is said that the first taste from the Grail is free and that it causes the heart to leap with joy and the mind to be filled with untold possibilities. It gives us a taste of what could be and creates a hunger that reveals our illusion of complacent satisfaction. It is part of the initiation. The second taste is another matter and comes with a price. For this we must enter into an unknown world in search of a dream of wholeness that we have learned to live without.*

I had begun in earnest my search for life and love in the only way I knew how. I explored the world. Yet the sensual energy of Africa was stored in me and I would later rediscover it – within my soul. Perhaps my travels did have an important role to play. As far as love was concerned, I would make many mistakes until the time came that I realized that true love is ordained, when the time is right. I was unable to properly understand love as I was blinded by my obsession to gratify my pain through immature sexuality and was either clueless or disinterested in the beautiful camaraderie that exists between two lovers that know they will ultimately express their deeper feelings in the sensual embrace and the sensuous movement that is the mark of true love making – like a serpent that winds its way around the body of another. I was cut off from the real benefits of relationship that springs from the sexual energy that exists between two people.

Perhaps that is why, on making the Eboga journey inwards, 7 years later, I was to encounter many potential and eager mates, albeit on a spiritual plane, as I was on the verge of discovering a part of myself that had not yet matured.

The Initiation Begins: Lucifer

I had begun the process of clearing out the debris of my past life, in order to once more taste from the Grail. And once more I was back in Africa, the cradle of humankind – a place whose energy I had long suspected could heal me. An energy that beats with the heartbeat of life. A raw energy, as raw as the red earth from which it comes.

So while enjoying the attention of the village women and the festive atmosphere of the village, I suddenly found myself in a large corral alone. It was at the lower end of the village and made with large wooden stakes stuck into the ground in a circular fashion. I imagine it could be used for keeping herds of cattle. There was one wooden door, the exit to a lane way, which opened to a nearby hut and to a lane leading up to the top of the village. I seemed to be the last one waiting. I felt I was like the runt of the litter. I didn't fit in. In fact, later I recall feeling what made me stand out was my attitude. *I am the one who breaks all the rules in order to show that the rules in themselves are not important.* It is the underlying reverence that counts and *that,* deep down, I have. What is true and real comes spontaneously from the heart and not the calculating mind.

This is when the process of initiation began officially. Apparently, all the other young men of the village had begun or completed their initiation process and I was the last one. I knocked on the door of the corral many times and eventually I found myself saying, "I demand acceptance into the tribe." I said this very spontaneously with a voice that I felt could only have come from Africa. It was very deep, from another part of my voice box. It was not something I had pre-planned. For a while they seemed to ignore me and then, suddenly, the door on the corral opened. Mr. Ebogaman was there to meet me. He took me to see the village chief. I stood before him on a platform located in the village communal area and asked for and was given my initiation name. He gave me the name Lucifer. I was a little surprised by this choice. In Roman astronomy Lucifer was the name given to the morning star (the star we now know by another Roman name, Venus). The morning star appears in the heavens just before dawn, heralding the rising sun. The name derives from the Latin term *lucem ferre,* bringer or bearer of light.

From there I went with Mr. Ebogaman to begin the initiation. The village itself appeared to consist of narrow streets with well-constructed tree-stake type houses, not necessarily circular, perhaps rectangular.

We went to the top of the village to a small building, which Mr. Ebogaman appeared to make his waiting point with some other elders from the village. He then sent me on my first task. He pointed to a stone on the ground. I made my way towards it. As I knelt down and began to read the inscription the stone melted away and a scene opened, depicting a situation from my past life to be faced and worked through. Once this was done I would once again be pointed to another stone, which I would once more read and watch as it faded away.

It seemed as I read each task that I knew at a deep level what it was concerning. I had a burning curiosity to register the text and tried hard to read it aloud to myself. But try as hard as I could it seemed that the attempt drew me further into my deepest self where all conscious thought disappeared, to be left with a deep emotional connection to some long forgotten part of myself. It was as if my conscious self could not know what I was reading as it might in some way try to bolt out of the situation. The deeper I sank the less able I was to maintain any conscious connection to what I was reading and my thoughts, like the stone, simply melted away.

I have very few detailed memories of these tasks except the form that they took. As the stone would give way to the scene it seemed I was looking at a grainy black and white film that in some way was alive and, with my focus on the scene, inside me would erupt a world of emotion. In one scene I saw my face covered with ice cream. In another I watched as my siblings played in the yard while in another I could see myself beside the beach. Each task and each scene seemed to draw me into an interior world I had long since shut down. Each scene was a reliving of a moment of past truth, a catalyst to focus on the stored illness represented by the scene. The content had very little to do with what one might understand a task to be in the normal sense of the word. You could say that each task was a challenge to go back and relive a set of thoughts and emotions long since buried. This process filled me with fear and foreboding, causing me at times to go into convulsions of pure white, sweat-filled, fear. At other times I would feel a deep sense of pain and loss. I would feel completely emotionally sick as though my emotional system was completely toxic. Often in agony I would attempt to throw up my guts. The clear light of Eboga illuminated the stored darkness within my soul and made it impossible for me to run away from my inner truth. Once a task was completed it was a relief to return to the security of the structure of the initiation under the watchful eyes of Mr. Ebogaman.

Thus as each task finished I found myself back in the village in a slight panic, looking frantically for Mr. Ebogaman. My thoughts were I needed to find Mr. Ebogaman quickly to begin the next task. I guess I was not sure how long this healing process would continue and I was keen to deal with everything I could possibly deal with. I was afraid he might abandon me and I would shout out, "Mr. Ebogaman, please give me my next task!" Then he would appear smiling and delighted to help me. This reassured me. I would go up to him and he would again point somewhere. I would run down an earthen path, seemingly marked out by small stones on either side and stoop down to read another inscription on a little headstone to see what the next task was. While I was doing this, as before, the headstone would melt away and a new scene would open up. I would find myself transported back in time looking at a TV screen of myself as a small boy in our back yard or at a scene of myself among my family or indeed any other situation of relevance. The scene would unfold and, as the truth of the scene dawned on me, my emotions would respond accordingly. It surprised me that whenever I addressed Mr. Ebogaman I found myself speaking with the voice of a black African. It was deep in my intonation as well. I was quite amazed by that. My heartbeat would deepen and I had to breathe much deeper to keep with its depth and rhythm.

In one of my visuals I saw sweets and vitamin pill bottles dropping before my eyes, which was a message for me to avoid them: I didn't need them. They were a kind of addiction I imagine. More importantly, they were probably bad for me. I certainly knew I had an unhealthy addiction to sweets, especially growing up, but the question of vitamin pills came as a surprise to me, as I had become obsessed with taking them for good health. I thought they served that purpose! Now I am glad I avoid them, as they now seem like a kind of poison to me.

I worked very hard to complete the steps as quickly as I could, each step being something from my past life that I feared or had hurt around and which needed healing and understanding. It was as if my life had been a path towards my initiation – clearly I had not been alone during those years. Each time I saw an image I had to work out what was going on, gaining insight into a part of my past. I also saw things which I could never have known and which have gone on to help me complete my healing in my own life after these sessions. Things which have helped me understand my personal family history in a way I could "never" have known. This has helped to free me from my past and to heal my broken relationships – through compassion.

It was all very clever and well-organized, not to mention humorous. It was as if the spirits were there to enjoy themselves as much as anything else, like kids on the one hand and completely focused adults on the other. Everything was choreographed and I thought, *This is so bloody professional and extremely clever!* There was an intelligence working, a super-deliberate intelligence! It was worked out in the most professional manner you can imagine and nobody slipped up. Nobody made a mistake. It was so intelligent that I knew that it came from a higher power. Not even my own subconscious could move with such fluidity and clarity, revealing only what is good for me, or indeed things it has no knowledge of! If it did come from my subconscious, this means my subconscious is far more clever and organized than my conscious will ever be. It was this realization that led me to accept the reality of the entities I was dealing with and to want to understand them better.

I then went through a period of feeling like a wanker (a fool) and I remembered how I had been stupid with a friend of mine when I was growing up. I vowed to write and apologize to him for my stupidity as a child. During all of this I asked for the courage to be a man and to be proud of being a man. I also asked to give my ego a holiday. I said, "Clear out, ego!" I really had no idea at the time what

I was saying in saying this. I just wanted to do what I could to help myself be successful. If I had realized what I was saying, I would have realized I was wasting my time saying it!

There was a period where I felt that I had been made a clown of and was an outsider at school. I also began to realize I did everything impulsively because I was afraid. While I was rattling on about all these negative feelings, I was told to shut up by a spirit. I said, "Mr. Ebogaman, please give me back my self-respect," which surprised me. I then told Karl I didn't want to talk, as I knew I was talking too much and anyway I had been asked to shut up. What "I" didn't understand at this time was where "I" came in to the healing process and where "I" should stay out. "I" had been so used to involving itself in my healing that it felt it had a role to play.

Needless to say, the different scenes which took place had a lot of emotional discomfort. My emotions were mixed. In fact, shivering with fear was one of the nicer, simpler emotions which brought with it relief. I felt like my life was being played out like a cartoon and I was really quite a helpless character. I felt a sense of deadness where we sit and wait out our lives, growing older, somehow disconnected from the real juices of life, our soul. I knew I did not want to go down that road and had to change my life to get it back on track. I had fooled myself into believing that somehow believing I knew better, I could someday get my life back on track. But the truth was it was off track and there was very little I could do in my power to get it back on – the road to hell is paved with good intentions! I needed the help of the strong Eboga energy to reach down inside and pull me back up before I died under the weight of my own self-imposed shutdown. I felt this was the situation for a lot of people who clung to their ego and I wondered how lonely and depressing that was. These were the hardest feelings for me to face and I did not like them one bit. They were a true look at myself, a true self-effacement. They were moments when I saw the confines of my ego and the darkness it imposed.

I continued to spend many hours in the throes of these strong emotions. My body alternated from being in complete panic, cold as ice with fear, to being in a cold sweat, shaking uncontrollably and throwing up. Throwing up seemed to make me acutely aware of my physically sick state as though in those moments I was brought closer to my normal self. In between there were brief moments of relaxation where I would get a respite to catch my breath and receive a little gift from my spirit helpers (mostly girls) such as flowers or some other delightful thing. During these moments I would gently shake, as though suffering from a kind of fever and overcome by all that was happening to me. My soul companions always remained in the background, acting as observers, as though detached from the main event facilitated by the Eboga spirit.

It was as if my body was undergoing some kind of African exorcism, as I shook throughout, overcome with fear for what was happening to me. It was something I did not understand and could only observe. At one point in a fit of shaking with cold fear, as the struggle within me between opposing forces reached its climax, my body gave one last heave and white emissions appeared rising up from my solar plexus. A moment later I simply relaxed – an interval to catch my breath! These experiences had a very humbling effect. There were also other moments where I saw smoke emissions from my body. They usually signaled the end of the issue I was dealing with and would be followed by a rainfall of gentle luminescent bubbles. Each time I completed a scene and succeeded in the task, including the learning, two or three girls would come out on the stage and flirt with me like dancing girls doing a little number in a cabaret of congratulations. I always commented to them how pretty they were and they genuinely seemed to enjoy my attention. I genuinely felt I was dealing with real souls expressing their own playfulness. How wonderful it was to be so cared for!

During the session Karl checked my blood pressure and pulse. I was not sure if my heart was up to this deep movement of blood it seemed to be undergoing. It felt as though a large quantity of blood was slowly flowing through my heart. Yet this movement was strangely pleasurable if not scary. It amazed me that, while I felt on the edge of death, Karl was calmly sitting in the corner of the room nonplussed, ready to assist when I needed him. Looking at him, he seemed to be in another world to the one I was in, as though I were looking through a glass window.

Each time I came up to a heavy emotion I would hear the drums starting to beat. If I came upon an emotional block I would feel the spirit of Eboga rising up through me like a large snake agitated. My breathing would deepen and my voice drop to what sounded like the voice of an African tribesman. I would go into a hyped state and then I would either attempt to throw up or go into shakes and/or cold sweats, each change occurring in a split second.

Sometimes the compeer would show me things behind my eyes or he would point up to the ceiling where I would see a little ant mound forming like a rising hill of grainy sand with something pushing through. The mound would open out and a small television screen would appear. Then suddenly out of nowhere, someone would come out and do a little jig. It was like a small intro to what was coming up next for me to deal with.

Some years later the TV screen ceased to appear in my sessions and this seemed to coincide with my own growing lack of interest in watching TV. I began to realize that the frequency of the appearance of visuals embedded in a TV screen in Eboga sessions reflects our addiction to TV as a society. Hence TV is also being dealt with as a sideline addiction within a session.

I went through feelings of being useless and then learned that I was a healer, a natural healer. I don't fit into the tribe. Perhaps that is why. Perhaps that is a prerequisite to being a healer? (Perhaps that is why I was waiting on my own in the corral and had to demand acceptance into the tribe?)

I asked Mr. Ebogaman to take fear away and in desolation said, "I am an utter, fucking fool." I went through my fear of asking women to be with me and said, "Just get me out of my prison. I am super cheese!" My prison (not the only one) was my broken sexuality, which frightened me. My obsession with the removal of fear was to appear throughout all my sessions. I did not understand that fear only goes once the underlying causes have been healed. It doesn't disappear in a magic puff. However, not understanding the process properly, I was to keep asking for its removal in case that was the thing to do!

Then something very strange happened. I saw spaceships, thousands and thousands of spaceships coming towards the Earth. At the same time someone I knew was being described to me as an alien. I took this to be more of the cosmic sense of humor illustrated. The significance of this scene was somewhat lost on me. Later it was to become more revealing and left me with many unanswered questions, the answers of which I hoped to find out in time.

I was then told that the earring I wore was for the finger and not for the ear, "That is what a ring is for, the finger and not the ear." So I shouldn't wear one in my ear and also I should have a beard! How strange that they should care about these things. *What has that to do with my healing*, I thought?

I was then given a series of lessons on how "not" to be naïve. A number of different scenes were presented to me. As I lay there, each scene was played out and we went through it together. I was given a series of quizzes and questions and I answered. If I got it wrong they would say to try again. Then they would say, "Yes, you got it right." Naïveté was one of my problems and they were reprogramming my (ego) mind not to be naïve. Each time I got the answer right I received a round of applause and a couple of pretty girls would come out and do a little dance.

There was a moment where I entered a state which I can only describe as my deepest self or inner witness. I felt very relaxed and very much myself in a deep and altogether real way. I thought, *This is perfect. I want to always be like this.* I encountered Mr. Ebogaman during this state on a village path where I stood in front of him in complete attention and then there occurred a moment of blankness as if I was receiving some instruction which was not to be remembered by the ordinary me. It felt like we were on a very deep connected level within my soul. Perhaps he wanted to probe my deepest self to see what I was really about or advise me in some very deep way. Or maybe there was a part of me that wanted to talk to him? Whatever the case, this knowledge could not be made available to my ego, not yet anyway, as it would not know how to deal with it or it might try to jeopardize whatever it represented. This may have happened to me more than once. A short time after this session I had a dream where Karl is in a room of girls. He tells me that I died twice during the session. I actually asked him once some time after the session if he had said that, not sure if I had dreamt it or not. Later I found the dream entry in my journal.

My journey continued and I ran around the village as fast as I could, as I was eager to start the next task, the next step toward initiation. I did not want to leave any stone unturned. Perhaps this eagerness stemmed from years of trying other forms of therapy and having to work damn hard. Here was an opportunity too good to miss. In a short period, I could achieve what would easily take a lifetime to achieve. In fact, achieve what, quite possibly, could never be achieved on one's own. After each step, if I could not find Mr. Ebogaman, I would say, "Please, please Mr. Ebogaman, give me the next task now," and if there was something that came up that I didn't like I would say, "Please, please Mr. Ebogaman take away my fear or take away this thing," and each time he was only to happy to help me. As usual he threw his hand off to some object, invariably a small headstone which is where I would have to go next. Each time, as I began to read, it would melt away and the next scene would open up before my eyes.

While all this was going on it seemed everyone in the village was waiting in their homes in quiet expectation for the outcome. This I felt was my moment; my chance and I lapped it up. It seemed I had the village to myself as it had a total atmosphere of initiation and respect. I was the last one to be undergoing initiation and the village pathways were empty. This was clearly an important tribal moment. I felt part of a long-forgotten initiation process practiced by our forefathers many millennia before in Africa. Later, when the initiation was over, I felt the atmosphere in the village relax and return to normal. It was as if the single mind of the village had returned to being many minds. I suddenly felt at a loose end and uneasy in myself as though I didn't know how to fit in to normal life without upsetting someone. I had excelled in carrying out my individual tasks, but I was not as confident when confronted with ordinary, communal reality, the ego mind. Then a surprising thing happened. I was told I should paint.

At different times I could hear voices trying to speak to me, which I could not always make out. I took them to be my three soul companions in the background. I would strain myself to hear what they were saying but the street noise made it very difficult to do so. The lighting at times was also problematic, as I strained to see the images on the ceiling. It needed to be very low, barely perceptible to allow the images to appear.

The issue of my fear of falling from a height also came up. It was to appear during many of the sessions I later undertook. It was as if I was being slowly desensitized to this fear. It was real, live behavioral psychology at work. This fear went back to a time when an older, sadistic youth who I was playing with held me by the legs over the castle tower used in olden times for dropping tar. I had asked him to do this on the understanding it would only be for a few seconds in order for me to get the sensation. He then took the opportunity to torment me after I had put my trust in him, threatening to let me drop. It was just one example of my crazy stunt-taking as a child.

I was then given a number of life tasks to undertake. They told me to go back to Ireland immediately and to sell my apartment in London. I said I did not want to go. I felt if I was to do everything they told me I would have quite a transformation in my life, but I was not sure that I wanted to follow their advice, as I already had wheels in motion to buy another property and felt very insecure about backing out. I was afraid of upsetting all the parties involved; my fear of upsetting them was greater than my concern for my own well-being! I was then told many practical things, from how I should travel to lessons in professionalism and appearance. I was also told that no job was too small.

The village itself was beautiful. I kept seeing this African countryside, red earth and huts. It was all very pleasant. Everyone was very happy and the women were clearly looking for men! It made a welcome difference, having had a history of failed relationships and unsuccessful attempts at deep connection: one of which was to lead me, in part, on a wild goose chase to the other side of the planet: Australia. A journey that was partly inspired by a last ditch attempt to find a sense of freedom – a freedom that would only come when I was focused inward, not outward, prepared to face the demons that lived there and raised their heads at the slightest sign of danger.

Journal: Australia 1992 – 1997

It was while I was in Frankfurt, I decided to make a trip to Berlin where I met Kelly, a blonde Australian backpacker. We met in a hostel. She was sitting alone at the breakfast table when I spotted her. My own need for being mothered immediately drew me to her. Later, when I knew her better, I realized I had had a dream some time before, written into my journal, where I was talking to a blond girl with her head sticking out of a yellow VW Beetle situated close to the beach. As it turned out, she had a yellow VW Beetle and her father a house by the beach with magnificent views. In an act of desperate faith I decided to quit my job, now that I had saved some money and return to Australia with her on the basis of a friendship with the possibility of more. I reasoned that I should put the possibility of love and life, not to mention surfing, before the boring and seemingly pointless accumulation of money. Another reason for my interest in Australia was the sense I had of the energy that existed there and as yet was unknown to me. I felt it would in some way expand my inner world and give me a more complete feel for the world as a whole, being as it was a part I had yet to experience: Australia/Asia.

Beforehand we traveled together to visit my parents in Ireland. My visit home was one of the few times I saw my family together again. On leaving my parents I pulled my car over to the side of the road and cried into Kelly's arms. I missed them terribly. It seemed I was going further and further away from everything I loved in pursuit of a dream I hoped would make sense of everything and liberate me, so that in the end I could return as I truly was, the real person I wanted my parents to know. But for that I had to leave them. Unfortunately I had chosen a girl with a short temper and I needed her. The thought of being alone scared me. It never occurred to me that I could make my own way. I was living my life through her world. I was a prisoner to her insecurities as well as my own. I was also a prisoner of dark forces I was unable to defeat.

Kelly was from Brisbane, so that is where we headed. I had heard it was a little provincial but that didn't bother me too much. I was looking forward to the heat and the waves. While living there, from time to time I would visit the area called the Valley where the Aboriginal people could be found hanging around, aimless, sometimes drunk, basically broken. Many Australians had little time for them and looked on them as a bunch of losers. But the real story, I soon discovered, was a lot different.

The Australian Aboriginal culture is defined by its emphasis on clanship and their belief in the spiritual significance of the land and its natural features. They have been in Australia for at least 40,000 years. Art is an integral part of Aboriginal life. An intimate knowledge of plant harvesting and the behavior of animals ensured that food shortages were rare. When the first British settled in Australia, it is believed there were some 300,000 Aborigines. White settlement saw many driven from their land by force and their way of life destroyed. In Tasmania practically all full-blooded Aborigines were wiped out. In Australia the settlers rounded them up and hunted them down. Many looked on Aborigines as a form of wild animal. For many years few Europeans were prosecuted for killing Australian Aborigines. Citizenship was not bestowed until 1967.

An assimilation policy in the 1960s took almost total control of the lives of the Aboriginal people, including dictating where they could live and whom they could marry. The idea being that they would adapt to European culture. Missionaries set up settlements to house and educate the children and place them in service as a kind of white Aboriginal. Children whose fathers were non-Aboriginal could be taken by force from their mothers. It led to families being torn apart. Their natural ways of existence were destroyed and as a result they became culturally and spiritually disorientated. Australian Aborigines suffer terrible social problems within the family and within the community, including drug and alcohol abuse. Today there are enormous health problems, indicating a huge discrepancy between Aboriginal and non-Aboriginal Australians.

It is therefore understandable that many Australians today see Australian Aborigines as a social nuisance. For me, one of the most beautiful aspects of their culture is the idea of the "Dreamtime." Such a gentle way to describe the spirit as it passes through the land and the people, creating a world just beyond our ordinary senses, beyond our ego.

The first six months of my stay I was unemployed, living on my savings while waiting for a work permit on the basis of a de facto marriage with Kelly. It was a ploy to get a work permit. However, I was desperate and sinking. The relationship was not working and I could not survive on my own. Eventually the work permit came through and I found work with Queensland Railways as a contract analyst programmer, earning less than half of what I had earned in London. I had hoped the youth and energy of Australia and the possibility of a life centered on the outdoors, including surfing, would be the tonic I needed to get going. What else could I do? I had tried everything else to overcome my demons.

My work in IT was simply a means to an end, an end that looked increasingly out of sight. Inevitably the relationship failed. It was a telling point that I worried more about Kelly being unfaithful than about the life we shared together. Yet I painfully hoped in some way to connect deeply with her, if only to prove to myself I was capable of doing so. I knew I had to learn how to do this if I was ever to find joy in a relationship. Unfortunately I was simply unable to do so. It escaped me. I had lost touch with the real meaning of relationship and friendship. My demons were my jailers.

One of the deciding reasons that had brought me to Australia was the fact that Kelly's mom was involved in rebirthing, a form of breath work. She knew of a three-month live-in facilitator's course, six days a week, focused on all the contemporary methods used for emotional release therapy. The course, costing Aus$3,400, was held in Kempsey, a small community near the coast of New South Wales. It involved Holotropic Breathwork or Rebirthing, Sand Play, Dance, Group Therapy, Dream Work, use of Mandalas, use of Mythology and other bits and pieces. It was set in a country house where the group of almost 16 women met each day beginning with breath work and emotional release. I reasoned that this could free me. It had been part of my reason for leaving Germany, as I had saved enough money to afford this odyssey. It was what gave me the strength to up and leave all I knew, believing it could finally be the cure I needed. I had been very optimistic on my way to Australia. I reasoned that if things did not work out with Kelly, I would have the strength to handle the situation on my own. Besides, she had agreed to be my friend and to help me get settled. I felt that perhaps we both wanted more, but for the moment it suited us both to pretend otherwise. During the course, I stayed with three women in a bungalow close to the coast.

Part of the course involved the study of myth by James Campbell, a highly regarded American mythologist. I found this intriguing, in particular I enjoyed the myth's of *The Hero's Journey*, *Psyche and Amor* (romance) and *The Goddess*. Each day we would gather as a group and begin with breath work which involved hyperventilation to break down the emotional armor, leading to inner connection and then release. Stanislof Grof had developed this method after working with LSD, which became a banned substance. The course led to a certificate in transpersonal psychology, later redefined as emotional release therapy. On one occasion when hyperventilating, I felt I had an experience of being a lion in the African Savannah. However, for most of the course I felt blocked, unable to connect to my inner frustration and anger. I was simply too afraid to connect to any real anger. I did however have one major experience of an uncontrolled outpouring of grief, as though I had opened a door on myself and partly watched as I felt myself empty. I connected to the love I once felt for my parents. I cried for their dignity and my respect for them. I prolonged this healing experience using simple techniques I had learned from primal therapy, i.e., I kept the emotional valve.

The course was clearly not a failure as I had two very unusual experiences. Lying in bed one night I could feel energy begin to rise from the base of my spine. As it rose towards my sternum and filled my body I realized I was having a Kundalini energy release. From what I had heard of this process on the course I panicked and it stopped. It did not return. On another occasion, while running into the chill, crashing waters at Kempsey Beach during the mild, sunny winter, I felt a shock course through me. I was with a girlfriend and her little boy. Suddenly my inner world changed. I felt distinctly like an early, primitive man, strength coursing through me, a mind fixed and set – my woman and child on the beach looking on, somehow separate but yet a part of me. It was powerful, exhilarating and liberating. My girlfriend called out to me and I tried to reply but I couldn't connect to her somewhat different existence. I was definitely in an altered state, like I had been some years before while gardening. As I replied, my consciousness shifted back (from my soul), the spell broken by my attempt to connect to her (from my ego). Still I was left in no doubt as to what I had experienced. I had accessed early man. This experience mirrored my frustration. I was living a life like a weasel and yet inside was all this untapped energy kept down by experiences I had no control over.

For me this course was the most creative and useful form of therapy I had undertaken. Steve and Patricia, both ex-clergy, gave the course. On the course I was told the reason why I was struggling with therapy was because my child had me by the balls. I balked at this, as it was the child I sought to protect, but I had no way to explain this. I really did not understand the Jungian idea of the shadow (a psychic repository of all our repressed dark feelings and experiences) and I had no intention of humiliating my own inner child in any way, a child who had suffered far too much humiliation and subjection. This I believed I would have to do if I was to stop defending myself in the way I did while on the course. I wanted healing, but I also wanted to protect a part of myself I perceived the world was seeking to annihilate. I was not interested in becoming a well-adjusted adult if it meant looking down on a part of myself I had long sought to save. It was my fear of loss of my true self that made me at times stubborn and difficult in therapy.

One of the fantasies I brought with me to Australia was my desire to surf. I bought a mini Malibu board, my pride and joy, a beautiful board and the perfect companion. I lived in Brisbane, which was not far from the gentle waves of the exclusive Noosa Beach on the Sunshine Coast. I loved to sit on the waters, lying on my board waiting for a wave, watching the light glance off the sea. Yet, as hard as I tried, I could not master surfing. I was simply too afraid; like with so many other things in my life, including women. I was deeply frustrated with myself. Everything I wanted in life seemed beyond me, especially my passion for singing. All because I had a vulnerability I could not overcome. Yet I knew deep down there was a part of me that was strong, able and talented. I knew this and

I pursued every possible path and avenue open to me to connect to it. From time to time, though, I felt I was trapped. I feared that ultimately I would not have the strength to take the path I needed, even if I were able to find it.

There was a time in my childhood I did not hesitate, anything was possible. Now I lived in a jail, an invisible jail and I was fully aware of how absurd and ridiculous it was. Yet I could not overcome it. It was a monkey on my back and, like a demon, it would not let go. My ego, struggling to cope with the emerging pain, cracked the whip harder and harder in the only way it knew. It imposed fear and dominion over my soul. I rejected the outlook of certain healers who tried to convince me to accept my lot, a mentality I saw as ignorant and defeatist. That is why I broke from certain forms of therapy, as they seemed to keep people in their cages, not free them.

In my healing journey I refused to submit to anyone. I was not going to allow myself to be humiliated by what I considered to be ignorant – even if well-meaning – therapists. Unfortunately I contributed to the force of my own problems. I refused to pretend anything to myself, mostly due to the influence of Krisnamurti and Janov, as well as my own stubbornness to be whole and free. If I felt bad I preferred to look at it and try to resolve it, not to find reasons to feel good. Perhaps I was hoping that, like a boil, I could bring my problems to a head. Unfortunately I was unable to resolve anything properly. I thus fell at every fence, every opportunity, while at the same time I empowered the bad feelings and not the good. And that really is not a good thing to do, is it?

On returning home to Kelly after a long trip of about four months to visit my parents, I found a photo of another boy on the mantelpiece. Even though Kelly and I had been experimenting with an open relationship while I was away, this shocked me. Before I left, things had not being going well between us.

I had decided to visit my parents to see my father, who was confined to a wheelchair. During this time I truly felt I had made a good connection to him, which meant a lot to me. On one of my earlier trips home I was surprised when my father expressed an interest to visit Australia. Unfortunately that was now not going to be. Too many years of smoking were beginning to take their toll. While I was at home, as it happened someone had hired out the old lofts and put a music studio there. So during my visit I recorded probably my most joyous song ever, one I had written before leaving Australia called "What Lovers." It was very upbeat and very happy and expressed a state of being I longed for. It grew out of a song I had in a dream where I was sitting at the kitchen table in our Queenslander Cottage with Kelly and some of our friends happily singing.

We made love once more. Kelly decided it was not going to happen between us and ended the relationship there and then. I remember how she stood looking at me, kissed me, thought for a moment and said to herself, *No*. Of course she was right. I just didn't have the courage to admit it myself. However I was very upset and stunned. She made a passing remark about how her new boyfriend had said he felt like he needed to have a fight. She knew my weakness and, it seemed to me, hoped to use it to scare me off. In a state of panic I went out and bought her a huge bunch of red roses which she looked at and took from me without any emotion, as though I had just handed her the shopping. For the next few days I was in complete shock and started to cry uncontrollably. I even rang the Samaritans. It was as if I had cut myself off completely from everything I knew and the one lifeline left was simply cut. I felt like I was sitting on a rock in the middle of a great sea without land in sight.

It was not long after in the depths of my despair that I concluded that no lifestyle, no country, no person could give me what I needed.

I had to face the facts. I had grown up with a love and ache of singing, not to mention dance. If I had any chance of happiness, it had to be through this. I had lessened my desire, but now I realized it had to once again become the center of my life. I began to write melodies and again hit the same walls, fear and lack of self-confidence. I simply could not push myself forward in these areas.

I was, however, still determined to succeed and managed to write a number of tunes. Eventually I decided that Australia was too far away as it meant losing contact with home and Europe. I reasoned that, even though life was much better in Australia, I did not want to lose contact with the heritage and culture of Europe. I also longed for a circle of trusted friends and I felt the cultural gap was too great for me in Australia. I was not prepared to be someone I was not. Meanwhile, I made contact with an agent in Dublin. At the same time I turned down the offer of a Green card from the United States government. I had had enough of going around in circles.

There was also another important event that happened at this time that gave me a sense of urgency. One morning, while lying in bed half-asleep, I could hear a voice saying my father wanted me to let go. I replied, in tears, he could go if he wished. I was told that the best was yet to come. So now I was keen to return, as I was not sure how real this omen was and how long my father had left to live. I wanted the opportunity to heal the years of mistrust that had developed between us and had made good progress on my last visit.

It was vital, therefore, that I should return to Ireland, as I felt a deep need to heal the past between my father and me before he passed for good from this life. Once again I was living my life close to the edge, only acting when I clearly had no other choice. Fortunately, life was looking after me.

So I decided to return home and left behind the golden beaches and crashing white waves of Australia, along with the music of 4

Non Blondes and Midnight Oil, among others. I was running out of options. I had spent three years in and out of Australia with occasional trips to the Far East. Yet not much had changed for me. This I realized when I visited Sydney before leaving Australia, where I stood in the Academy of Music and longingly wished I could be one of the students I saw there chatting happily away. However, life is a line of continuity, much like the generations that tie our ancestors together. Until that line is fixed all our present actions are overrun and undermined by a past, which seeks to heal itself.

Earlier I had begun to think I needed my own apartment. I thought maybe this would give me the courage I needed. Somewhere I could simply close the door and call home. Somewhere I would be safe. I decided Australia was not the place to buy one. The agent I was in contact with found me a contract position in a deeply Protestant part of Northern Ireland, Antrim. At first, returning home was a bit of a shock, as life in Australia had been much more comfortable. But I reasoned that I needed to spend time back where I came from if I was ever to get to the roots of my problems.

I spent the weekends at home and was glad for the time I had with my father. One moment in particular stands out. I was helping Mom move Dad in the bed and he let out some wind. All three of us laughed together. That was a moment to cherish and remember.

It was not long after – about three months later – that my father passed away, on 15 September 1994. The weekend before I had attended a healing weekend in Wicklow, where I sat in the middle of the room and told everyone I had no wish to talk about my father on that occasion, as I felt reconciled to him. He passed away the following Thursday. When I arrived home to my parents' house the following evening I had an experience where a rapid stream of images of my father's life started to flood through my mind. Afraid, I stopped them. On reflection I should have let them flow. They did not return. Within a few days I was back at work, afraid that the edifice of my life would collapse around me were I to pause and absorb what was happening to me. I had only one possibility left in my life and that was to grit my teeth and go forward and somehow make my dreams come true.

Not long after I moved to Dublin where I found work. Luckily, I soon bought an apartment in the city center just before the economic boom took off. I was sad my father had not lived to see it. That was 1996. Shortly after buying the apartment, I wondered if I was not simply digging a bigger and bigger hole for myself. How on Earth was I ever to enter the music world? I hoped to be able to make enough money to take time off and, using my apartment as a base, attempt to make music in Dublin. It was a pipe dream, because my hidden demons would not allow me. Fortunately I had bought an apartment below a guy called Séan. It was a lucky encounter, as he was genuinely a good person and a good friend. I also made friends at work, but I was looking for friends on a different wavelength but was too insecure to find them. The nightlife was inviting but threatening if you are on your own. I was unable to find someone to explore it with. Once I had saved enough money I quit my job to try to pursue music. This, of course, left me without my regular contacts.

Around this time I went to Spain and spent nine days on the pilgrims' walk, El Camino de Santiago, in the north of Spain, covering the last 270 km. of the trail. I arrived just as the door to the office that issued certificates was closing for the weekend. Had I been a few minutes later, I would not have received this testament to my little pilgrimage. When I arrived I refused to make the traditional visit to the tomb of Santiago de Compostela, believing that this was to recognize something which at the time I philosophically disagreed with. It was not the reason for my trip. The other pilgrims I traveled with did make the visit and were a little bemused by my attitude as I stood at the door of the Cathedral watching each in turn mark the final part of their journey. It was a little silly, I suppose. But at the time I was totally in earnest about doing the right thing, even if I was not sure what that was.

I had hoped the walk would clear my head after breaking up with my most recent and short-lived girlfriend in Luxembourg. Instead, as I walked, I could not stop my mind from chattering. It was endless. In the silence, I found only noise.

Unable to sort out my mind I decided instead to sort out my body and focus in on my music. Surely this was something I could do! But even here I hit a brick wall. And after a very expensive and unsuccessful Harley Street back treatment I was once more looking for work as I needed money. Well, at least I did produce a tape but I never promoted it. It lacked the spirit I was looking for.

So, time went by and another effort to change my life met with nothing. It seemed the old adage applied to me, one of many I learned from my mother, "A fool and his money are easily parted." That is for sure. Another important phrase she taught me, and I have never forgotten it, is, "Your health is your wealth." I made the mistake of forgetting the first one. I wanted to believe in anything that could improve my life and I had the money to do it. Yet money was not solving my problems. Perhaps I had yet to learn that while I believed it would, it in fact would not. You could say it was blood money and it had little real value for me. I derived little pleasure from what I bought with it. Further, my encounters with the medical profession left me in disbelief at the supremacy of money over any real effort to heal people. It seemed to me that the very last reason one should be a healer (money) was for many the very first reason. Because of this they were unable to heal others properly, as healing comes from the soul.

There was a time when I was willing to rely on the support of comfortable institutional surroundings. But that day was now past and the time of reckoning had arrived. I wanted life, nothing less and singing was the one thing that lit up my soul. I could not tolerate my sense of alienation any more. I also realized I would never be able to sing properly until I had allowed the floodgates of my emotions to open. And this I was not yet prepared to do. The same place where my sense of beauty and ecstasy lived was the same place where the wells of my emotion were guarded. Something was fundamentally wrong with me and I had to find out what. The energy spent in endless pursuits was monumental and in the end would be the death of me. I was frustrated beyond belief. I could prove my ability and could feel my potential. Yet I could not realize either in a way I desired. My early boyhood became a curse, as it was filled with the memories of what I had dreamed of, but could not now attain; like the man who regains his sight only to lose it again. Yet my past became more and more a blank to me. In the end I could only conclude it was not possible to escape life. The only option is to face it and change it.

Deep down, I did not want to grow up until I was healed, as I was afraid I would lose my link to my childhood and to who I felt I truly was. In the same way I did not really want to achieve until I achieved something that truly came from my own soul, something that I could really be proud of, afraid that any other kind of success would be the death of my dreams and the death of the real me. However, I seemed to be living in a daze, an altered state of mind. So I chose to believe in the light, in the hope that I might find my way out of the dark.

If ever the motto "If at first you don't succeed, try, try again" applied, it applied to me. I lived it in every bone of my body. As a result I was to taste the greed, dishonesty and cynicism of my fellow man. However, every time I was knocked down I got back up again.

I had no other choice. I simply knew I had to find what I was looking for if life was to have any meaning for me.

However, I had a hidden agenda to which I was subject. Many choices were made from the logic of the mind and not the wisdom of the heart. It would not be so easy to escape its control. Yet, I wanted to live my own life before it passed me by and not live to look back and mourn what could have been. This I wanted with all my heart.

You could say that I was, in some ways, an accidental tourist. I was tired and I was worried about my own mental health. I was not sure how much more disappointment I could take. Clearly, I was running from something and all my efforts to date had not helped me uncover what it was. If I had gone to this much effort and failed, then the writing was on the wall that I was heading for serious problems. This began to scare me. Also it seems I was not the only one to suffer from this time period, as I heard of others from my childhood who were also having difficulty in their lives. It was perhaps as if something strange had happened in my small town all those years before and its effects were now beginning to show.

Perhaps I was simply a small part of a bigger picture?

There was a song my mother sang some words of to me as a boy when she could see I was troubled:

> "Walk tall, walk straight, walk the world right in the eye.
> That's what my mamma told me when I was just a boy.
> Walk tall, walk straight, walk the world right in the eye."

I certainly wanted to walk tall, but I was not sure how. One thing was for certain: I was probably prepared to die trying if I had to and it was the dream that kept me going. Perhaps I had to learn what the hero Parcival in his search for the Holy Grail had learned. The answer lies not in doing what you suppose is correct, but what you "know" to be right. Otherwise, if it were all so simple, there would be nothing to learn. However, I had yet to have my mind opened to the wisdom of the heart and the subtlety of the soul. And for that life would keep knocking me down until I had.

I adopted the phrase "Follow your Bliss" from Joseph Campbell as a guide to light my path. Later I refined it to a search for happiness, believing each happy person makes the world a better place. No one could argue with that, as many argued with the other. In this I decided, in a last attempt for healing, to actively open my heart to try to discover the meaning of compassion and not just simply view life from a self-centered perspective, driven as I was by my ego: the Great Dictator.

As Leonard Cohen sings so beautifully, "The heart has got to open in a fundamental way." If I was to ever overcome my sense of alienation I had no choice. And at some level, it seems, I must have made that decision as I was about to have an experience I had long forgotten, a natural inclusion in something greater than myself: community. It was something I had inadvertently shunned, as my inner self felt threatened by it. The existence of both together had become a contradiction for me. I was to learn otherwise.

Coming of Age & Tribal Acceptance

With my lessons in deportment and the tasks assigned to me completed it seemed my initiation work was done. I had come into the session as an outsider looking for my place in life based on the integrity of my true self – a contradiction I was not sure I could resolve. And so I was pleased to have come this far and yet still remain connected to that sense of self.

Then without as much as a word I once more found myself part of a larger group. This time a group of young initiate men. We were brought into an open area with a low lying staked wall along one side. We each had a girl waiting for us. Mine seemed about 16 and I remember how natural it felt as I completed that part of the initiation. It seemed this was a form of mate-ship that followed once one had completed one's initiation to manhood. I wish now I still had my little girl from the village. She was beautiful and I felt for her. There was a special aura of calm, simplicity, beauty and depth about her. I missed her afterwards, the same way I missed my gentle angel earlier.

Once the tasks of initiation had been completed and the mate-ship ritual was over we were all brought together (perhaps 100) as a group in what looked like a square, bamboo-style compound. Each of us was holding what looked like a traditional African shield in one hand and a spear in the other. We stood in lines of formation, absolutely still, absolutely as one. You could hear a pin drop. In that moment nothing else existed. It was as if time and space had become one. All at once we gave out a cry and knelt on one knee. This was a sign of our tribal link and in that moment I had the greatest sense of community I have ever had in my entire life. I felt I belonged to this tribe in a way not explicable in words and yet I was entirely myself. In no way was I lessened by this state of being. In fact I was validated by it. I knew in that moment that if the call came to support this group I could without question and yet I still felt I was not in any way undermining myself, as the group and I were indeed one. In that moment I was fully connected and felt myself a part of pure community. I understood the real meaning of loyalty. It was a true feeling of initiation, a call to something higher, a place you can only wonder about unless its door has been opened to you. After all, is initiation not the movement to a higher ground?

Finally we were taken in groups of three before the chief, where we were acknowledged as initiated. In my case, I looked down and saw myself in the foot straps of a windsurfing board. This was a celestial joke referring to my training to become a windsurfing instructor where the final task, which I had yet to complete, was to be seen planning with your feet in the foot straps – once that is done, the requirements are officially met and one becomes accepted as an instructor. This I had yet to do. However, for now in this world at least, I knew I had been accepted and thus initiated.

I then returned to the theatre of my session, but now it was all closed down. It felt like the show was over and I was standing there alone, all the players gone. The curtains closed. I saw the party balloons and curly paper strings lying around. I asked, "What now?" One of the girls came out and threw her hands up saying, "That's it." I wasn't sure if I had bottled out from going further, or if that was all for now. On reflection that was all that I was ready to handle.

They then told me to check the results! I am not sure which results they were referring to. Prior to the session I had undergone some prerequisite physical tests.

I felt a sense of sadness and wished my encounter with the villagers could have gone on longer. I would also have liked to have spent more time with my new partner!

Anointing with Oil

Even though I could feel the strongest part of the Eboga experience finishing, it was not yet the end.

I could see what seemed to be angelic beings, almost translucent, very close to me, holding what looked like a small ceremonial jar made from gold or silver, with which I was anointed on my head with some kind of healing agent that went from the top of my body and seemed to work its way through me. I then felt it going into my heart, where suddenly it seemed to take away a little twitch that was there before. Perhaps that is what they meant by checking the results?

In these moments I felt I was undergoing a profound physical healing throughout my body and was healed in ways I may never know. Who knows? Perhaps it was not a physical healing but instead some kind of spiritual blessing?

I then had an image of children running around and playing in a playground. One of them shouted out to me and cried, "Lee! Lee!" as though we were all playing together. I took this to be my new nickname. Something I had always wanted, but never seemed to get right. It was like a parting gift!

Ego Mind Reeducation

It was clear at this point that the emotional odyssey, in large part, was completed and I seemed to turn inward to my mind's eye, where I met someone who came to me, sat down with me and said, "Let's go through these different things now." It was like a quiet, safe little classroom in the center of my mind where we went through many, many things together and worked them out. This second part was possibly a review and a reeducation based on the first part. In normal life, when we overcome a trauma, we have a period of relearning. With Eboga, it is as if everything is speeded up. During this second phase, I was taken step-by-step through all kinds of things for me to know and learn. It was as if my mind was like the spring of a clock that has been wound too tightly and now was rapidly releasing itself in some kind of instinctive self-ordering process, each lesson a part of that self-ordering process, a kind of mental unwinding. The session was an insight into how the brain can simplify itself and find answers quite readily when allowed to. Unfortunately, most of us are unable to take the necessary steps to move forward personally in our own lives, trapped as we are by our ego which we have developed and manipulated to protect us from our pain. So we go into a kind of closed-down state, unable to summon up the self-ordering processes which can heal and sort out the mind.

During this phase of the session I thought, *the ibogaine is wearing off.* Now I realize it was simply moving to a different stage of its life cycle. I was going through a period of what Howard Lotsof calls "massive thinking," which went on for hour after hour and left me feeling mentally exhausted. I imagine there were many items related to phase one covered. It was overwhelming the vast amount of material one needed to deal with and process and it left me with little interest for conventional therapy. How could anything compare to this?

I felt like I was in a mental sprint to keep up, each lesson delved out in a matter of seconds, the next right on the heels of the last. How could I have so much to learn and how was it going to affect me? Did these lessons represent the vast storehouse of knowledge the ego needs in order to exist harmoniously with the soul? Or was I perhaps learning what I had failed to learn as a child growing up due to my exclusion from normal life? Perhaps I was unlearning all the negative things I had taken on board resulting from my childhood traumas? Had I not already received mental reeducation in the first part or was the material simply being reinforced?

As the amount of material in the second phase was so overwhelming it seems to me it somehow related to the detail in the underlying issues which had been uncovered and in part healed. I imagine all kinds of ego unwinding and simplification took place.

I received lots of lessons on a very deep, inner level. Perhaps a level that we are not normally conscious of, but which we use to live our lives through (our ego). Perhaps also, many of the IRMs (Initial Response Mechanisms) that Joseph Campbell talks about were also being unraveled and replaced? (Initial Response Mechanisms are learned responses in a child up to the age of 12 that become hardwired into the subconscious of the mind unlike animals who are born fully wired.) It seems as though the ego, which until now had been kept at arms length, was been taken under the wings of the Eboga teacher and been given much more attention than it could handle.

Even though it seemed the power of Eboga to create images had dissipated, its power to teach had not – the eboga plant is, after all, a teaching plant. However, I was still able to see myself (in my mind's eye) sitting in a classroom with someone writing all kinds of things on a blackboard for me to learn. The visualization was on a very much reduced, almost dreamlike, level compared to the visualization in the first part of the session, which was quite powerful and expressed many emotions. The need for visualization in this part of the session being less important than in the first part.

I may have missed out a little during this phase as I was utterly exhausted and felt I had done what I had to do already. So I was perhaps not as enthusiastic as I could have been. In fact I was so tired I just craved for sleep. Eventually, I did fall asleep. It was a short regenerative sleep. When I awoke I felt a little bruised and a little disappointed that I had not been able to stay awake.

However, I did have a deep sense of relief and accomplishment that I had achieved something quite incredible and beyond my wildest dreams. I had tapped into a source of healing far more powerful than anything I could possibly have known. I was chuffed with what I had managed to put myself through.

A Time for Coffee

Karl came in to see how I was doing. I felt the need for some kind of gratification – like a cigarette or some other thing to give me a sense of freedom, to savor the moment, to mask any discomfort I felt. So, after 18 hours, while still in the energy of the session, I got up and went with Karl for coffee. I was a little shaky on my feet, but after walking around for about ten minutes I was reasonably steady.

I was feeling a little pained and wanted some kind of fix; something to alleviate the remnants of the pain I was feeling.

I felt a need for outside stimulation. The session had been very demanding. To get up and leave early is not something one should do but it is understandable, especially if a lot of pain has been uncovered. So, we had coffee in a sidewalk café with the table close to the edge of the pavement. I felt as though I was on the street almost and that the coffee table was elbowing itself into position, in spite of the cars. It was a battle between normal and abnormal life. The passing cars seemed like a brutal intrusion. I, however, was in my own world, the energy of Eboga clearly making me much more sensitive to my surroundings. Karl and I talked at length about the session. In fact I was still in it. I probably did most of the talking; as it is something I have found comforts me. I indulged myself with cigarettes. After all had I not done something great for myself? A little vice at this stage was surely acceptable. The first cigarette did little for me, but as I continued to smoke, I managed to get the hit that I knew in some way would alleviate the soreness of my exposure.

When we got back to the apartment Karl asked me if I would care to write down what I had experienced. I began, but could not bring myself to switch my mind into laptop mode and the need to struggle with keys and files. I gave up and took out my recorder, lay down on the bed and recorded my thoughts. I felt as though my life had just been saved from drowning. I simply could not believe the enormity of what had just happened to me. It was unbelievable and I felt very, very privileged. I lay on my bed as the energy moved into its final moments, much like a lover fulfilled in love, reflecting on the profundity of everything and the sheer good fortune to be in such a special place.

In these moments my ability to look inward was still strong and my fear to look lessened. I had been freed in some way: my mind opened up. My imagination was somewhat less intimidating to me, as before I had been afraid my ego would take over and throw up all kinds of rubbish that might scare me. Now my imagination was flowing.

As I lay there, in my mind's eye I could see an image of a small boat on calm waters making its way towards a headland. As it went round the headland I saw something I did not expect to see.

Have we Met Before?

Karl and I spent some of the day talking in between my resting and recuperating. Later that evening the doorbell rang. I did not realize he had been expecting visitors. It was his girlfriend Maria and her sister Paula. Maria entered the room followed by Paula. Immediately my world lit up. She was beautiful and dazzling; tall, strong-featured, with beautiful hair. As she entered the room her face was lit up in a smile from ear to ear. Her tall stature lent her an air of nobility and strength, her movements slow and graceful. I was thrilled to meet her. We sat around the table and talked awhile. I was unable to keep my gaze from her. I am not sure what she thought of me. I guess I was a novelty.

We decided to head downstairs to the pizzeria for something to eat, real Italian pizza. It was the kind of place I liked. Excellent home-cooked food, served generously in surroundings that called for no pretension, cozy and familiar. We huddled around the table, Karl facing the door, Maria and Paula facing us, Paula opposite me. I told her a story about the angels I had met and how the most beautiful and sweetest beings in God's kingdom are the little ones, for they are the most gentle. I was telling her about my experiences in an indirect way. She had no idea about what I had just been through. It never occurred to me that perhaps I was meeting the little angel I was so fond of in real life or that the nervousness the little angel had shown in flying away was possibly an attribute Paula shared. It also never occurred to me that perhaps my encounters with my soul companions were a foretaste of what was yet to come. So much was going on, I was oblivious to it.

Paula listened with her shoulders hunched, leaning forward, attentive with a smile on her face. She seemed to enjoy every moment. I was entranced and delighted. We left the pizzeria and headed off to a charity fair. There were many different stalls. As we walked around, we came upon one that caught my attention, a classic ball-throwing stall. Taking center stage, I won a teddy bear shaped like a koala bear. I duly gave him the name Mr. Ebogaman amidst a lot of fuss. To say I enjoyed the attention would be an understatement. However, soon the time came for Paula to head off to be with her friends. I felt a great loss in that moment. I sensed she had been enjoying my company and was perhaps also a little sad to part. I put my feelings down to being simply needy after a tough and emotionally bruising session. However, in that moment I knew that any session was worth going through to be able to one day connect with such beauty. I hoped I would meet her again as I was sad to see her go.

The following day Karl, Maria and I headed off into the country to have lunch with some friends of Maria's who had a weekend cottage in a small, protected park. I was still feeling the effects of the session and did not like to say very much. We decided to take a bike ride around the park. While cycling, Maria and I talked at great length about the many things I had experienced. It surprised me how seriously she took what I had to say, as I imagined it would seem a little crazy to most normal people.

The next day I found myself invited to the family home for dinner and was treated with the utmost of respect. It was all a little odd for me as I had arrived there, I imagined, little better than a drug addict in the eyes of Karl and now I was in some way a guest of honor. I guess the family simply assumed I was a friend of Karl's and, in the meantime, I had become a friend of Maria and an acquaintance of Paula. Dinner was served in the front room with all the gentility of an Italian setting.

The father, a friendly man with a grasp of English, worked in computers and so was interested to talk about the work I was involved in. It was hard for him to grasp how little interest it had for me. However, I was happy to talk to him as he exuded an air of paternal warmth. The truth was I was more interested in getting to know his daughter and whenever we did get a chance to talk he always seemed to appear on the spot. I could not decide whether it was because he was starved for someone to discuss his technical background with or whether he was protecting his daughter from an unknown quantity. It was hard to be annoyed with this man. After all he was friendly and, more importantly, he was her father. Perhaps he was a little concerned at the interest she showed in me?

Paula shared a love of Ireland, having been there a number of times to study English. So we had a few areas upon which to build a friendship. She also appeared to like windsurfing, which I was also very enthusiastic about. We even joked that I might teach her. Yet this conversation was not enough to build a link. It seemed that every time I came close to making one, her father was always there to prevent it. Karl, Maria and I became friends that weekend. A friendship with Paula would prove to be very difficult.

However, the truth that my feelings for Paula uncovered made me realize I could not live with myself if I did not realize my full potential as a person, capable of giving and receiving love. She became an inspiration for me, a light shining in the darkness. Regardless of whether I had any earthly possibility of being with her, she inspired me to prepare myself for someone equally beautiful. To do otherwise would have been to remain in a state of perpetual discontent. *The first taste of the Grail brings initiation. The subsequent tastes bring transformation.*

Thus it seems, with my initiation, I drank once more from the Grail Cup, as love flows the waters of eternal life and its saving grace. Perhaps I had my first sip when, as a 13-year-old boy, I looked into the emerald eyes of my dark-haired beauty or perhaps my first real taste came many years later in a Madrid nightclub in a moment of inexplicable union with all. Whatever the case, this was different, as a spell had been cast and it brought with it the pain of being truly alive. Without knowing it then, it was to give me the strength to bear what lay ahead, as love bears all things.

10. The Field of Adventure

We are kings in search of our Kingdom.
If we do not find it we live in the shadow of our souls.

I have written about my past, not to become a prisoner of it, but to be free of it. In so doing I hope to show a new way to others, a way that requires looking back with an open heart and not a closed mind. A way that only succeeds when the intention is pure and is born of a vision of love.

Little did I know what lay ahead for me in the next 24 months. This was to be a very hectic time indeed. My inner travels involved another three Eboga sessions as part of my Process, as well as three professionally guided MDMA sessions. It was also to be a time of great inner turmoil and worldly concern. I certainly needed to simplify my life but I seemed to be moving in two opposing directions at once. A conflict was raging between my ego and my soul – suddenly my soul's agenda was on the table too.

In *The Hero's Journey* the belly of the whale represents the final separation from the hero's known world and self. It is the point of transition between worlds and selves. It comes after the call to adventure has been taken up whereby, with the help of spiritual helpers, the hero has actually crossed into the field of adventure, i.e. has crossed the first threshold. It signifies that the experiences that will shape the new world and self will begin shortly or may have already begun. Entering this stage shows that the person is willing to die to himself or herself, i.e., to undergo a metamorphosis. Given what I was about to undergo, it seems my soul was intent on dragging me there – whether I liked it or not. First, however, I still had many tasks to undertake within the field of adventure before that separation would be complete and I would finally begin my metamorphosis, i.e., enter the belly of the whale. My initiation had set me firmly on that road enabling my soul to guide me where I needed to go.

My outer travels took me back to Ireland and then on to Italy, Spain, South Africa, Botswana and finally to Brazil where I underwent my fourth and most climactic session, described in the second book of this trilogy, exactly 33 months to the day of my very first session. The circumstances surrounding this session were completely unexpected and the events which occurred, remarkable. It was a session I most certainly did not expect, as my own motives had been rather simple. The choice of date was entirely accidental and circumstantial. The Process however had its own agenda, which led to a period of revelation that has enriched my life since, revelation that has helped me to better understand the nature and purpose of our humanity, my own humanity and the future that lay ahead of me. Unaware of its true significance, with this fourth session, I fully entered the belly of the whale.

You might be forgiven for thinking that the worst part was over. You might also be forgiven for thinking I had taken leave of my senses when in fact all I had taken leave of was a pained ego that had caged me in. It seems that through my initiation session, I underwent some kind of reorientation within myself to redirect my focus and thus empower me to greater success. By that I mean prior to the initiation I was focused on healing my wounds, driven by my desire to reach my dreams. Love was always a part of those but I never focused directly on it, as it was generally too painful. But it is the pain we have to face. Now it seems from this first session all the elements needed for a successful quest were being put into place. Like Parcival I now carried a love in my heart. I was unaware of how fundamentally important that would be to bring me through what lay ahead. Just like the knights of courtly love, love created for me a vision of what I could become and made the pain easier to bear. In fact I welcomed it as it was a sign that I was fast approaching my goal. It also served to keep me open to the unknown which I was about to encounter and which sought to reveal itself to me. My world was about to become much larger while my ego would become much smaller and the universe much closer than ever I possibly imagined.

Paulo Coelho asserts in his book *The Alchemist* that, "Everyone, when they are young, knows what their destiny is." Mine, I had hoped, was singing. In truth I always harbored a secret desire to unlock the mysteries of man, to experience life to the full so that ironically I could truly be part of this world, someone who belonged here. At the same time I did not want to lose the divine experience that singing gave me. It was the dream that kept me going. Now it seems my horizons were being expanded to include my love for others and the joy and appreciation of being a part of life.

Many people have no dreams. They do not follow their bliss but instead harbor ambitions of power and material wealth, the only dreams an over-burdened ego can comfortably live with, a perversion of the true wealth and power of the heart and soul. They rely on the baser aspects of the animal. They have placed their true heart in an emotional prison along with all their dark secrets and thrown away the keys. They profess that life is meant to be full of pain and that one should simply see it all as illusion, allowing the mind to rise above the body. In this they reject the body as they reject the body of man. They are the Fisher King, but unlike the Fisher King they do not know how to heal themselves. You could say, in many cases they have unwittingly made a pact with the devil.

Then there are those who have developed a romantic attachment to the idea of their own suffering, like a captain going down with his ship, preferring this rather than the obvious pain required to rise above it. They prefer stories of struggle, pain and failure, as they draw comfort and reassurance from them. They do not like stories of struggle, pain and triumph as it threatens their cozy equilibrium. They are martyrs to themselves and do not seek to be healed. Instead they suck in the gullible to their little world of suffering, where they place themselves on a cross for others to worship. "Look at me. See how much pain I am in and yet see how loving I am!" Be careful you don't fall off!

Someone who genuinely suffers does not boast about it.

We all have secrets. The problem is we tend to forget them and, as each secret is compounded onto the next, we arrive at a state of confusion as we find ourselves full of contradictions, unable to apply the reasoning of our ego to the whole picture. It is as if the wires in our brain have become fused and melted into one glob. The good news is, once uncovered, it is surprising how easily this glob reforms into a simple, functional, coherent whole. The key to a riddle is usually something quite simple. Put two riddles into one and two simple answers become extraordinarily difficult to decipher. So too the mind which holds onto its secrets. We all have done things we are not proud of and may indeed do things in the future we will also be ashamed of. However, that is our path and our way to deepen our understanding and compassion for ourselves, for others, for life and ultimately for God.

In his wonderful book *The Alchemist* Paulo Coelho states, "Every search begins with beginner's luck. And every search ends with the victor being severely tested. The darkest hour of the night comes just before the dawn." He also says, "At a certain point in our lives, we lose control of what's happening to us and our lives become controlled by fate. That's the world's greatest lie."

I think the saddest part of turning our backs on ourselves is this: When we see horizons that others reach for and which we have turned away from, it fills us with pain as we remember what once was possible. We remember the greatness life has to offer and what we have thrown away in pursuit of things that, in the end, mean "very little." We also see how much of our lives we waste by all the little ego games that we play with others which are of no consequence in the end and simply blind us from the wonderful gifts life has to offer. In acknowledging these mistakes we reassert our soul and return to our path. We rediscover a new way to find our bliss. It is never too late.

In the end it is faith that counts and not creed. And faith is something the ego can never prove. It can only recognize the divine by its presence and the way it fills our being. In so doing, in an act of faith, we let go of the ego by the action of the heart and allow the divine to enter, opening a channel to a greater life. In the end the lion lies down with the lamb and together they exist harmoniously, each one playing its part. The choice is simple really: either we grow in the spirit or we die in the body.

There is only one thing we are called to do in this life and that is to be truly happy. Life is for living, nothing more, nothing less. Live it, love it and find your "way" to enjoy it.

The Eboga Process

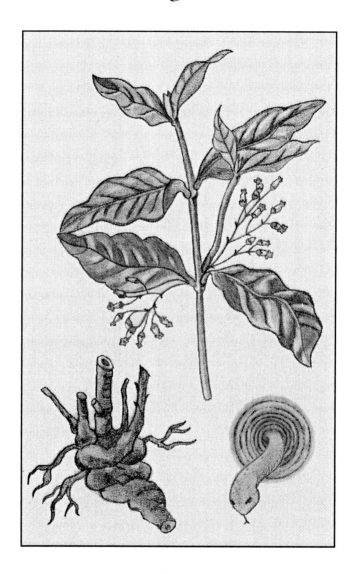

Tabernanthe iboga.
Root, Plant & Serpent.

Ibogaine is the principle alkaloid of the eboga root.
The Eboga spirit is carried by a serpent.

1. The Three Phases of "The Eboga Process"

If one part of your brain makes no sense,
You can at least try and develop the other.

1.1 The Soul Mind, The Ego Mind & The Emotional Body

To better understand the healing mechanism of Eboga we can think of the soul mind, the ego mind and the emotional body as forming what we consider our "whole" being, where our actual conscious awareness is made manifest in the Seat of the Mind (see below 1.3). I have developed this theory to help improve understanding of the Eboga Process. It is based on my own experiences. I will explain my theory in greater depth in the next book.

The ego mind can be thought of as a purely animal mind. It is what we normally take to be our conscious mind. I could not have written this book without it. It can manipulate our response to each event, i.e., it has a mental toolbox. The ego (mind) is an organic reality. When I refer to the ego I am referring to the ego mind. I call it a mind as it clearly operates from some part of our physical being. It does not exist in thin air. Also, it is important to note, it will never be perfect.

On the other hand the soul mind (the inner child) is the physical expression and manifestation of the soul – its temple. Like the ego mind, it too is an organic reality. The maturity of the soul, starting out as an animal spirit, is paralleled by the evolution of the species. (I will explain in detail why I believe this in the second book of this trilogy. It is based on visions I have had during one of my sessions.)

The purpose of the path then is to strengthen the soul and understand our relationship to God, to All, as a means to transcend the limitations of the earthly existence. When I refer to the soul I am referring to the soul mind, or the actual soul itself which can exist apart from the body. We undertake our path with the help of the ego which is our interface to the physical world and our interpreter of experiences.

Through free will we can choose to heal the soul mind (and thus the soul) or rely on the ego mind to sedate its pain, i.e., pervert the real purpose of the ego. When we heal, the soul is empowered, i.e., the power the darkness held over the soul is transformed and transferred to the power of the soul. Which leaves the emotional body.

The emotional body stores the emotional pain of what has happened to us and the years of pain it has caused. This is unavoidable as the emotional body is the source of great joy in the healed person. Thus it must also be the source of great pain in the unhealed person. I believe its center is close to the stomach, which is why eating, drinking and smoking can be used to offset the pain that is there.

"Cosmic Man" lives from the soul (mind) using the ego (mind) as an interface to the real world, as it is built for the purpose of interpreting physical reality and the many learned responses we need to know to live. It serves the same function in all animals. It is a teacher.

The emotional system manifests our joy.

1.2 Healing Is an Ordered Process

The primary objective of Eboga is the healing of the soul and the alignment of the ego to its wishes through self-awareness and reconditioning of the ego mind. That essentially is what the first phase of the Eboga session is about.

In the unhealed state the soul or spirit of the person is in a state of disturbance. A pure soul will be in harmony. A disturbed soul will not. This imbalance can be thought of as a form of possession. Thus in removing these demons the body experiences emotional trauma in the session as they resist removal – like parasites. This still leaves the affected ego mind and the affected emotional body. Both still affected by the original trauma. The original trauma is thus stored spiritually (its essence or spirit in the soul mind), psychologically (in the ego mind) and emotionally (in the emotional body).

In the second phase of the Eboga session we move to a period of intense mental activity. This is not the hallmark of the soul as the soul is the experience of essence. Hence we have moved to the healing of the ego mind. I suspect the instruction received in this stage is directly connected to the demons which have been eradicated in the first phase. Clearly in this phase the ego mind is being unraveled due to the endless storage of erroneous impressions, ideas etc resulting from the underlying problems. This phase can also be viewed as an "Ego Unwinding" as explained in the earlier chapter on Eboga, i.e., unresolved ego material is resolved. Any ego mind instruction in the first phase I therefore view as behavioral modification and awareness enhancement which in part rely on responses not associated with the second phase.

Of course we continue to exist through our ego mind, once the soul mind has been healed, but the ego mind needs to operate and adapt to its new foundations that reflect the new soul mind and which allow the soul mind more freedom to be. In time, through integration, the ego mind is restructured and the emotional system healed. In this way the session itself does not focus on emotional release specifically, as this is also handled through the integration process.

The period of integration can last for up to a year and beyond, whereby the ego changes in its choices through its new interaction with life based on its new mental and spiritual base, in conjunction with the freeing of the emotional body. All areas still need integration into the ego mind and emotional body, much as an infant discovers its surroundings for the first time. The emotional body also discharges related emotion during this time and can be an indicator of a persons preparedness for another session. Emotional release therapies can play a useful role during this integration period.

1.3 The Seat of the Mind

It seems to be that the actual crucible of consciousness is the "Seat of the Mind." This is where the sum total of our conscious awareness manifests. I have created this term to describe this phenomenon. In effect, a full session forces the ego (mind) out of the Seat of the Mind and allows the soul's experience to be by default. It is when the other is not. In doing so, the unhealed state the ego was keeping hidden and pacified, is exposed, as the soul does not hide its secrets, unlike the ego. In exposing the soul the essence of the trauma is revealed and Eboga links its release to the stored memories in the ego mind. However only those traumas one can deal with at the time, are revealed. Eboga controls and handles the energy of one's soul (mind) in an intelligent and protective way. With each session it goes deeper.

The Seat of the Mind is like a chamber within which our experiences are interpreted and transmitted to us via the interface of its walls. While it is occupied by the ego (mind) burdened by hidden pain and trauma, the awareness of our soul mind is practically wiped out as it demands virtual control of the Seat of the Mind. The soul still "acts" through intention.

The ego (mind) is like a program that is triggered each time there is a sense of discomfort or a need to analyze reality. In a wounded person, the ego is constantly caressing the wounds each time they are sensed, through a form of mental stroking. That is why we are unable to be in an ego less state, because we are afraid to feel the pain this mental stroking avoids. We do not want to lose touch with the wound as that would lead to a momentary panic as we search for it again. The ego knows the wound and what works to allay the pain. In the unhealed state spontaneity is almost impossible as we need the ego mind to maintain our equilibrium and also to prevent us from doing anything we might regret.

Unfortunately we are so used to relying on our ego it has become stuck in place and we are unable to drop it, as a child often does, to allow the soul to simply be. In effect we are addicted to the ego's ability to sedate our pain via way of thought and emotional manipulation. Hence with each gap in the ego's presence our awareness of pain emerges and thus the ego jumps right back in to allay this pain. In this way we do not know any other state other than the ego mind state and have lost almost complete touch with the childhood state. The soul can only be experienced properly in the healed person or the person whose ego is controlled by another force such as Eboga. Meditation in the unhealed state, in my own experience, is at best extremely difficult and perhaps is not the best use of one's time, as the ego is very determined and abnormally developed. Separating from it is horrendously difficult unless one is able to enter directly into one's heart. In the unhealed state one can focus on what I call, "Life Meditation" (reflection on life appropriate to the ego, one's intuition and one's healing). In the healed state we can move to what I call, "Soul Meditation" (reflection appropriate to the soul), and enter into the garden of the soul.

The ego enters the seat of the mind in an active way, the soul in a passive way: it is when the other is not. We cannot survive without the ego mind nor can we survive without the soul mind. This then leaves the third eye for paranormal reception.

Thus, healing is operating on two levels: the spiritual and the physical.

In time I will try to clarify these matters further as my understanding matures. No doubt my ideas will evolve and change. However I expect their essence will remain the same.

1.4 The Eboga Process & Session Phases

From this perspective we can describe the three phases of the actual (full) session as follows:

- Phase 1: **Unseating of Ego & Soul Exposure**
  Or Eradication of Demons
  & Behavioral Modification
  & Awareness Enhancement.
  i.e. "The Crucible of The Process."
  (Also, for Initiates – Regression or Submission).
- Phase 2: **Ego Cleansing or Reeducation**
  Or Period of "Massive Thinking"
  Or "Ego Unwinding."
- Phase 3: **Ego Release**
  Or The Coming Down,
  Or Period of Quiet Reflection and Recuperation.

In the first phase the person doesn't know what has hit him or her, as the true mind has been exposed and the ego has lost its ability to control it and thus, how a person feels – one feels the things one sought to avoid as a child through the development of the ego. The person has thus suffered a great shock due to the exposure of the soul (inner child) mind without the protective ego and so in phase 3 the ego apparatus is slowly restored into its mental position to play its important and central role in our lives.

For those who undergo the full initiation, the initiation commences in phase 1 once the person has undergone a regression to the childhood state of dependence. Events leading up to this point are designed to bring this about – one is reduced to the childlike state of mind through fear, desperation or any other method deemed suitable by the Eboga spirit, i.e., one gives up control of one's mind.

Here we can possibly see why psychotic breaks, i.e., where one is fixated in one mental state, usually preclude people from taking a session. Eboga (often) unseats the ego mind and as the person's usual coping mechanisms won't work, it may cause a possible psychotic break. Some apparently normal people may have a psychotic break much to their surprise. It is not necessarily a major problem. In this regard it is very common to be concerned about abnormal mental behavior as we all (from time to time) are concerned about the nature of our thoughts and feelings. This is more a symptom of stress (due to underlying problems) than it is of serious mental illness. It simply illustrates a need for some form of healing and is not a reason to turn away from Eboga. In fact quite the contrary.

In the first part of the session the therapist should also ensure the person does not fall asleep and perhaps reassure the person that this phase does not last indefinitely and that the physical experience is as expected, nothing more. It is probably worthwhile during the second phase of a session for a therapist to become more actively involved, as the possibility of going to sleep is more likely, due to exhaustion, than in the first phase, where the energy is much stronger. It may be important to encourage the person undergoing treatment to stay awake to learn the lessons being given to him or her while in this receptive state, prior to the full restoration of the ego mind, which has been disabled or unseated in the first part of the session.

If the person goes to sleep during the second phase the ego mind, I imagine, in some way closes down and the opportunity for reprogramming it is possibly lessened. However, the tendency to go to sleep is very strong, as the most physically demanding part of the session has been passed. Apart from helping the person to stay awake, the therapist should not interfere, as this is a very rapid inner process. Going to sleep in the third phase is part of the recovery process.

The session also has another phase not normally discussed:

Phase 4: 24-hour Pick-me-up: The first 24 hours following a session can be characterized by a 24-hour relaxation period where one feels just fine, as though one does not have a problem in the world. It's like a little present from the gods. However, this is not always the case and it certainly was not the case for me because I still felt pain after my initial session.

An holistic approach to the Eboga Process itself consists of three phases, of which the Eboga session is phase 2:

- Phase 1: Preparation Prior to a Session.
- Phase 2: Eboga Session.
- Phase 3: Period of Integration.

Phase 1: Preparation Prior to a Session.

Intention is very important, as is any actual work done to prepare oneself in the preceding days, weeks, months and years. An "Eboga Journal" should be kept, detailing dreams, thoughts and feelings. This centers the mind, preparing it for the work to be carried out in the session. It is also very important to continue this journal after the session. In fact it should become a lifelong means to focus and arrive at Selfhood. I have discussed the journal elsewhere and mention it again in the section on tips for a good session.

Phase 2: Eboga Session.

Phase 3: Ego Restructuring & Emotional Body release.

This is a period of time following a session and appears to have noticeable points at the three-, six- and nine-month stages and, to a lesser extent, with the ongoing passage of time. It is useful to think of healing as being limited by the necessity of the ego to change with time in tandem with changes in the emotional body, although the ego's basis has been altered within the session. The ego's self perception or awareness does not change instantaneously. It is a structure that has its own intelligence and does not change easily. It is very sensitive to the mental well-being of the person and requires special handling. It has until now defined our sense of self.

In particular, where deep issues exist in the emotional body, they require the passage of time to be eventually recognized as no longer a threat. They can then be released in one emotional manner or other. At the same time the ego resolves and frees itself from a role in which it has been overused causing it to become tied up tightly, frightened to change. In time, after a session, a gradual ego catharsis can occur or at times a sudden catharsis through the final release of fears (in the emotional body). This leads to a change of perception, which the ego is better able to cope with – the ego and soul foundations being healthier. Thus, the new reality being tested in day-to-day life slowly feeds itself into the ego's structure to bring about its change in accordance with its own laws. This is tied to changes in the emotional body. The ego will remain suspicious until the emotional body is properly healed.

Immediately after a session the ego, in many ways, expresses itself like before – as though it has a resident memory profile of how things should be. However, it is more malleable to change as it has been displaced and reeducated, but with time it can return to its rigid state as we begin to depend on it once more.

Some ego changes are almost instantaneous, many are not. An example of a sudden catharsis might be a dream which relives an old fear, but comes with the knowledge that the fear is not real. It is simply being relived, like a final notice of the exit of the fear. We should take notice of this, as dreams expose our true state of mind.

This is a completion of the chain of cause and effect that allows the ego to let go of that issue which before it was unable to do, as the fear was trapped in the emotional body. This is part of the period of integration or ego restructuring / reordering / reprogramming or, if you like, a mental simplification and reordering process which coincides with emotional body release.

1.5 The Process of Selfhood

The ultimate goal of the Eboga Process is self-actualization or self-realization, what I call Selfhood. When one overcomes one's prejudice to the presence of a spiritual world and the fact that as a whole person we are inextricably bound to it (as we are inextricably bound to the earth), one can then begin to complete the necessary process towards Selfhood.

In my own case, I seek to do this via what I have described and called the Eboga Process. Of course I imagine there are other ways. The universe is a creative phenomenon and so to be limited to one way would seem a little uncreative. What makes the Eboga Process so appealing is that it builds on existing perspectives in modern psychological thought and is therefore more accessible to the Western mind. I practice the Process from a Christian perspective (which includes the divine feminine), i.e., suffering as a way to soul growth leading to transcendence, as that is the tradition I come from. However I also employ any ideas which help to convey the idea of wholeness and unity in the spiritual and physical dimensions.

While Eboga leads relatively quickly to self-knowledge there is a huge difference between this and self-acceptance (or true self-awareness) which is an important step towards self-actualization. Self-acceptance (i.e., an integrated ego) takes time and is arrived at via adherence and faith in the Process which is working in tandem with events in the universe. Each moment of self-acceptance can be characterized by an opening of a door to the soul (mind) resulting in a powerful force entering, which can result in an unpleasant shock of self-awareness for the ego. This door is only closed when there is something we seek to avoid. Otherwise it is open. Hence the greater our self-acceptance, the greater will be our access to our soul (our true mind), resulting in an ego and soul which are in harmony, coexisting simultaneously. This comes about by the ego choosing not to block out something that it perceived as too threatening before, i.e., it allows the truth to be known within full ego awareness leading to ego acceptance arriving at what is called the tamed ego or the non-interfering ego. In this state the soul can properly manifest alongside the ego.

It is quite possible that once the ego mind is completely healed and no longer threatened by what lies in the soul mind, the cumulative essence of the soul's experience can emerge in a synergistic whole leading to what can be described as a true awakening or enlightenment. This would be in line with a complete opening of the heart and an awareness of the More.

The major stumbling block to self-actualization as I see it, is the unwillingness to face oneself and ones problems. From the onset of puberty the individual relies more and more on his ego. If the individual has outstanding problems from childhood, then the growth of the ego can become overbearing. However, the development of the ego is very important as the ego is a teacher and teaches us among other things how to coexist in human society at large. We could not manage as a species without it. Therefore, the ideal aim for good ego development is to heal oneself by the power and intention of the soul so that ultimately a tamed ego emerges, driven by the wishes of the soul (inner child) with which it coexists. It is a circle: first we have the child (soul), then we have the ego development and then we return to the child (soul) with a tamed and developed ego present. Once we arrive at this state of balance, we can then enjoy the wonderful gift that life is, as a happy child does, but with the expanded possibilities of the adult.

Those who turn their backs on healing rely instead on the ego, resulting in behavior more characteristic of the desperate animal state from which we derive, which leads to a hunger for power and a greed for material possession. The more one enters this way of being the more one's view of life is limited by the purely material and talk of the divine seems absurd as it is only the soul that can sense and appreciate what that is. Our challenge as the primary and chosen species on this planet, is to recognize our special divinity and create a harmony between our ego-body and our soul, i.e., to transcend the limitations of the ordinary animal. You could say that the human soul is an animal spirit that has been chosen to become a sentient being within the universe – see next book. The soul grows via the path it undertakes. The body is the temple or carrier of that being.

Unfortunately, or perhaps fortunately, our society is making this development more and more difficult as the ways of the ego are allowed to drive people's life experiences more and more and thus it is harder to balance the ego with the soul. However, there is a positive side to all this, as it ultimately leads to dissatisfaction and a crisis of self which can precipitate an ego meltdown and an emergence of Selfhood. Some call this a "Spiritual Emergency." As it is caused by an overdeveloped ego, it can perhaps lead to a more highly developed sense of self. Perhaps the present difficulties in modern life reflect how advanced the human soul is becoming and that a new dawn is fast approaching.

The key to ultimate success towards Selfhood lies in holding onto what you truly valued in yourself as a child, as that is the essence of who you are in your soul. It is this essence that drives the process toward Selfhood. In other words, as Joseph Campbell says, "Follow Your Bliss."

2. Thoughts on my Process

When you know how little you know,
It is then that you know a lot.

2.1 The Session Itself

The Eboga session itself lasted for 36 hours, which is the normal length of time. The first part prior to the period of intellectual evaluation or "massive thinking" lasted approximately seven or eight hours. Time was very deceptive as I was initially intensely aware of what I was going through and the first few hours seemed an age. Then it seems this awareness of time dropped away and suddenly I arrived at hour five or six. Earlier I had serious doubts I could survive for 36 hours. It seemed very, very daunting. How can I last this long, I thought? I knew, but didn't realize, that this first part lasted for about eight hours and it would have been comforting to be reminded of this at the time, as I somewhat panicked I might not be able to keep up or my heart would not be strong enough to last. I felt as if I was hanging on for dear life, as though on a roller coaster ride.

During the period of mental evaluation, I was mentally exhausted. I fell asleep at some point in this phase and woke up in what can be described as the third or final part of the session where I remained with my own thoughts. I felt I had somehow missed out on part of my Process. In this part I still felt under the influence of Eboga. A mild form of light stayed with me and seemed to permeate my senses. It surrounded me. Suddenly, after 36 hours, it was as if someone slowly switched off the power and I just returned to my normal state.

It seemed to me that the session dealt with the major soul charges surrounding my childhood traumas. It was as if the session was a major soul catharsis that happened so quickly and suddenly I did not have the power to resist it. The suddenness of the experience was the perfect opportunity to reach down deeply into my inner being and take out whatever cancer was living there.

It felt as though the psychological backlog on my life was being downloaded in one massive inner encounter. I was wafted along as though in a slipstream. Whenever I tried to hold on, the force of the flow would pull me away and back into the stream, i.e., I was forced to leave an issue and move on. I saw things I would simply never have considered in my own psychological enquiry and indeed would have rejected were another to suggest them to me. How then could traditional psychotherapy have worked for me? Suddenly I knew how much I didn't know and the years of confusion and self-argument and counter-argument began to dissipate into a knowing whole. I also realized with a shock how in our eagerness to find an explanation for our problems, in collusion with our therapist, we often create explanations which are at best only partly true and at worst downright misleading, leading to a reactionary relationship to life and those around us. We remain blind to the real source of our problems which, when uncovered, always comes with a sense of understanding and simplicity.

I now realize that to undergo the same experience twice is highly unlikely as it is the element of surprise that makes it work, as the ego is a very adaptable animal. Much like the first time one undergoes therapy for an injury. Subsequent treatments may not go as deep, as it is much too painful. However everyone is different and it is possible that a series of mini-sessions could act us a buildup to a major session. (Such an approach has certain intrinsic advantages.) This is an area I am still considering. Of course everything depends on a person's needs. For me it would still take much more work to complete the healing process and that could not be handled in the same way. However, in one sense the hardest part was over. In another it had only begun. But the worst was yet to be revealed and I later wondered if the malignant power of it had not already been removed during this session, also unknown to myself, as I had experienced very powerful forces of what I can only describe as "exorcism." My subsequent sessions took on a completely different character and feel.

Instinctively I had chosen a session with the sense of the child. I could have chosen something else. In that sense I created my own reality as we all do every day, often leading to living in a dark, illusionary world. The world is like celestial putty waiting for us to mould it in our likeness. Believe in a world of doom and gloom and you will find it! I genuinely felt during the session that I was in a very holy place and so it is good to acknowledge and respect that.

I was given many tasks to complete, which were in the opposite direction to where I was currently taking my life. Would I be able to complete these? It was as if my soul had been released and now I had its agenda to attend to along with my ego's. A struggle was certainly about to ensue. For now I was not going to make any immediate change. I needed time to grasp what was going on and, being in the grip of my own fears, I felt I needed to carry on with my plans. Time would see. For now, my ego wanted to maintain control of my life as it up 'til now had maintained control of my fears. Somehow I knew I would turn this juggernaut of my life round, but not right now. I knew that I (my soul) sought happiness and would in the end do whatever it took to arrive there: ultimately I (the ego) would not stand in "my" (the soul's) way. One of the odd things I was told to do was to return to Greece by plane. Karl even went as far as to make inquiries. I didn't really understand why. For a moment I thought maybe there might be an accident with the ship. On reflection I believe it was a hint to start looking after myself better and not to keep putting myself through needless strain. However, I didn't fly back. I took the ship as I was not yet prepared to do everything I was told to do. In this case to spend a lot of money on a plane ticket I felt I didn't need.

Occasionally during the session, I became distracted and forgot what it was I was working on. I would say to myself, *Okay, I've got to remember now*, and then I would get the memory back like one gets back an elusive dream one is trying to remember. I chased after each of the issues. I didn't want them to get away. In that sense perhaps there is a certain amount of effort required in a session in the form of intention to confront and become aware of certain things, things you might otherwise choose to ignore. Perhaps the force of intention keeps us connected to the issue and aids the Eboga energy in keeping the ego de-empowered.

This session taught me to trust the Process and to realize my own limitations. Whenever I tried to pursue something that was too deep for me to uncover I started to throw up. The ibogaine would go into reaction if I stepped too far where I should not go for now. It had a strong sense of being regulated. Thus, while it was very powerful, it seems to me it was very safe. Nothing was happening that I could not deal with in one way or another. In one particular case, after trying to force open an issue, when it was actually time for me to let go, I started throwing up and saw clouds of white smoke leaving my mouth. I actually thought I was seeing the powder of ibogaine leave me. I later asked Karl if he had seen the white smoke and he said no. I thought it was visible in the real world. It was as if the ibogaine was being kicked out of me by the strength of what I was trying to uncover, acting in its own self-defense. It was as if it was being forced out by the darkness of what was being exposed. In that sense Eboga is limited by the depth of the disease that it seeks to uncover and thus heals little by little through subsequent sessions and the integration that takes place in between. It is not that Eboga does not want to uncover and heal the deepest ills. It is that regardless of the amount of ibogaine we take, Eboga is still limited by the depth of the disease as to what can be achieved in a given session. There is a limit to what one can take in one session. Yes, dosage is important and this session would not have worked in the way it did on a low dosage, but it does not follow that the more we take the more we can heal in a given session. In fact, to get carried away with the dosage is abusive.

What we can take away from this is that if we try to force an issue we are not ready for the ibogaine in the bloodstream seems to regress out of the blood and we have an urge to throw up, i.e., it takes away its power from us. There is a balance. The more we push, the more it regresses. There are some things it chooses not to do directly and that is where time and synchronistic coincidence play their part as we move into the situations that allow us to explore, open and remold our emotional storehouse. In this way we have a period of relearning and integration on a normal human level. The first major session appears to pave the way for this. However, there is no way to predict how a session will work out. Each person is different and has different needs. Others have had a similar session to mine. Many have not. The type of session one has is not necessarily a judgment on the character of the person. It is most likely a reflection of one's needs in that moment.

As I write this now, some five years later, I cannot help but feel that the Eboga entities I was dealing with are the souls of "transcended" people who carry out different tasks such as assisting other souls to make the same journey that they have made in this time-honored tradition.

I was shown many things that I would not have thought about. And this is a very important point. Often in traditional psychotherapy we can become prejudiced as to what the source of our problems is and remain blind to the real source. Indeed, we may correctly identify problem areas but these could be just spin-offs from the real problem area. We then become lost in the spin-off, which perhaps we can unravel, but what is the use of that if the underlying problem remains unresolved?

I learned many lessons during this process. The most valuable I learned was the sense of being related to people while at the same time being true to myself. That fundamentally is what initiation to adulthood is: a process of communion with the group while maintaining one's identity. However, it takes time after a session, especially one of this magnitude, to fall in line with what has been taught (i.e., to allow your soul room in your life and to start realigning to it) and to fully benefit from the healings gained through their full integration into the body and mind, which thus leads to a greater presence of your soul in your body. Initially after the session, I did not apply what I learned here. Eventually I realized, as my soul presence grew and I felt in conflict with it, that I had no choice if I truly wanted to find happiness. And happiness is what I was seeking!

For an overview of what an initiation ceremony is like within the Bwiti, please see appendix 1: Bwiti Initiation Rituals.

2.2 Man's Progression

From this experience it becomes apparent to me that man progressed in part due to the ingestion of various plants that he encountered on his journeys. The early groups of man lived with turmoil and pain and these plants were a respite from that pain and in the case of eboga, a way to heal that pain and make sense of existence. It is therefore not surprising that Eboga spirituality is linked to the ancestors. In this sense it's amazing how much our forefathers have done for us and how arrogantly we abuse this planet and dismiss our elderly. The reason, of course, for doing this is that we prefer the "easy" way of the ego rather than the way of the soul. The ego, however, is blamed for a lot when in fact it is simply fulfilling a very important animal role that becomes hijacked when we refuse to take our path.

Other plants, I believe, also helped to enhance the development of the human form as well as perhaps offer a respite from the hardships of everyday life. Early man would have placed great value on these plants and over time would therefore have sought to discover more.

In this day and age, we have lost our roots in a past filled with the customary ingestion of various plants and the widespread use of mythology and symbolism. We are as a species very much poorer for that. We deny ourselves a rich storehouse of knowledge and access to spiritual realms based on the ego mentality that everything must be put in front of the scientist or made by the scientist. Only our scientists can be trusted to produce what is good for us, regardless of the profit motive involved. Unfortunately, science cannot prove that which is outside its scope and so we checkmate ourselves on the path to personal growth and consciousness.

Because of certain drugs which are a source of self-abuse, we have a largely reactionary and misinformed response to all drugs. We are hindering our consciousness growth in our ignorance. It is like living in a small bubble inside a huge balloon which we never see into. It does seem to me that there is a treasure trove of hidden powers within our psyche and our forests, which together can herald a new era for man, where possibly all man's physical and emotional needs can be satisfied without producing any of the toxic side effects associated with modern drug therapy.

However man's emotional needs will never be met while he maintains an attitude of use and abuse. "Primitive" man already knows this. These powers exist at the level of the soul, the child. If we put our energy into pursuing these possibilities instead of creating costly commercial pharmaceuticals, maybe we would achieve a lot more for a lot less. Unfortunately the amounts of pharmaceuticals we ingest, which poison our body, seem to suggest that our drug policies are based on the maxim: if it pollutes the body it is okay, but if it opens the mind it is not. Pharmaceuticals have their place but to my mind they are, in part, a form of legalized drug pushing and drug abuse.

Why then do we not put our huge resources into understanding what we already have instead of trying to create poor substitutes? If Creation gave us something as wonderful as this Earth, could it not have given us many more wonderful things? The answer of course is simple. You cannot patent and charge for something which exists naturally in nature. Not only do we cut ourselves off from our spiritual advancement by doing this, we also destroy untold precious gifts waiting to be tapped, gifts which have been handed down to us from time immemorial by the Divine.

Obviously not all drugs are bad, particularly those derived from natural sources, which have been shown to have spiritual properties without physical drawbacks. Penicillin cannot be described as bad. In the same way ibogaine *is not a recreational drug* nor is it bad and by definition cannot be addictive as it is a force that is working in harmony with our own best interests. It heals us and the more healed we are, the less addicted we become. It also makes us realize how vulnerable we are, as it is through our vulnerability and "exposure" that we are healed.

While we readily accept the use of medicinal plants for physical healing we are blocked in their acceptance for mental and spiritual health. It seems that we have placed a taboo around plants that can heal the mind. When did this happen? Clearly shamans in traditional societies do not act to destroy mental health with their use of traditional plants for psychological and spiritual problems – problems which they recognize as being interconnected. Why would nature choose to provide natural healing for the physical and not also provide it for the mental and spiritual? Obviously man is intrinsically bound to nature. Surely a natural mind is a mind in harmony with nature and what it provides to heal us on all levels?

It does seem that we are deeply ignorant of nature's goodness because the truth is: we are deeply ignorant of nature.

2.3 A Pact with the Devil

In the next book I will attempt to explore in depth the nature and function of the ego and how it relates to the Self. What I can say now is this: many people's egos are scared shitless. Because of this, they place incredible strain on the ego (mind) as it seeks new and more devious ways to avoid the whole system of the ego, body and soul, a Holy Trinity which needs to be in total harmony in order to arrive at a state of self-awareness and fulfillment, to become what I call "Cosmic Man."

This strain is self-evident in forgetfulness and general ill ease in the body. It leads to premature aging and, eventually, a dull listlessness. It manifests in depression, mental disturbance, erratic behavior and personal inner death. Those who hold on in this way by clinging to daft beliefs are doing themselves a great disservice and are inflicting great pain on those around them. Of course they are scared. We are all scared of the dark, but when we befriend it, we draw on its strength. The darkness is the way to the light: not by imitating it, but by acknowledging it and passing through the fear it poses for us.

Many people in their perversity seek to imitate the darkness and many in their perversity do so because they believe life is an illusion and thus should not be taken seriously. Without realizing it many of us have made a pact with the devil by pinning all our hopes on the overburdened ego and resisting any influence that will bring us into direct contact with our souls and of course our unhealed state, our path to God.

3. The Eboga Process – Considerations

The way back is the best way forward.

While there is clearly much to explore, my present focus is on the mechanism and meaning of the healing process.

3.1 What Do You Seek?

Those who come to Eboga simply because they have been pushed into it, but do not have any real interest or desire for change, or people who live a life full of avoidance and distraction without serious intent for change, will quite possibly experience very little. The most important tool on the path to freedom is a positive mental attitude as it aligns you to the light and away from the dark. One of the major stumbling blocks is unquestioned, unexamined, built-in prejudice from childhood. Unlike animals, humans are born without all their basic instincts fixed. I refer to these from time to time as IRMs, Initial Response Mechanisms (see Joseph Campbell), i.e., in the formation of a child up to a certain age they make many mental associations such as other religions are wrong, other nationalities are bad, other religions are good, life is meant to be tough, I am worthless, God is a controlling God, God is a loving God, certain foods stink, etc. They are hard-wired into the brain in a similar way as basic human instincts at birth are already hard-wired. Hence why so much prejudice is virtually impossible to overcome in the mind of someone unwilling to look and question. Much of our scripture teaching is based on a punitive understanding of God and not a realization that real spirituality is a freeing and liberation of the soul, a return to the spontaneity of the child, a realization that a relationship to God is one of independence, interdependence and self-understanding. It takes a determined soul to overcome these prejudices. Many are afraid to look inside their own program as they over-identify with the program, the ego. But the good news is these prejudices can be overcome and altered through deep healing. Too many fail to seek healing or succeed in healing because they harbor many negative views they are unwilling to challenge, as it is too close to the bone for them and, thus, too scary. They simply lack the imagination to dream as they have already fixed into their minds the whole circumference of their world.

So, the mentality of a person undergoing treatment is very important. Often addicts do not give a rat's ass for a spiritual experience. They are in pain and simply want help to kick their habit, naturally enough! Many later relapse, as they are unwilling to do the personal work necessary to effect change and thus the pain returns. It would be fair to say that follow-up treatments for addicts, where underlying issues are confronted, are pretty much mandatory for an eventual cure. Therapy may not be enough without sufficient inner connection. In that sense, to my mind, therapy works once the issues have been uncovered. The uncovering is the hard part and, in my experience, often fails in the normal therapeutic context. For this further Eboga sessions can be very beneficial.

In preparing for a session it is very important to know what you seek and, to this end, making a list of every issue in your life you have a concern about is very helpful. This can also be part of what I describe as an "Eboga Journal," which helps to focus the mind and should begin immediately. Many of the issues will dissolve into one common issue or may be resolved within a session to one common source. To begin with, though, make your list freely. Over a period of days, reconsider it and put it into some kind of order. Don't worry if your list is very long. Although it is better to focus on a few detailed areas. However, I made a list of 100 items before my last session in Brazil, recounted in my next book. Now my lists are usually a few items under one heading, e.g., Sexuality and Woman. I do however add any questions I might have. You may be surprised how much of the list emerges in your session. I certainly was. There are other considerations for the preparation of a drug addict. In this respect I recommend Web sites which deal in more detail with drug addiction, in particular *www.ibogaine.org.*

Generally speaking, a drug user is advised to reduce the number of drugs used, in an effort to be on the verge of withdrawal by the time the session begins. Once the session has begun the eboga takes over and the withdrawal symptoms are significantly, if not completely, reduced.

Eboga is an energy that needs to connect with the person's own energy and willingness to learn and change. In that sense it is a teacher plant as well as a healing plant. Intention is everything. Think of Eboga as an engine for soul change seeking to restore as many souls as it is able to, i.e., help is out there waiting for those who ask! Little by little the engine can move forward once the cog or soul of the person is engaged. However, at first it can only make small movements using the cog of the person, as the person's cog will disappear due to it being overwhelmed, tired out, or simply unwilling to work due to the weight of its illness or its basic lack of intention. However, the engine will remain, waiting to click into gear, sometimes going into neutral as it observes the need of the person to catch his or her breath. With time, as the person gets stronger, it can work more deeply. Eboga will not miss a beat to help that person in any way open to it, but it also needs the person to connect to it and this one does through intention. Intention is everything. Everyone benefits to some degree, but that does not guarantee arriving at a stage of completion unless persistence and hard work are applied.

There is a lot of fear around the taking of eboga and the experiences that follow. In my own experience the presence of fear towards the taking of eboga with regard to the inner revelations that may unfold, is in itself a strong indicator that there is unresolved fear in the person and therefore is a good indicator of the need for self-confrontation and healing if what one seeks is wholeness in oneself.

3.2 Set & Setting

Many Eboga sessions are held in clinic settings, which vastly increases the costs involved. No real case has been made for the absolute need to conduct Eboga sessions in a hospital environment if proper precautions are taken. If anything such an environment would tend to create an almost sterile and anti-spiritual atmosphere. In the few cases where death has occurred, the client appeared to either fall outside the guidelines on the basis of a health check, in particular an ECG heart test or else acted inappropriately during the session, such as taking heroin, which is amplified by the effects of ibogaine, leading to a drug overdose. In any case a doctor should always be on call if problems arise. "The main concern should be to attend to the client in case he or she should vomit and is unable to move, as ibogaine usually restricts movement." Also it is important to remain still, as movement induces vomiting. Pulse and blood pressure are also important indicators to watch.

As with all inner voyages, set and setting are important. The presence of a reassuring but non-interfering person in a room that has a sense of comfort and quietness is very helpful. I have found, particularly for a mini-session, that looking at colorful, integrative images moving and transforming (such as the kind which come with music software on the Macintosh, for example) combined with gentle, spiritual music or even a CD of the sounds of the rainforest is a good way to wait for the onset of the eboga as it calms the mind and helps bring the two halves of the brain together. These kinds of considerations do not really exist in a hospital session and it seems absurd that the absence of hospital facilities should bar many poor people who could benefit from its use.

3.3 Following Treatment

Following treatment, the help of an open-minded, trustworthy friend to share one's experiences and to talk about what one has undergone, is very worthwhile and indeed, very important. There is a period of time after a session when one is able to alter one's behavior pattern, i.e., put into practice some of what one has learned. Our brains appear to be more "pliable" in this stage, i.e., less dominated by the ego and more open to the soul. It is as though one can feel the link to a better way of existing and the awareness that goes with it and the lie in the way we have existed. After a period of time the normal weight of our other problems becomes a disincentive to holding onto this awareness and so it is more difficult to apply the lessons as the link becomes forgotten or ignored. Also, the ego becomes nestled into its usual position. It is therefore worth making an effort for change during this early time period.

3.4 Eboga & Therapy

Often we come to therapy as a result of the confusion we feel towards events in our life. We don't understand why we react the way we do. Effectively we are in a state of denial and thus we try to control our personal world to avoid that which troubles us. However sometimes even the smallest thing upsets us and as we cannot link it to anything specific we tend to place the fault on those nearest to us. This is because the pain is so great and our need for relief very pressing. We imagine there can be no other explanation as we are unaware of the true source of our problems. This is a combination of denial and projection, which adversely affects those around us. In this state it is not uncommon to have suicidal feelings as this way of dealing with personal feelings simply does not work and can lead to moments of complete desperation as we have closed ourselves off from relationship out of anger and hurt. It is quite natural to harbor a lot of self hatred for our behavior. And that's the sad part because in truth the fact that we are looking for the cause often implies we are someone of a high order with a wonderful but broken heart. We have a duty to resolve these problems for our own good and the good of all.

In my experience the most genuine form of therapy around these days is Transpersonal Therapy, also known as Holotropic Breathwork or Rebirthing, combined with various other modalities such as Sand Play, Myth, Dance, Dream Work and Emotional Release Work, typified by the Primal Therapy approach. These therapies explore our inner world and allow us to express hidden emotions. I am sure there are other equally valid forms of therapy available which I have not encountered, but in my own personal experience I find Breathwork to be an effective way to open a person up and the Primal Therapy approach a valid way to deal with those feelings. Don't be surprised if once you begin a therapy, such as Holotropic Breathwork, events in your life take a turn for the worse. This is because once you begin to access the soul by undermining the ego, life does what it can to help the process, i.e., events unfold to further undermine the ego so as to expose the underlying unhealed state in order that it can be accessed for healing. You might call this "The Dark Night of The Soul," which so many seem to experience prior to effective healing.

A surprising aspect of Eboga is how many of the issues we access and consider healed through Eboga return shortly, as though to emphasize their meaning and to drive home the lesson to be learned. We may believe we have learned something in a session. Yet we still encounter it some months later, i.e., we are somehow made conscious of the issue again. However this time with a new, cleaner soul and mind reality, the ego can adopt new and better ways to deal with the situation – ego restructuring. Intention, again, is very important, as intention directs the ego in these new choices, i.e., it allows the soul to be heard and to influence the ego via a window of opportunity where the ego is malleable to change. Without intention, it can choose to hold onto the old ways. In that sense, the period of integration can be called "ego restructuring." It is not necessarily a walk in the park!

A period of integration following a session is very important and appears to work in stages. However, there is no reason why someone cannot have a subsequent session if there are pressing issues to be dealt with, leading to an overlap in the period of integration as well as progressing the integration; much like a toe can be fixed while a finger is mending – although as mentioned elsewhere there is a natural limit to the number of sessions one can effectively undergo within a given time period. The use of conventional counseling or the company of trusted friends can be very helpful during this period of integration to examine and understand the experiences better. Part of the process of integration is helped by the use of imagination or creative visualization whereby one imagines and senses a new way to approach an old issue: a path of least resistance. By visualizing another way, which is in harmony with the sense your newly discovered soul gives you, it helps to bring it into being, i.e., you begin to build a part of the mind which up till now has remained undeveloped. It is not about reusing the old but about discovering the new and for that Eboga opens the door to the untapped potential lying dormant within. Eboga is a tool for self-creation.

A lot, of course, depends on the person. Also, a point may arrive in this sharing with others that the negative and ego-orientated attitudes of others are closed to the full benefits of the experience.

In this case a certain amount of self-analysis and self-reliance may be called for in order to progress past an impasse which others may see as simply a normal fact of life, but which in fact is an impasse created by our ego- or materially-oriented society. I believe a pure heart, similar perhaps to Parcival in the myth of the Holy Grail, has the greatest chance of success and talk of loss of material advantage is simply the talk of a brainwashed society that does not understand the ways of the soul or the spiritual laws of abundance. Basically you know when something rings true. Needless to say the length of healing is clearly different for everyone.

It seems that what we learn from Eboga is how to see the situation with new eyes and thus alter our relationship to it on an everyday level, i.e., the healing and learning process proceeds on many levels. For example, one may be naïve in how one accepts a certain kind of person, allowing the person to take advantage of you. In a session you may be made aware of this and reeducated. Yet months later one can walk into the same situation again and wonder how did that happen? However, this time at a very conscious level one wakes up to one's behavior, one learns to be wise and to adapt new and more wholesome ways of handling the situation, i.e., the relearning process is not over just because you were educated in an Eboga session. It is as if, in a session, the ego is opened for relearning as though it somehow is tied into the very fabric of one's emotional system and needs to be reeducated at all levels. Full integration appears to require a rerun of the situation later for the benefit of your normal ego mentality. It works best with an attitude that you have no wish to be in conflict with life or those around you. At the same time you seek to express yourself. Don't stop the flow, but don't seek to inflict damage. Sometimes it is best to lose the battle but win the war. It is surprising how many pious beliefs are challenged and debunked during this period: beliefs that contribute to our own well-meaning but at the same time personally dangerous naïveté. The elimination of these forms part of the elimination of the psychological toxins in our body.

An interesting aspect of the integration period is when one finally accepts the futility of an old behavior pattern designed to fulfill a broken need. In such a moment there is a sense of defeat, acceptance and openness to something new. This is in part an ego death and is also in part a release of the soul, which then uncovers a new part of oneself dormant and waiting to come to life. As it does the ego is reorganized and reformed on a new holistic and reduced level to properly meet ones changed needs. The ego is therefore a vessel to support the new way and is in effect a simplified and tamed ego. One could say that more of the soul mind has been engaged, replacing the part of the ego mind that has been disengaged.

In that sense there is a benefit in counseling following an Eboga session to help see the processes and the dynamics of the processes as they occur. When we encounter personal problems after a session, it is not that some blame does not rest elsewhere, but that we walked into a situation we should have known better to avoid. Fools rush in where angels fear to tread! However, there was a reason for allowing the situation to manifest and so eventually we have to acknowledge the true feelings behind our actions. The Eboga work normally should have revealed this. It marks the turning point to the integration of an original problem. The turning point in the healing of a serious trauma can also be preceded by days of intense self-hate and anger as the full effect of the trauma emerges. Thus, counseling can be advised to assist in this overall process.

This process can take months before one realizes what is going on and what one's true feelings are. It may also take time before the hurt that emanates is integrated. This can lead to a temporary rift in some relationships while one comes to terms with the situation. Further "mini" sessions can be very beneficial to the Process.

A stumbling block to the Process is when our ego, feeling bruised, wants revenge. This is characteristic of low self-esteem, as high self-esteem realizes the bruising of the ego is not due to the present situation, but to a past situation and thus the associated hurt will only go away when the past situation is fully healed and not by engaging in present-day brawls. High self-esteem values the importance of not hurting the innocent. Also, high self-esteem realizes that who we are is a soul in an ego-containing human body and not simply an ego in a soulless body. We judge ourselves by the state of our soul and not the state of our ego. Knowing this, it is easier to let go of the present problem that is triggering a past hurt and return to a contented state.

Sometimes this is almost impossible to do without the help of further mini-sessions, as further pain needs healing and further facts about oneself need facing. This is hard to do, as each fact brings with it the very feelings of low self-esteem we seek to avoid. However, by adopting practices of awareness we quicken the healing process, as we are minimizing the creation of new debris and instead are channeling our energy towards wholeness. Wholeness in return channels itself towards us.

To be able to trust oneself means not to undermine oneself and not to jeopardize what one is doing. In order to obtain this state of being, I believe one must heal any self-hatred that exists and realize one's self and one's part in this life. Then self-respect is a natural thing, as low self-esteem ceases to be a problem. The inner nugget of vengeance and hatred is melted away and ceases to sabotage one actions at the very moment one is close to something good and beautiful.

There is a difference between counseling and the emotional release therapies I have spoken about. The former helps in understanding what is going on and learning new ways and choices while the latter helps in dealing with residual emotional material resulting from the Eboga healing, leading to emotional release, relief and better clarity. During the period of integration these are useful tools. However by themselves, I am afraid that on balance neither is much good at uncovering the deep truth other than to create a mud map to work from. However, reprogramming the ego to a better way of behaving can expose some of the causes underneath and in this respect it is a useful therapeutic tool, i.e., in Primal Therapy terms: we stop acting out, feel the feelings and have the insights. These feelings make the work of Eboga easier.

I am left with the unshakeable belief that a deep spiritual healing experience is needed to bring about fundamental change in a person and so, while books which offer advice on how to live are well-intentioned, they can do little if the underlying forces are held firmly in place by trauma. Just like the alcoholic or the drug addict who does everything to recover while the underlying causes keep recurring. Like a sleeping snake disturbed they can suddenly bite when least expected. This I see as the main problem with treatment programs. The addict must constantly be on guard against the thing he is addicted to. To forget is to leave the door open to being taken by surprise. That is not a healed state. That is a prison sentence. Hence, a cure for drug addiction or alcoholism should bring the person to a state where he no longer needs or desires these drugs – not where he has them under control!

Finally, trauma can have a hidden function that is overlooked: it puts us into an altered state of mind. From this altered state we lose touch with consensus reality and, if you like, we open a door to another world, a world where our soul can guide us on our path. Much of what happens in this altered state is possibly part of the path and it is in a sense a world of illusion. However, in finding our way ultimately out of this world of illusion and darkness, we engage and empower our soul to rise above it, we progress along our path as we have overcome and integrated the darkness. In this way our soul grows so that the darkness holds no power over it.

3.5 How Many Sessions?

The beauty of Eboga is that you only remember what is appropriate at the time, so that the healing process is gradual and in the proper order necessary to ultimately heal the person. Like building a house, different areas are dealt with when the time is appropriate and the gradual strengthening of the person over time is used to reach the deepest areas ultimately. From the point of view of drug addiction rehabilitation, the first session can give the opportunity to start again, as it removes the craving for the drug and the physical addiction while at the same time healing some of the root causes. However, the learned patterns of the addicted state have to go, as do the underlying causes that brought them about.

As far as psychological rehabilitation goes, there needs to be more than one session to do justice to the needs of a person's psychological process. To try to push a person through on a single session is naïve and a little bit harsh, insensitive. Also, as came out in my own first session, there were things I was not ready to deal with, which indicated that the healing process required time and patience to allow the psyche to recover and repair organically as well as spiritually, thus strengthening it to undertake the deeper work.

Initially one can undergo a number of full sessions but there comes a point where they are no longer advisable and a serious of small or mini-sessions are in order. Basically, like a person recovering from multiple wounds, a major operation can quite possibly reopen the wounds unnecessarily. A mini-session however, under the right circumstances, can act to advise the person in their integration, alleviate certain sticking points in the integration process and also alleviate pain, i.e., the dosage acts in different ways. For example in a mini-session one can be given insight into another individual that allows you to let go of any age old prejudice and move past a major emotional stumbling block. This is entirely different to confronting the hurt and pain which that person may have caused you. The actual timetable for mini-sessions varies depending on the individual. Like a car engine that needs to be overhauled, some parts move swiftly, others very slowly. Hence, mini-sessions can occur frequently or infrequently depending on the nature of the problem.

There are two levels of healing: the soul is one level while the physical, emotional body is another. The physical, emotional body requires more time, as it is linked to our ego, which can find it very difficult to accept the truth and to change. So while the soul may have found healing or renewal in the first session, the organic body may require more time to strengthen before it can accept and integrate the full truth and in time alter its ego.

There may be a temptation to undergo numerous mini-sessions and this is where we see the anti-addictive nature of Eboga emerge. If sufficient underlying issues have been exposed, the emotional system can become overwhelmed by the amount of residual emotion to be integrated. This then leads to sessions where practically nothing occurs as one is simply too tender to absorb any further and undergoing a session is a reminder of that. This is the cut off point in the Eboga experience. It is the point where one realizes that the purpose of Eboga is not eboga itself. However, where a person is in serious emotional pain due to the previous release of deep issues, Eboga can be advised as a mini-session to relieve the pain.

3.6 The Best Way to Take Eboga?

In the time following the events described in this book I was to have many more experiences, each one solidifying my knowledge and dispelling any misconceptions I may have had. I was to take ibogaine in various different ways: namely dissolved in warm water, dissolved in warm water mixed with honey, in capsule form and, finally, anally. I also was to take eboga in both forms available, namely ibogaine itself and secondly as an extract of the plant purportedly containing all the alkaloids present, called the Indra Extract. I was to take both in varying concentrations and once as a mixture. The first time I took ibogaine dissolved in warm water – it does not dissolve very well – I was disgusted by its foul taste. The next time I took it mixed with honey followed by chewing on sweet gum to clear the taste from my mouth. The third time I took it in capsule form and I found that for a full session (high dose) this method was the least effective. I think the main problem with capsules is they contain too much, i.e., once the capsule dissolves the ibogaine is deposited in one lump, as it does not dissolve easily. Given that one is likely to feel sick at some point in a session, particularly if one encounters a sickening experience, which abuse is, any lumps of non-dissolved ibogaine aggravate the experience and are thrown up. It can remain as a lump for some hours. I imagine a sudden movement with a lump of non-dissolved ibogaine can have a sickening effect.

For a small-dose session or when a large quantity is not required, capsules are excellent but they should never, in my opinion, be packed full, i.e., 250 mg. Capsules of 100 mg. are preferable. In one session, some hours after ingesting the capsules, I threw up and lumps of ibogaine appeared. As I was in the deepest part of the session, the thought of re-ingesting more was out of the question as my system was repulsed at the thought. Also the depth of the experience put me off seeking to prolong it. This is a natural reaction. I believe the problem in this case was that the capsules were packed too full.

Further, throwing up is an inevitable event in the vast majority of cases. It is almost like a ritual cleansing. If the ibogaine is not fully dissolved, then it will be ejected. For this reason, to take it dissolved in warm, sweet water is a better option as it lines the tract leading to the stomach and the uptake is more assured and requires less time. However, the presence of ibogaine throughout the digestive tract is not a pleasant experience and for this reason the best and most effective method for taking ibogaine in a full session is anally, i.e., if the body is completely empty. This solves many problems and is purported to be more effective. However it requires a different dose. By taking it this way one does not experience any of the vomit-inducing effects of the taste. It is tasteless although one is aware of its presence as a low-lying flavor in the system. When one does eventually throw up none of the ibogaine is lost. Initially there can be a stinging sensation followed by a throbbing effect in the anal region. However, it bypasses the sensibilities of the body and gives greater comfort physically.

There is also the question of self regulation, i.e., does one throw up because the dose is too high? Does taking the dose anally make it impossible to do this? In my own experience the act of throwing up is, at times, a form of throwing off the Eboga energy and does not actually involve the ejection of the physical eboga itself. Refer back to discussion of white smoke during my session.

3.7 Physical Sensations

The physical sensations in the beginning are not very pleasant. I recall once, when at the age of 20 I went to Germany to work for a summer with IBM in Sindelfingen I became very drunk one night in a nightclub. I retreated to the toilet and stayed there. I was overcome by the most harrowing feelings I had ever experienced. It was as if I had unwittingly opened up the doors to my suppressed feelings, which included a sense of illness similar to receiving a blow to the emotional system, where one feels one is about to die or pass out.

Not only that, but one also feels genuinely horrible, like the body is in revolt on an emotional level. I had the same feelings the first time I took eboga. With Eboga these feelings will likely emerge as we experience the true feelings behind the effect of poisoning the body with repressed emotions. These can, in some cases I believe, lead to cancer as the body turns in on itself. However, physical pain associated with past trauma is not usually re-experienced. Eboga is not about re-traumatizing the person.

I was to reach a point where I felt I had a very personal relationship with Eboga and so the nature of my eventual sessions were quite different from the experiences I describe in this book. I can now safely say that Eboga does not frighten me, as I feel I am working with it in a benevolent way, having gone through the most harrowing part. Because of this I believe it has enormous, untapped potential for those willing to persist in applying its lessons and moving on with it. I believe its power is only limited by our belief in what is possible and our willingness to ask. However, the experience does not exist in a vacuum and requires changes in the external world also brought about by our greater insights into life and ourselves. The dosage also needs to be calibrated depending on the needs of the person and these usually reflect the stage of the healing process the person is at.

3.8 Safety Issues & Prerequisites

What follows are but a few of the considerations taken from a purely medical point of view. For those who wish to investigate ibogaine from a purely scientific viewpoint and to better understand the use of ibogaine for drug withdrawal, I refer you to the excellent Web site *www.ibogaine.org.*

No medical testing is the norm for many persons receiving ibogaine therapy. As I approach ibogaine as a spiritual practice, I believe the likelihood of problems, once precautions are taken, to be small. However, anyone who undertakes an ibogaine session does so at his or her own risk. A heart test (ECG) and blood test are the absolute minimum one should undergo and I would not support anyone who chose to take a session without these basic checks. On top of this the dose should reflect the stage the person is at in their healing journey. Having said that, heart and blood tests are sufficient for the vast majority of people as the real concern is to be able to process the ibogaine (with a properly functioning liver) and to avoid heart problems, as ibogaine also acts to lower blood pressure which can be problematic for those with heart conditions. What follows, then, is a brief outline of the medical precautions that should be taken.

1. It is advised to have a blood test to show that the person is in good health and, in particular, that the liver is functioning properly.

2. An electrocardiogram (ECG) is the most important consideration, particularly when the dosage exceeds 8 mg/kg. Heart conditions rule out an ibogaine session, as a full-length ibogaine session can be very physically demanding and induce a heart attack as ibogaine lowers blood pressure. Of the known recorded fatalities (at least 3 persons – lowest dose 8mg/kg., 40 year old woman) heart conditions and the use of drugs during a session have been considered the contributing factors.

3. Pulse and blood pressure should stabilize during a session and observers should have training in cardiopulmonary resuscitation and be prepared to call a hospital or emergency medical services should the patient's pulse drop below 50 beats per minute. These are good indicators to watch. A hospital should be called at any time if a person loses consciousness, i.e., is not communicable in any way. A person can and often will be in a distant and wiped-out state. That's normal. The emergency number to be called

should be available to all provider personnel at all times. It is best that a doctor is on call and made aware of what is taking place.

4. The main concern should be to attend to the individual in case he or she should vomit and is unable to move, as ibogaine usually restricts movement. For this, it is important to remain still, as movement induces vomiting.

5. An antidote exists among the Bwiti of the Mitsogho. Atopine suppresses all signs of ibogaine intoxication as well as ibogaine's arousal and inotropic properties but it is only administered in a hospital environment – see full text of appendix 1.

There are some other prerequisites before undergoing treatment. A person should satisfy the following:

1. General good health.
2. No past psychotic breaks.
3. Not be pregnant.

I am open-minded regarding the inclusion of those with certain mental health problems, as I believe it is possible to use ibogaine also in these circumstances when sufficient is known about its action and the services of a competent professional are at hand. While abnormal psychological activity may unexpectedly occur during a session, it is (I understand) usual to recover one's normal state.

There are apparently other things to consider, such as some gastrointestinal problems. There is a recommended follow-up period of exercise, therapy, drinking lots of water, etc. Personally, after my first session I just went back to my normal life. I think that the whole question of medical suitability to a session is mostly common sense within the main guidelines of heart and liver function and general good health.

3.9 What are the Risks?

During the past 20 years, two fatalities happened under medical supervision. The first was a German lady who underwent the treatment in Holland and died during a period when she wasn't observed by the staff. After careful examination of the data, Dr. Ken Alpers from New York defends the theory that the woman managed to leave the treatment facility and took heroin while the ibogaine was still very active in her body. Hence, she overdosed on heroin, as ibogaine re-sensitizes the body to opiates.

The other death occurred in Switzerland during a treatment given by a psychiatrist who administered ibogaine to a patient in spite of a serious heart defect (and may also have used MDMA concurrently). I have also heard anecdotal reports of a recent case where a woman died who also had a known heart condition.

However, it is important to put this into perspective. I have not heard of a case where anyone following the standard safety protocol has died. On the other hand according to a recent study by the University of Liverpool, up to 10,000 people per year in England alone could be dying from the taking of commonly prescribed drugs. The researchers estimated that adverse reactions to prescribed drugs causing hospital admission were responsible for the deaths of 5,700 patients a year in England. Taking into account incidents occurring while patients were in hospital and admissions together, the figure could be greater than 10,000 a year.

Clearly it is important to observe the safety protocols in taking ibogaine, which, generally speaking, are designed to deal with high dosages of ibogaine. The risks are obviously linked to the dosage – the higher the dosage, the higher the risk. In that sense there is an argument to begin ibogaine treatment at the lower end of the dosage scale. I strongly recommend the reader to read the document,

"Manual for Ibogaine Therapy, Screening, Safety, Monitoring, & Aftercare," available from *www.ibogaine.org/manual.html.* This has been developed specifically with drug users in mind. It does, however, deal with the same safety issues that apply to all users of ibogaine.

3.10 Healing & Awareness of Dose

It is important to realize that the link between dosage and experience is linear except when there is nothing to experience. The reason for this is that the Process is controlled by the Eboga spirit, the power of the ego and one's intention. Thus, while the necessary energy for an intense experience is in the body, it does not follow that one will have an intense experience. Hence, the real question of dosage becomes one of safety (i.e., calibration according to weight) and location on the healing journey axis. Another consideration is this. I believe dosage is perhaps less effective when the body is saturated from the by-products of previous sessions, i.e., too many sessions held close together can become ineffective.

There are those who take small amounts of eboga regularly and have, over the years, ingested very impressive amounts. You might be forgiven for thinking they are very healed. Quite the contrary. A "very" small dose does not displace the ego. Instead, it quite likely engages it, manifesting in imagery reflecting the ego's defenses, leading ultimately to self-avoidance and even greater ego defenses. Such people need a large dose to displace their ego as it is intent on controlling the situation and has no intention to submitting in humility to healing. However, small doses, if taken correctly, can be a useful aid in remaining drug free after a full session has cleansed the body. Small but reasonable doses can also be useful for continuing inner work or perhaps as a precursor to major work. It is the intention that counts.

Experimenting on oneself with small amounts without proper direction or preparation is ill advised. Questions asked in this state can evoke feelings which can be misinterpreted as answers. Real answers are generally symbolically revealed as required – dosage is important. Also a person can sometimes be mistaken in what they believe they have learned, only to rediscover they had more to learn and understand before the real answer was revealed. This they do via the mistaken answer.

Claudio Naranjo, in his book *The Healing Journey* (see Web site references for online versions of his work with ibogaine, appendix 2), states that he believes there is nothing that can be achieved via drug therapy that cannot also be achieved via conventional therapy. He says this because he worked with small doses in people who had not been given any previous ibogaine. Also, he then used the emerging imagery in a Jungian way to resolve what lay beneath it. In that sense, what he did was correct and useful. However, he was using (if you like) the outer parts of the ibogaine substance and not the very active engine within it. On the other hand, as he was a trained therapist, he was able to channel the imagery positively and thus avoid the problems of delusional thinking and negative ego strengthening.

For those who seek to work with ibogaine on low doses from the beginning the help of a therapist working in a manner similar to Naranjo can be very positive as it can exploit the ability of Eboga to open new perspectives. For those who are at an advanced stage and have built a relationship with the Eboga realm, such assistance at low doses is not necessary as the Eboga realm acts as a guide and therapist and builds on a person's journey up to that point.

Another writer states, "Ibogaine does not come with significant emotional connection." This depends on what you consider an emotion to be and it also depends on the dosage taken. If I fill a

Mercedes-Benz with a half a gallon of petrol I will be lucky if I get the engine to start. Further, instant emotional connection to a freshly retrieved trauma is not necessarily what Eboga healing is about. Eboga is a gradual process that in part depends on the ability of the emotional body to heal itself with time – it paves the way for this. Eboga is about self-knowledge revealed in a timely manner. These revelations ultimately (after a session) lead to emotional connection. Also, if we analyze the nature of the demons, we see that they exist in our soul as their counterweights, fear, pain, anger and hate, are anchored in our emotional body. When a demon is eradicated there is a profound emotional connection equivalent to the discharge of an electric current. However, the emotions that one normally associates with healing do not manifest initially, i.e., the kind we associate with the final stages of healing and acceptance. That's part of the integration and growth of awareness. The primary aim of Eboga is to release the spirit of the trauma and reeducate the ego.

Eboga also works in many other ways. For instance, in a mini-session it can bring your attention directly onto a problem and give you full emotional and ego awareness, thereby catalyzing change. This is useful for people who are in the course of changing their lives, based on self-awareness and are experiencing difficulties linked to the traumas that have been exposed in a full session. Eboga is an intelligence and it knows what it is doing.

I should also add that, while before I was nervous of a "mini" session without a sitter, I now see a "mini" Eboga session as an opportunity to learn and grow and generally do not fear it. However, each Eboga session comes with some nervousness until the major part of the darkness that lies hidden is revealed. It is only then that you do not need a sitter for a session. You only need your "Self."

Eboga healing is akin to deconstructing an old house and using the best parts to build a new one. The house is engineered with all kinds of interdependencies. You don't begin by removing the cornerstone (the core of the problem), as that would be ferociously difficult and lead to a collapse of the whole structure, damaging much of the good. The cornerstone is the last to go and by that time it is simply a matter of "picking" it up and walking away. This requires relatively little energy than to remove it in the first place, i.e., less dosage. In the same way, when decorating a house, you do not paint all coats at once as well as lay the floorboards and all the accessories. That would not be common sense.

3.11 Eboga & Drug Addiction

I have had the opportunity to observe the use of eboga/ibogaine for opiate withdrawal and it seems that, in general, drug addicts in their first session do not tend to experience much in the way of visuals. It appears that the energy of the Eboga is taken up with cleansing the body of the opiates. In this, methadone, a clinically prescribed substitute for heroin, is much harder to eliminate than heroin. Subsequent sessions held with addicts who are open and willing, do lend themselves to the kind of experiences that I have had.

In the West the Eboga spirit is used principally for opiate withdrawal. It seeks to return the body to normal, healthy function and this it does, among other things, by helping the individual explore and resolve their past. According to Howard Lotsof, who pioneered its use in the U.S. as an anti-addiction therapy as well as campaigned tirelessly for its use and legalization, opiate withdrawal is pretty much a done deal. However, it is essential that this is followed up by suitable counseling or personal inner work and that subsequent sessions are undertaken whereby more of the underlying issues can be revealed and worked with. Failing this a relapse into addiction often occurs. Addicts need to become aware of who they are and why they are behaving the way they do. Eboga is a teacher and helps in this. Those who have no interest in change or self understanding will relapse into drug addiction or else maintain a high level of inner pain.

According to one source, as of March 1999 there were 140 scientific papers on ibogaine's anti-addictive properties. Fifteen years earlier there was only one. Ironically, ibogaine is scorned by the medical profession and starved of commercial backing. There are many conspiracy theories as to why.

My own interest has grown out of dealing with my own problems and in particular the treatment of childhood trauma. However I seek to work with the Eboga realm directly, which requires doses higher than what Naranjo used for one-on-one therapy and lower than what Lotsoff recommends for drug addiction treatment. In this, it also acts as an anti-addiction interrupter, although the addiction is a dysfunctional behavior pattern rather than a substance. Much of our behavior is addictive until we can explore its causes and, subsequently, change our behavior.

3.12 The Corruption of Addiction

One of the characteristics I have noted in drug addicts is the manner in which many have their soul subverted by the desperate need to get a fix. In this regard integrity can be wholly corrupted. Yet one does not have to look to drug addicts to see this. Among those whose sexuality is broken, we also see this. The need to get a "sexual" fix leads to men and women willing to say anything or do anything in order to be satisfied. While we are under the forces of an addiction our true selves are subverted and we live in a state of self-hate.

With this in mind our drug policies are clearly a source of great and unnecessary suffering. No law makes any difference to the need for a drug fix in the same way as the Catholic Church's suppression of sexuality did nothing for sexual abuse except to foster it. Just as someone commits suicide to stop the pain, they take drugs to at least function from day to day. Drug laws in most countries are horrendously cruel, as well as deeply ignorant and reactionary.

The real effect of drug laws is to fill our jails with huge numbers of drug-related crimes at an exorbitant cost to the taxpayer. On top of this, house burglaries are mostly drug-related, as addicts seek to pay for their fix. These burglaries create enormous waste with items sold for a fraction of their cost. To my mind the laws solve nothing except to create more pain and crime. The enormous sums of money wasted could be used for helping people, not punishing them. As things stand the real problems regarding drug issues are not born of drug use, but of the laws used to suppress it. Unfortunately our government is held to account by reactionary forces that are unwilling or unable to be enlightened. They are afraid of what they do not understand. Without realizing it they themselves are addicts. In this case: addicts to the ego mind.

4. Good Practice Observations

Whatever you need is given to you when you need it.

The Process works with us, not against us. What I write here are simply my present observations for discussion among interested parties and are not meant to be a do-it-yourself guide.

Think of a session as containing five elements:

1. You.
2. The setting.
3. The sitter.
4. The higher beings assisting you.
5. The eboga root extract.

To gain the most from a session, the presence of a good, loving sitter provides the earthly support, should it be needed. It also goes a long way to comforting the person undergoing the session. Remember, the most important consideration is you and your preparation in general. The higher beings clearly want to help anyone they can but, as the saying goes, "God helps those who help themselves."

If these considerations are well taken care of, then the session will open you up more, knowing that you are supported on the physical level. Think of the higher beings as the ones who decide what you get from a session and do so based on how well you, the setting and the sitter are prepared.

A good sitter is vital. It is possible to have a low-dose session without a sitter but I do not advise it, as it is a cruel experience to be alone when you are dealing with hidden pain. In that sense it makes it less likely that such an encounter will be successful. The presence of a reassuring, caring sitter gives the person the confidence to go deeper and creates an atmosphere more conducive to healing. To have a full-scale session alone is out of the question for the safety reasons mentioned above, particularly the possibility of vomiting and being unable to move, leading to choking.

The recommendations here apply to a large-dose session where the Eboga spirit has practically full control. For example, in a low-dose session one might use music which evokes the heart and lifts one up. In a high-dose session there is no music and preferably no background noise.

Remember that there is a huge difference between the two types of eboga available at present. First there is ibogaine, a highly purified extract of the principal alkaloid of the eboga plant. It is my preferred form of eboga, as its action is easier to predict. It is an off-white with a tinge of orange, grainy powder. Most samples of this product are 95% pure ibogaine. Then there is the Indra total alkaloid extract, which is darker, deeper in color and comes as a brittle lump. It contains a reported 15% total alkaloids of which 8% is ibogaine. As the other alkaloids in the Indra product are active, this material is viewed as having a 15% potency. However, its science is largely unknown and for this reason I do not recommend it. Given that eboga is a precise catalyst which opens the portal to the Eboga spirit, I believe it is best that it is precise and that it is pure.

Taking everything into account, I suggest the following:

1. Think of a session as the second phase within a three-phase Eboga Process. In the first and third phases, i.e., before and after the session, an "Eboga Journal" is very important. A daily write-up of insights, dreams and feelings of ill ease or anything relevant should be recorded. These writings, which act as a form of active meditation, should become a focus for your thoughts, leading to a centering of the mind onto the issues in your life within a session. After a session, these writings should continue.

Someone who has been severely abused may require up to six years for full recovery or more. However, the rewards are heavenly for those who persist and once one realizes what the rewards are one cannot turn back without remaining in a state of permanent discontent.

2. Initially, as the session proceeds, try and connect with the spirits through inner dialog. After a while any active mental process may become impossible.

3. The room where the session takes place should be considered the womb of your inner world. Nobody should be allowed to enter unless you have made a request for them to do so or there is a medical emergency. Eboga has the effect of exposing your deepest self. You cannot take care of anybody else's needs in this state. Sometimes a loved one will seek assurance as they may be threatened by what the session will reveal. They should not be allowed to interfere. It is your space.

4. Before you take the eboga/ibogaine, take a moment to yourself and give thanks for what you are about to receive and what it will do for you. A session is not about going in, sitting back and walking away. It is about a relationship where you are aware of what is about to be bestowed on you and receive it with respect. It is also a collaborative process between you and the Eboga spirit.

5. A test dose of 100 mg. can be taken 48 hours before to check for an adverse reactions. It also has the advantage of facilitating a movement inwards and provides a preliminary connection to the Eboga energy which can help create a more relaxed ambience inwardly and outwardly.

6. It is best not to eat until the 36 hours are up, as it interferes with the flow of the energy and probably works against it. In any case, it is difficult to do so as one is very sensitive to everything one

eats. Start with something simple and natural, as it is difficult to eat anything processed or prepared.

7. The same applies to alcohol or any other mind-altering substance such as marijuana. As the energy is moving into its final stages such substances nullify its action.

8. A suitable form of sedative, natural or medicinal, can be taken beforehand if required.

9. Remain on a supported bed for the 36 hours, as the muscles in the back can become very flaccid and cause back damage. In some cases, it is acceptable to get up and walk around.

10. During the session it might be a good idea to have a flask of warm water mixed with a little honey to absorb the taste of the ibogaine, especially if one has taken it orally and not via capsules.

11. As explained before, anally is possibly the best way to take ibogaine – it requires a different dose. Failing that, mixed with sweet or honey water. If capsules are to be used, then they should not be packed full – 100 mg./capsule is optimum to avoid excessive loss due to vomiting.

12. If taking the ibogaine dissolved in water, use sweet, warm water and keep some for after to help clear the mouth before and during the session, as the taste can become overwhelming. In any case, it is a good idea to have a little water and a little sweetened water available during the session. (Flavored chewing gum can also help before the ibogaine takes effect to clear the mouth of the taste.)

13. Normally one cannot move without being overcome by nausea leading to vomiting, as though one is disturbing a large body of mercury finely balanced within oneself. For this reason one should lie perfectly still. In subsequent sessions this sensation lessons considerably.

14. If and when you feel sick, it is important to breathe deeply. Practice deep breathing beforehand, right into the stomach. The sickness feeling will pass as quickly as it came – sometimes it is overpowering as something deep has been exposed. In the first two to three hours try to avoid being sick, as some of the ibogaine will be lost.

15. The session should be conducted in a quiet, gentle, darkened room, ideally with a lamp on a dimmer switch and not light from the ceiling. The reason for this being that the session may externalize images onto the ceiling. Usually these images are also seen behind closed eyes, but for some it can be more comforting to view them externally as it is less threatening. In this case "very" dim light is required to view these external images.

16. Ideally the room should be close to a natural environment, e.g., a house in the country, or surrounded by lots of plants and vegetation, etc. This is a question of energy. Urban stress is not edifying for the person undergoing the session. Similarly the environment should not be noisy or intrusive and it is best that it has an atmosphere of safety and reverence. Burning a little incense beforehand may set the stage as well as cleanse the air. This can be accompanied with a candle in the corridor as a sign of the intention at work.

17. A recording system can be set up during the session, especially for the first three or four hours. (In most cases however a person will be unable to talk.) Coming back to these tapes months later can have a very powerful, cathartic effect. One can have little desire to write after a session, especially after a first major session and so recordings are very useful for later on.

18. Once the session is over it is a good idea to tape any thoughts, memories, or reflections of the session. For this, a magnolite and

a journal by the bed are also very useful, especially for recording any thoughts, insights or dreams (which can be analyzed later) which emerge during the night. It may be easier to have a handheld tape recorder.

19. It is best to start your session at the time of day that is your physically strongest and not simply at a time that suits your sitter. Try to schedule a time that comes close to meeting your needs while taking into account the needs of the sitter. For myself the second half of the day is the best.

20. Dehydration can become an issue. It is recommended to drink plenty of purified water in the days leading up to the session. This also has the effect of preparing the body. Once the session is over remember to re-hydrate, as a lot of water is lost from the body during the session – at least 3 liters of water per day is recommended by one author.

21. Prior to the session a healthy regimen consisting of diet and exercise will assist the outcome of the session, as it increases the efficacy of the ibogaine significantly. This is due to the stress reduction in the body along with the improved circulation and mental attitude. A week by the beach prior to the first major session, swimming each day and eating fruits, good food and drinking natural fruit juices is an excellent preparation.

22. It is recommended to fast at least 12 hours before, to allow the body to clear itself. Small amounts of liquid can be taken, but this, too, should be refrained from in the six hours leading up to the session. (One can gargle water during this time to kill the dryness in the mouth – a few drops is not a problem.) A session often leads to continuous bowel movement until one is empty. Hence if taking ibogaine anally it is very important that one fasts beforehand. Also, as one normally cannot move (particularly in a first session), going to the toilet can prove extremely difficult.

23. In regard to the previous point, in some cases it may be wise to use whatever methods are at hand to clear out the digestive system prior to the session especially if taking ibogaine anally.

24. It is a good idea to arrive a few days early to be rested before the session, as it is very demanding.

25. Ideally a week should be allowed for recovery after the session.

26. Know what you SEEK! Use common sense. Make a list.

27. INTENTION is everything, i.e., self-awareness aligned with purity of heart. What you seek should mirror your intention.

28. It is important to agree on guidelines with your sitter beforehand. If you do not wish to talk they should be aware of this and respect your wishes. Conversely, if you need to talk, they should be open to listen and make the absolute minimum of response. They should not engage you in argument or conversation! A sitter needs to be aware of what this state is like and be sensitive to your needs. Remember, the session is for you and you only. It is an internal process and any external engagement breaks the flow of the session. The session is not for the benefit of the sitter. The first 24 hours after a session is also a time to be used as you see fit. If you feel like talking about your experience, great. If you wish to stay by yourself and reflect, even better. The sitter needs to be aware of your needs in this and not be driven by their own curiosity.

29. The session is about going in and any attempt by the therapist to engage you is going to take you out. Basically any reason for the person undergoing the session to think a response for the therapist is an ego-oriented action and unhelpful in the first part of the session which is functioning from a reduced or disabled ego state. Therefore, in the first phase of the session in particular the therapist should do little to interfere, other than to keep you awake and to reassure you that what is happening is as expected

and will pass. In the second phase the therapist can engage you if they see you are tiring and falling asleep. The therapist may at some point question you to establish which stage you are at and what action on their part is appropriate – that is reasonable interference.

30. Step dosing will not produce the same effects as a complete dose as the spiritual energy has its own life cycle which begins at the moment the eboga is introduced to the body. However, for drug addiction treatment step dosing may be appropriate.

31. A bowl of freshly cut fruit after a session is a must!

32. Like images in a rearview mirror, predicted future events in a session may not be as close as they appear.

Appendices

The Spiral Galaxy M33.

1. Bwiti Initiation Rituals

Apparently an Eboga session is much more of an ordeal for the Bwiti and therefore it takes them longer to recover. We can be much more effective, with less strain or damage on the body because the preparation we use is easier to ingest and contains only the active part that is required.

In my own first session, I had coffee 18 hours after I took the ibogaine, going through the same steps as the Bwiti using a relatively high dose. As far as I know this is unheard of in the Bwiti. Also, only about 25% of the Bwiti actually have the initiation experience, according to Fernandez. We can do it much more safely with a higher degree of success. I would also add the following from Nick Sandberg of *www.ibogaine.co.uk:* Westerners are not advised to travel to the region to undergo the Bwiti initiation ceremony. He states: "The Bwiti initiation ritual, as this 'rebirth' ceremony has come to be known, has in recent years attracted the attention of some Westerners who find themselves romantically drawn to the notion of travelling to the region and undertaking it themselves. Anyone considering doing this should be aware of three things. Firstly, that both the Cameroon and the Democratic Republic of Congo, two of the three countries where the Bwiti are located, are now regarded as being acutely dangerous for Westerners (Zaire especially). Secondly, that in Gabon, the remaining country, only the least reputable groups would usually consider initiating Westerners and then almost certainly only undertake the task for financial gain, likely in a half-hearted fashion. Finally it should be remembered that each year some local initiates are believed to die during the ceremony, bizarre court cases between parents and priests frequently resulting."

Apart from these reasons, it can be a very brutal experience, as it is tied up in local custom that is much, much tougher than

Western practice. The Western approach is much gentler. It is worth remembering that local custom is not paramount to the Eboga realm. The Eboga realm is paramount to local custom.

The following extract should give some idea of what an initiation ceremony is like among the Bwiti. It is important to remember that the Bwiti is the name given to the religion practiced by the Mitsogos and the Fangs, two distinct tribal groups in Gabon. In the words of one writer, Rene Bureau, "Gabon is to Africa what Tibet is to Asia, the spiritual center of religious initiations."

I have chosen the part that deals with the Bwiti of the Mitsogos, as I found that description in this article the more straightforward of the two, reflecting better my own experience. The Bwiti of the Fang is a later development in Gabon and is interlaced with many newer influences, such as their memories, their traditions and ideas and rites that came from Catholicism. Unlike the Mitsogo, they initiate both men and women. They appear to have come from central Africa, fleeing from Islam.

Currently the "primitive" Bwiti (as it is described by one author) of the Mitsogos is on the decline while the Bwiti of the Fangs is expanding. However it is losing some of its initial purity. This can be seen by the fact that the Bwiti of the Mitsogos are much more conservative in their approach to eboga.

P. Barabe describes the Fang as being eager to receive that which is new, convinced that they can integrate all techniques and ideas into their own culture. He says it was therefore just a matter of time before they would take possession of the primitive Bwiti of the Mitsogos and modify it.

The following extract has been reproduced with kind permission from the ibogaine dossier www.ibogaine.org/bwiti1.html, which has an extensive library of documents, from the article:

Pharmacodynamics and Therapeutic Applications of Iboga and Ibogaine.
By Robert Goutarel, Honorary Research Director;
Otto Gollnhofer and Roger Sillans, Ethnologists, C.N.R.S.

(French National Scientific Research Center)
(Translated from French by William J. Gladstone)

Psychedelic Monographs and Essays, Volume 6:70-111, 1993
Subsection: The Gabonese Rituals of Iboga, Bwiti of the Mitsogho.
Author: Robert Goutarel (Footnotes 1,2,3)

The original Bwiti or Bwiti of the Mitsogho arose among the Mitsogho when they reached the territory that is now Gabon. In the remote period, the Bwiti itself was a product of a syncretism made up of ancestor worship enhanced by the discovery of iboga (perhaps imparted by the Pygmies of the equatorial forest) and of cultural elements acquired during the migrations of the Mitsogho.

Among the Mitsogho (and the Bapinzi) the Bwiti is strictly for males and those who have been initiated are considered as Masters and sole custodians of the mystery of the *visual knowledge* of the beyond given to them by iboga, the "miraculous tree".

This initiation is indispensable for social promotion within the tribe and any individual who is unable to join the Bwiti becomes an outcast and is considered by one and all as a girl.

Iboga brings about the visual, tactile and auditory certainty of the irrefutable existence of the beyond. Through his spiritually immutable substance, man belongs on two planes of existence with which he blends, knowing not where birth and death begin. Physical death loses all meaning because it is nothing but a new life, another existence. "It is Iboga that conditions the several existences."

Iboga does away with the notion of time, the present, past and future blend into one, as in the super luminous universe of Régis and Brigitte Dutheil (footnote 4): through the absorption of iboga man returns to the birthplace whence he came.

In order to be admitted to the Bwiti Society the candidates must submit to a series of trials or rites of passage that begin in an enclosure strictly reserved for the initiates.

Each candidate has a "mother," who is an old initiate; this is a man who sees to it that the initiatory ceremony is conducted properly.

This ceremony consists essentially of ingesting scrapings of iboga root (Tabernanthe iboga H.Bn. var. ñoke and mbassoka).

This "chewing of iboga" is supervised by the "mother" who constantly checks the dosage of the drug according to the physiological reactions of his candidate who must take a very large quantity of root bark and stems of T. iboga.

This chewing is preceded by abstinence from sex and food the day before. The rite is very strict and each manifestation has great symbolic value.

Over a fire, the elders roast squash seeds. The sound they make as they pop symbolizes the release of the spirit – which supposedly leaves the body through the fontanelle – on its mystical journey. The candidate's skull is struck three times with a hammer to help free his spirit.

The neophyte's tongue is pricked with a needle to give it the power to relate the visions to come.

Since the chewing can last several days, the disincarnation and the reincarnation of the neophyte are reenacted before the visions appear.

The candidate is led to the river and a miniature dugout canoe made of a leaf, bearing a lit torch of okoumé resin, is set upon the waters. This rite represents the journey of the spirit downstream, toward the West, the setting sun, death and symbolizes disincarnation.

A stake surmounted by a diamond-shaped wooden structure is planted in midstream: it represents the female sexual organ, which the candidate must go through (in a fetal state) against the current, thus swimming upstream from the East, the rising sun, from birth.

For the enactment of this initiatory birth the neophyte's head is shaved and is sprinkled with a red wood (padouk), as is done with the newborn.

Finally, as soon as the neophyte's psychological state after the chewing is considered satisfactory, he is led into the Temple where he is placed on the left side, symbolizing womanhood, darkness, death. He remains in the Temple on the left side, absorbing iboga leaves until the normative perception of the visions occurs.

During the chewing the effects of the drug begin to be manifested twenty minutes after the first absorption of iboga by violent and repeated vomiting: "The belly of the neophyte (banzi) is emptied even of its mother's milk."

To go to the beyond one has to die; the body remains on the ground with the elders, the soul departs.

The physiological manifestations begin with drowsiness, followed by motor incoordination, strong agitation, tremor, crying and laughter, partial anesthesia with intermittent hypothermia and hyperthermia, panting that may go as far as choking.

To assess the progress of the intoxication and to adjust the dosage, those in charge take the pulse, listen to the heartbeat, check the temperature simply by touching the body and evaluate sensibility by pricking with a needle at different times. According to the physiological state, the "mothers" regulate the dose of iboga up or down from time to time.

The oneiric effects do not begin to be manifested until after about ten hours during which time the aforementioned rituals take place, partly in public with dances and music.

Among the Mitsogho the subjects under the influence of iboga go through four stages to reach an image content corresponding to the required norms. The candidates are constantly questioned by the initiated elders as to the content of what they perceive. The elders are the ones who make a judgment as to the initiatory value of the vision described.

The first vision consists of hazy, incoherent, disordered images devoid of religious significance, whose authenticity is often questioned by the neophyte.

The second stage is characterized by a series of apparitions of menacing looking animals that sometimes break apart and at times form together again rapidly.

In the third stage the oneiric vision clearly progresses toward the mythical stereotype. The neophyte grows more and more calm, a sign of a pleasant, peaceful vision that dispels his doubts as to the objectivity and factualness of the image perceived.

The neophyte feels himself enveloped by a wind that carries him off in the twinkling of an eye, to the sound of the Ngombi harp, to an immense village without a beginning or end.

We ought to say a word about the symbolic value of the musical bow whose melodious sounds accompany the ceremony. It represents a link between the village of the men here on Earth and the village of the father in the beyond. The musical bow symbolizes the road of life and death.

On the way over voices are heard: "Who is it that you seek, stranger?" And the traveler answers: "I seek the Bwiti." The voices suddenly take on human forms that ask the question again and then respond in a chorus: "You are looking for the Bwiti. The Bwiti is us, your ancestors, we constitute the Bwiti."

The vision tends more and more to become normative. The initiates then tell the candidate: "You are on the right path, the Bwiti will soon be here. Go further on. Look and you will find it. You must not forsake the images; take up where you left off."

A voice gives the candidate his initiatory name. The neophyte is watched constantly by his "mother," who regulates his psychophysiological reactions to prevent him from letting terrifying phantoms interfere, for they would lead him down the wrong path, down the road of death.

The fourth stage, of vision (the one that ethnologists refer to as the stage of normative visions) is the one marked by the encounter with higher spiritual entities.

After a dialogue with his ancestors the neophyte suddenly finds "his legs immobilized, before two Extraordinary Beings" who disclose that he is in the "Village of the Bwiti" (village of the dead). They ask him why he has come to this place.

After hearing the answer of the neophyte the "Fantastic Beings" speak again. The first one says: "My name is Nzamba-Kana, the father of humankind, the first man on Earth," and the one standing to his left says: "My name is Disumba, the mother of humankind (wife of Nzamba-Kana) and the first woman on Earth."

Suddenly the "Village of the Dead" is covered with increasingly intense sparks, a "ball of light" takes shape and becomes distinct (Kombé, the sun). This ball of light questions the visitor as to the reasons for his journey. "Do you know who I am? I am the Chief of the World, I am the essential point!" This is my wife Ngondi (the moon) and these are my children (Minanga) the stars. The Bwiti is everything you have seen with your own eyes."

After this dialogue the sun and the moon change into a handsome boy and a beautiful girl. Without any warning the moon and the sun resume their original forms and disappear. The thunder (Ngadi) is heard and calm returns everywhere.

The wind wraps around the neophyte for a second time and carries him to Earth among the living. The elders greet him with pride: "He has seen the Bwiti with his own eyes," and invite him to take his place on the right side of the Temple, the side of men and of life.

The candidate has become an initiate by discovering the Bwiti in another reality, that is, in the other life stemming at once from physical death and initiatory death. Through the waking dream he catches a glimpse, in the present, past and future of his own being, of man, immutable in his spiritual essence and living on two planes of existence.

However, after the rites of passage the new member will be isolated from the outside world for a period of one to three weeks. During this time his meals will be prepared and served by a young woman who has recently given birth because he is considered as a newborn.

The initiate has seen, he knows, he believes, but as a Mitsogho he will only make this journey twice: during the initiation and on the day of his death. It is out of the question for him to take iboga again under the same conditions. From then on the sacred plant will only be used sparingly, to "warm the heart" and to help him "in physical efforts or discussion."

We can learn several things from this study of the Mitsogho Bwiti.

First of all there are some striking similarities between the Bwiti initiation and the freemasonry initiation rites. The end result is the same, the knowledge of the mysteries of the beyond, which the masons call the "sublime secret." Freemasonry initiation is preceded by the candidate's retreat, during which he is assisted by one who has been previously initiated. The latter will convey to him, as he makes him pass through a narrow door, that the initiation is a new birth.

But most astonishing in the masonry ritual are the three blows on the head with a mallet, in remembrance of the assassination of Hiram, the architect of the Temple of Solomon, by three of his companions to whom he refused to reveal the "sublime secret." The only difference between the masons and the followers of the Bwiti is that the latter have the certainty of knowing this secret.

The Bwiti initiation among the Mitsogho, concerns essentially the passage from adolescence to manhood, hence the necessity of eliminating the epigenetic elements of childhood and adolescence in order to reprogram in the young man a new ego corresponding to the cultural norms of the tribe.

To achieve this the Mitsogho call on the instrumental deprivation of sleep, as the initiation lasts for days without sleep or food, as well as on pharmacological deprivation through the chewing of iboga.

The result is a waking dream without psychotic manifestations during which the subject remains perfectly conscious and can communicate with those around him, being at once an actor and a spectator of his visions.

What is remarkable is the fact that iboga intoxication is very gradual, which makes it possible to observe several stages during these visions. Ethnologists were able to follow in the field the progression of this intoxication and to distinguish four characteristic stages during the initiation. In the first three stages, the visions correspond essentially to what the psychoanalysts call the subterranean world of Freud. The fourth stage is referred to by the ethnologists as the stage of normative visions corresponding to the collective and cultural image of the tribe (cf. Jung).

While in the Bwiti ritual we did not fail to bring out certain similarities between the Bwiti initiation and the Freemasonry initiation, we are compelled likewise to draw analogies between certain aspects of the vision resulting from the absorption of iboga and what certain persons see at the time of clinical death. We have discussed this topic in the conclusions.

The neophyte will have to face initiatory (or real) death that will enable him to gain access to the things of the beyond. He can do so only if he has been properly prepared and, especially, if his motivation is sufficient. For various reasons – poor preparation, inadequate motivation, fear, psychosis, neurosis – certain subjects are unable to get past this critical phase. They fall prey to evil genies who veer them off onto the road of death.

The elders will then decide to stop the initiation by means of an antidote whose composition is not known. We should note that the pharmacology of ibogaine has shown that atropine (an acetylcholine antagonist) suppresses all signs of ibogaine intoxication as well as ibogaine's arousal and inotropic activities.

The Ombudi (or Ombwiri, among the Fang) is an initiatory order reserved for women who belong to the therapists among the Mitsogho and the Fang.

The women take iboga in smaller quantities than the ones taken in the Bwiti initiation. In their case the visions do not go beyond the third (Freudian) stage during which genies, good or evil, communicate to the women that they are in possession of the causes of the affliction or illness for which they were consulted.

1. Binet, J.; Gollnhofer, O.; Sillans, R. 1972. Cahiers d'Études africaines vol. 46(Xii/195):253.
2. Gollnhofer, O. & Sillans, R. 1985. Usages rituels de l'Iboga au Gabon (Ritual Uses of Iboga in Gabon). Psychotropes Vol. 2(3):95-108.
3. Gollnhofer, O. & Sillans, R. 1983. L'Iboga, psychotrope africain (Iboga, an African Psychotropic Agent). Psychotropes Vol. 1(1):11-27.

4. Dutheil, R. and Dutheil, B., L'Homme superlumineux (The Superluminous Man), Sand Publ., 1990.

2. Books, Web Sites & Eboga Resources

2.1 Referenced Reading

The Holy Grail, by Ingrid H. Shafer online at *www.myeboga.com.*

The Da Vinci Code, by Dan Brown, Doubleday.

A Class-Book of Irish History, by James Carty, 1966, National School Program, Standard V.

"The Riotous and The Righteous," New Internationalist, issue 255, May 1994, Bill Rolston.

The Alchemist, by Paulo Coelho.

Man & His Symbols, by Carl Gustav Jung.

The Awakening of Intelligence, by J. Krisnamurti.

The Power of Myth, by Joseph Campbell.

The Hero With a Thousand Faces, by Joseph Campbell.

The New Primal Scream, by Arthur Janov.

The Drama of the Gifted Child, by Alice Miller.

Spiritual Emergency: When Personal Transformation Becomes a Crisis, by Stanislof Grof.

The Secret Chief, by Myron J. Stolaroff, Conversations with a pioneer of the underground psychedelic therapy movement.

The Ibogaine Story, Report on The Staten Island Project, by Paul De Rienzo, Dana Beal & Members of The Project.

IBOGAINE: Proceedings from the First International Conference, by Kenneth, R. Alper (Editor), Stanley D. Glick (Editor).

An Introduction to Ibogaine by Nick Sandberg, *www.ibogaine. co.uk.*

2.2 Eboga / Ibogaine Cultural & Religious Perspective

www.myeboga.com – Author's web site: "my eboga" stands for the development of understanding in the area of spiritual advancement and personal growth via the use of eboga or ibogaine.

www.iboga.org/us/ – French (and English) site on the Bwiti.

www.ibogaine.org/opinion.html – Newspaper and magazine articles.

www.ibogaine.org/forenaranjo.html – The Healing Journey, foreword by Claudio N. Naranjo.

http://www.cures-not-wars.org/ibogaine/iboga.html – Dana Beal's site. *The Ibogaine Story* online.

www.mapinc.org/drugnews/ – Use this link to search for recent articles in the press.

2.3 Eboga / Ibogaine Provider Names

The listing of a name should not be taken as an endorsement. Many of these providers are oriented towards drug addiction. Anyone who undertakes a session does so at their own risk.

www.ibogainetreatment.com – Karl Naeher's ibogaine provider site. (US$1.5k, approx. Nominal amount for 2nd session.)

www.ibeginagain.org – Eric Taub's ibogaine provider site. (US$900-$2,500, approx.)

e-mail: sara119@xs4all.nl – Sara Glatt works mostly with the Indra extract from her family home outside Amsterdam.

e-mail: wardconn@hotmail.com – Edward Conn, ibogaine practitioner working in London, England. Tel: (+44) 0207 833 3327 *e-mail: marc@cannabisculture.com* – The Iboga Therapy House, Vancouver B.C., Canada work with highly motivated individuals who have an after-care program in place.

www.iboga.org – Treatment with Tabernanthe iboga in either the Cameroon or France. (US$1.3k, approx.)

www.ibogainetreatment.net – Brian Mariano's ibogaine provider site. (US$1.8k, approx.)

www.ibogaine-therapy.net – Medically supervised ibogaine treatment near San Diego in Rosarito, Mexico. (US$2.8k, approx.)

e-mail: kabbas@brain.net.pk – Medically supervised ibogaine treatment at a hospital in Lahore, Pakistan, with Dr. Kalbe Abbas. (US$1.5k, approx.)

www.ibogaine.net – Dr. Deborah Mash's "Healing Transitions Institute for Addiction" provider site. (US$3-12k, approx.)

e-mail: ibogaine@chiriqui.com – Ibogaine treatment in a Panamanian hospital with Dr. Edgardo Della Sera. (US$15k, approx.)

www.ncbi.nlm.nih.gov/PubMed/ – Medline search page for details of clinical studies.

2.4 Eboga / Ibogaine Resources

www.ibogaine.org – The most extensive ibogaine site online.
www.ibogaine.org/manual.html – Manual for Ibogaine Therapy.
www.ibogaine.co.uk – U.K. based ibogaine site.
www.maps.org/news-letters/ – MAPS search engine.
www.lycaeum.org – Search page for psychedelics and select ibogaine.
www.erowid.com/entheogens/ibogaine/ibogaine.shtml – An extensive introduction to ibogaine.

About the Author

In a relentless search for freedom from lifelong problems and a burning desire to realize his dreams he spent 2 years in an Irish seminary, underwent intensive Primal Therapy, trained as a Emotional Release facilitator, explored the thoughts of Krisnamurti and finally in desperation forsook all belief.

He has an M.Sc. in Chemistry and is a qualified Systems Engineer and trained Windsurfing Instructor. He has lived, and traveled, through 36 countries and worked as a teacher in Africa. He completed his search through what he calls "The Eboga Process,"™ and embarked on a miraculous journey of self-discovery and reconnection to his inner self.

His interest now lies in the way to confront personal past history leading to self-discovery, happiness, fulfillment and one's own immortality.

Printed in the United Kingdom
by Lightning Source UK Ltd.
108436UKS00002B/97